PHP 7 Programming Blueprints

Learn how to exploit the impressive power of PHP 7 with this collection of practical project blueprints – begin building better applications for the web today!

Jose Palala
Martin Helmich

[PACKT] open source*
PUBLISHING   community experience distilled

BIRMINGHAM - MUMBAI

PHP 7 Programming Blueprints

First published: October 2016

Production reference: 2061016

Published by Packt Publishing Ltd.

Livery Place

35 Livery Street

Birmingham B3 2PB, UK.

ISBN 978-1-78588-971-4

www.packtpub.com

Credits

Authors

Jose Palala
Martin Helmich

Reviewer

Shuvankar Sarkar

Commissioning Editor

Kunal Parikh

Acquisition Editor

Chaitanya Nair

Content Development Editor

Onkar Wani

Technical Editor

Murtaza Tinwala

Copy Editor

Safis Editing

Project Coordinator

Ulhas Kambali

Proofreader

Safis Editing

Indexer

Rekha Nair

Production Coordinator

Melwyn Dsa

Cover Work

Melwyn Dsa

About the Authors

Jose Palala has been working professionally with PHP for at least 8 years. He has experience working with PHP frameworks such as Eden PHP, CodeIgniter, Laravel and Zend.

He has worked for Philippine-based IT companies for at least 8 years, working on projects ranging from internal corporate systems and CMS websites. In his spare time, he regularly contributes back to the tech community in the Philippines.

> *I would like to thank everyone at Packt Publishing, it's been great working with them since Day 1. Super thanks to all to my colleagues, friends and family who have helped me to become a better developer and have helped me become what I am today.*

Martin Helmich holds a Master's degree in Computer Science from the University of Applied Sciences in Osnabrück. He works as a software architect and specializes in building distributed applications using web technologies and Microservice Architectures. Besides programming in Go, PHP, Python and Node.JS, he also builds infrastructures using configuration management tools like SaltStack and container technologies like Docker.

He is an open source enthusiast and likes to make fun of people who are not using Linux. In his free time, you'll probably find him coding on one of his open source pet projects, listening to music or reading science-fiction literature.

About the Reviewer

Shuvankar Sarkar is an IT analyst and experienced in C#, .NET, PHP and web development.

He is a technology enthusiast and maintains his blog at `http://shuvankar.com/`. You can follow him on Twitter at `@sonu041`. He is interested in computer security as well.

I would like to thank my family for making my life easier and full of happiness.

www.PacktPub.com

eBooks, discount offers, and more

Did you know that Packt offers eBook versions of every book published, with PDF and ePub files available? You can upgrade to the eBook version at www.PacktPub.com and as a print book customer, you are entitled to a discount on the eBook copy. Get in touch with us at customercare@packtpub.com for more details.

At www.PacktPub.com, you can also read a collection of free technical articles, sign up for a range of free newsletters and receive exclusive discounts and offers on Packt books and eBooks.

https://www2.packtpub.com/books/subscription/packtlib

Do you need instant solutions to your IT questions? PacktLib is Packt's online digital book library. Here, you can search, access, and read Packt's entire library of books.

Why subscribe?

- Fully searchable across every book published by Packt
- Copy and paste, print, and bookmark content
- On demand and accessible via a web browser

Table of Contents

Preface

PHP is a great language for developing web applications. It is essentially a server-side scripting language that is also used for general-purpose programming. PHP 7 is the latest version, which provides major backward-compatibility breaks and focuses on providing improved performance and speed. With the rise in demand for high performance, this newest version contains everything you need to build efficient applications. PHP 7 provides improved engine execution, better memory usage, and a better set of tools allowing you to maintain high traffic on your websites with low-cost hardware and servers through a multithreading web server.

What this book covers

Chapter 1, *Create a User Profile System and use the Null Coalesce Operator*, we'll discover new PHP 7 features and build app for storing user profiles.

Chapter 2, *Build a Database Class and Simple Shopping Cart*, we'll create a simple database layer library which will help us access our database. We'll cover some tips on making our queries secure, and how to make our coding simpler and more succinct with PHP 7.

Chapter 3, *Building a Social Newsletter Service*, we'll be building a social newsletter service, which will have a way for users to sign in using their social login and allow them to register to a newsletter. We'll also make a simple admin system for managing the newsletters.

Chapter 4, *Build a Simple Blog with Search Capability using Elasticsearch*, you will learn how to create a blog system, experiment with ElasticSearch and how to apply it in your code. Also, you will learn how to create a simple blog application and store data into MySQL.

Chapter 5, *Creating a RESTful Web Service*, shows you how create a RESTful web service that can be used to manage user profiles. The service will be implemented using the Slim micro framework and use a MongoDB database for persistence. The chapter also covers the basics of RESTful web services, most importantly the common HTTP request and response methods, the PSR-7 standard and PHP 7's new mongodb extension.

Chapter 6, *Building a Chat Application*, describes the implementation of a real-time chat application using WebSockets. You will learn how to use the Ratchet framework to build stand-alone WebSocket and HTTP servers with PHP and how to connect to WebSocket servers in a JavaScript client application. We will also discuss how you can implement authentication for WebSocket applications and how to deploy them in a production environment.

Chapter 7, *Building an Asynchronous Microservice Architecture*, covers the implementation of a (small) microservice architecture. Instead of RESTful web services, you will use ZeroMQ in this chapter for network communication, an alternative communication protocol that focuses on asynchronicity, loose coupling and high performance.

Chapter 8, *Building a Parser and Interpreter for a Custom Language*, describes how to use the PHP-PEG library to define a grammar and implement a parser for a custom expression language that can be used to add end-user development features to enterprise applications.

Chapter 9, *Reactive Extensions in PHP*, here we'll look into the Reactive extensions library for PHP, and and try to build a simple scheduled app.

What you need for this book

You'll need to download and install PHP 7 from the official PHP website. You'll also need to install a Webserver such as Apache or Nginx configured to run PHP 7 by default.

If you are experienced with virtual machines, you can also use Docker containers and/or Vagrant to build an environment with PHP 7 installed.

Who this book is for

The book is for web developers, PHP consultants, and anyone who is working on multiple projects with PHP. Basic knowledge of PHP programming is assumed.

Conventions

In this book, you will find a number of text styles that distinguish between different kinds of information. Here are some examples of these styles and an explanation of their meaning.

Code words in text, database table names, folder names, filenames, file extensions, pathnames, dummy URLs, user input, and Twitter handles are shown as follows: "Let's create a simple `UserProfile` class."

A block of code is set as follows:

```
function fetch_one($id) {
  $link = mysqli_connect('');
  $query = "SELECT * from ". $this->table . " WHERE `id` =' " . $id "'";
  $results = mysqli_query($link, $query);
}
```

When we wish to draw your attention to a particular part of a code block, the relevant lines or items are set in bold:

```
'credit_card' => $credit_card,
'items' => //<all the items and prices>//,
'total' => $total,
```

Any command-line input or output is written as follows:

```
mysql> source insert_profiles.sql
```

New terms and **important words** are shown in bold. Words that you see on the screen, for example, in menus or dialog boxes, appear in the text like this: "Simply click on **Allow access** and then click on **OK**."

Warnings or important notes appear in a box like this.

Tips and tricks appear like this.

Reader feedback

Feedback from our readers is always welcome. Let us know what you think about this book—what you liked or disliked. Reader feedback is important for us as it helps us develop titles that you will really get the most out of.

To send us general feedback, simply e-mail feedback@packtpub.com, and mention the book's title in the subject of your message.

If there is a topic that you have expertise in and you are interested in either writing or contributing to a book, see our author guide at www.packtpub.com/authors.

Customer support

Now that you are the proud owner of a Packt book, we have a number of things to help you to get the most from your purchase.

Downloading the example code

You can download the example code files for this book from your account at http://www.packtpub.com. If you purchased this book elsewhere, you can visit http://www.packtpub.com/support and register to have the files e-mailed directly to you.

You can download the code files by following these steps:

1. Log in or register to our website using your e-mail address and password.
2. Hover the mouse pointer on the **SUPPORT** tab at the top.
3. Click on **Code Downloads & Errata**.
4. Enter the name of the book in the **Search** box.
5. Select the book for which you're looking to download the code files.
6. Choose from the drop-down menu where you purchased this book from.
7. Click on **Code Download**.

You can also download the code files by clicking on the **Code Files** button on the book's webpage at the Packt Publishing website. This page can be accessed by entering the book's name in the **Search** box. Please note that you need to be logged in to your Packt account.

Once the file is downloaded, please make sure that you unzip or extract the folder using the latest version of:

- WinRAR / 7-Zip for Windows
- Zipeg / iZip / UnRarX for Mac
- 7-Zip / PeaZip for Linux

The code bundle for the book is also hosted on GitHub at https://github.com/PacktPublishing/PHP-7-Programming-Blueprints. We also have other code bundles from our rich catalog of books and videos available at https://github.com/PacktPublishing/. Check them out!

Downloading the color images of this book

We also provide you with a PDF file that has color images of the screenshots/diagrams used in this book. The color images will help you better understand the changes in the output. You can download this file from `https://www.packtpub.com/sites/default/files/down loads/PHP7ProgrammingBlueprints_ColorImages.pdf`.

Errata

Although we have taken every care to ensure the accuracy of our content, mistakes do happen. If you find a mistake in one of our books—maybe a mistake in the text or the code—we would be grateful if you could report this to us. By doing so, you can save other readers from frustration and help us improve subsequent versions of this book. If you find any errata, please report them by visiting `http://www.packtpub.com/submit-errata`, selecting your book, clicking on the **Errata Submission Form** link, and entering the details of your errata. Once your errata are verified, your submission will be accepted and the errata will be uploaded to our website or added to any list of existing errata under the Errata section of that title.

To view the previously submitted errata, go to `https://www.packtpub.com/books/conten t/support` and enter the name of the book in the search field. The required information will appear under the **Errata** section.

Piracy

Piracy of copyrighted material on the Internet is an ongoing problem across all media. At Packt, we take the protection of our copyright and licenses very seriously. If you come across any illegal copies of our works in any form on the Internet, please provide us with the location address or website name immediately so that we can pursue a remedy.

Please contact us at `copyright@packtpub.com` with a link to the suspected pirated material.

We appreciate your help in protecting our authors and our ability to bring you valuable content.

Questions

If you have a problem with any aspect of this book, you can contact us at `questions@packtpub.com`, and we will do our best to address the problem.

1
Create a User Profile System and use the Null Coalesce Operator

To begin this chapter, let's check out the new **null coalesce** in PHP 7. We'll also learn how to build a simple profiles page with listed users that you can click on, and create a simple CRUD-like system which will enable us to register new users to the system and delete users for banning purposes.

We'll learn to use the PHP 7 null coalesce operator so that we can show data if there is any, or just display a simple message if there isn't any.

Let's create a simple `UserProfile` class. The ability to create classes has been available since PHP 5.

A class in PHP starts with the word `class`, and the name of the class:

```
class UserProfile {

  private $table = 'user_profiles';
}

}
```

We've made the table private and added a `private` variable, where we define which table it will be related to.

Let's add two functions, also known as a method, inside the class to simply fetch the data from the database:

```
function fetch_one($id) {
  $link = mysqli_connect('');
  $query = "SELECT * from ". $this->table . " WHERE `id` =' " .  $id "'";
  $results = mysqli_query($link, $query);
}

function fetch_all() {
  $link = mysqli_connect('127.0.0.1', 'root','apassword','my_dataabase' );
  $query = "SELECT * from ". $this->table . ";
 $results = mysqli_query($link, $query);
}
```

The null coalesce operator

We can use PHP 7's null coalesce operator to allow us to check whether our results contain anything, or return a defined text which we can check on the views, this will be responsible for displaying any data.

Let's put this in a file which will contain all the define statements, and call it:

```
//definitions.php
define('NO_RESULTS_MESSAGE', 'No results found');

require('definitions.php');
function fetch_all() {
    ...same lines ...
    $results = $results ??  NO_RESULTS_MESSAGE;
    return $message;
}
```

On the client side, we'll need to come up with a template to show the list of user profiles.

Let's create a basic HTML block to show that each profile can be a `div` element with several list item elements to output each table.

In the following function, we need to make sure that all values have been filled in with at least the name and the age. Then we simply return the entire string when the function is called:

```
function profile_template( $name, $age, $country ) {
  $name = $name ?? null;
  $age = $age ?? null;
```

```
if($name == null || $age === null) {
  return 'Name or Age need to be set';
} else {

return '<div>

    <li>Name: ' . $name . ' </li>

    <li>Age: ' . $age . '</li>

    <li>Country:  ' .  $country . ' </li>

</div>';
}
}
```

Separation of Concerns

In a proper MVC architecture, we need to separate the view from the models that get our data, and the controllers will be responsible for handling business logic.

In our simple app, we will skip the controller layer since we just want to display the user profiles in one public facing page. The preceding function is also known as the template render part in an MVC architecture.

While there are frameworks available for PHP that use the MVC architecture out of the box, for now we can stick to what we have and make it work.

PHP frameworks can benefit a lot from the null coalesce operator. In some codes that I've worked with, we used to use the ternary operator a lot, but still had to add more checks to ensure a value was not falsy.

Furthermore, the ternary operator can get confusing, and takes some getting used to. The other alternative is to use the isSet function. However, due to the nature of the isSet function, some falsy values will be interpreted by PHP as being a set.

Creating views

Now that we have our model complete, a template render function, we just need to create the view with which we can look at each profile.

Our view will be put inside a `foreach` block, and we'll use the template we wrote to render the right values:

```php
//listprofiles.php

<html>
<!doctype html>
<head>
<link rel="stylesheet"
href="https://maxcdn.bootstrapcdn.com/bootstrap/3.3.6/css/bootstrap.min.css
">
</head>
<body>

<?php
foreach($results as $item) {
   echo profile_template($item->name, $item->age, $item->country;
}
?>
</body>
</html>
```

Let's put the code above into `index.php`.

While we may install the Apache server, configure it to run PHP, install new virtual hosts and the other necessary features, and put our PHP code into an Apache folder, this will take time. So, for the purposes of testing this out, we can just run PHP's server for development.

To run the built-in PHP server (read more at `http://php.net/manual/en/features.commandline.webserver.php`) we will use the folder we are running, inside a terminal:

`php -S localhost:8000`

If we open up our browser, we should see nothing yet, **No results found**. This means we need to populate our database.

If you have an error with your database connection, be sure to replace the correct database credentials we supplied into each of the `mysql_connect` calls that we made.

1. To supply data to our database, we can create a simple SQL script like this:

```sql
INSERT INTO user_profiles ('Chin Wu', 30, 'Mongolia');
INSERT INTO user_profiles ('Erik Schmidt', 22, 'Germany');
INSERT INTO user_profiles ('Rashma Naru', 33, 'India');
```

2. Let's save it in a file such as `insert_profiles.sql`. In the same directory as the SQL file, log on to the MySQL client by using the following command:

   ```
   mysql -u root -p
   ```

3. Then type use <name of database>:

   ```
   mysql>  use <database>;
   ```

4. Import the script by running the source command:

   ```
   mysql> source insert_profiles.sql
   ```

Now our user profiles page should show the following:

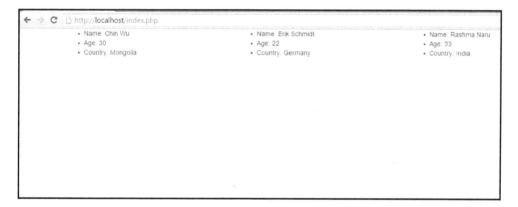

Create a profile input form

Now let's create the HTML form for users to enter their profile data.

Our profiles app would be no use if we didn't have a simple way for a user to enter their user profile details.

We'll create the profile input form like this:

```
//create_profile.php

<html>
<body>
<form action="post_profile.php" method="POST">

  <label>Name</label><input name="name">
```

```
<label>Age</label><input name="age">
<label>Country</label><input name="country">

</form>
</body>
</html>
```

In this profile post, we'll need to create a PHP script to take care of anything the user posts. It will create an SQL statement from the input values and output whether or not they were inserted.

We can use the null coalesce operator again to verify that the user has inputted all values and left nothing undefined or null:

```
$name = $_POST['name'] ?? "";

$age = $_POST['country'] ?? "";

$country = $_POST['country'] ?? "";
```

This prevents us from accumulating errors while inserting data into our database.

First, let's create a variable to hold each of the inputs in one array:

```
$input_values =  [
  'name' => $name,
  'age' => $age,
  'country' => $country
];
```

The preceding code is a new PHP 5.4+ way to write arrays. In PHP 5.4+, it is no longer necessary to put an actual `array()`; the author personally likes the new syntax better.

We should create a new method in our `UserProfile` class to accept these values:

```
Class UserProfile {

 public function insert_profile($values)  {

 $link =  mysqli_connect('127.0.0.1', 'username','password',
 'databasename');

 $q = " INSERT INTO " . $this->table . " VALUES ( '".$values['name']."',
'".$values['age'] . "' ,'".$values['country']. "')";
   return mysqli_query($q);


 }
 }
```

Instead of creating a parameter in our function to hold each argument as we did with our profile template render function, we can simply use an array to hold our values.

This way, if a new field needs to be inserted into our database, we can just add another field to the SQL `insert` statement.

While we are at it, let's create the edit profile section.

For now, we'll assume that whoever is using this edit profile is the administrator of the site.

We'll need to create a page where, provided the `$_GET['id']` has been set, that the user that we will be fetching from the database and displaying on the form. Here is how that code will look like:

```php
<?php
require('class/userprofile.php');//contains the class UserProfile into

$id = $_GET['id'] ?? 'No ID';
//if id was a string, i.e. "No ID", this would go into the if block
if(is_numeric($id)) {
  $profile =  new UserProfile();
  //get data from our database
  $results =   $user->fetch_id($id);
  if($results && $results->num_rows > 0  ) {
     while($obj = $results->fetch_object())
   {
          $name = $obj->name;
          $age = $obj->age;
        $country = $obj->country;
      }
        //display form with a hidden field containing the value of the ID
?>

  <form action="post_update_profile.php" method="post">
  <label>Name</label><input name="name" value="<?=$name?>">
  <label>Age</label><input name="age" value="<?=$age?>">
  <label>Country</label><input name="country" value="<?=country?>">

</form>

  <?php
  } else {
        exit('No such user');
  }
} else {
  echo $id; //this  should be No ID';
  exit;
```

```
    }
```

Notice that we're using what is known as the shortcut `echo` statement in the form. It makes our code simpler and easier to read. Since we're using PHP 7, this feature should come out of the box.

Once someone submits the form, it goes into our `$_POST` variable and we'll create a new `Update` function in our `UserProfile` class.

Admin system

Let's finish off by creating a simple *grid* for an admin dashboard portal that will be used with our user profiles database. Our requirement for this is simple: we can just set up a table-based layout that displays each user profile in rows.

From the grid, we will add the links to be able to edit the profile, or delete it, if we want to. The code to display a table in our HTML view would look like this:

```
<table>
 <tr>
  <td>John Doe</td>
  <td>21</td>
  <td>USA</td>
  <td><a href="edit_profile.php?id=1">Edit</a></td>
  <td><a href="profileview.php?id=1">View</a>
  <td><a href="delete_profile.php?id=1">Delete</a>
 </tr>
</table>
This script to this is the following:
//listprofiles.php
$sql = "SELECT * FROM userprofiles LIMIT $start, $limit ";
$rs_result = mysqli_query ($sql); //run the query

while($row = mysqli_fetch_assoc($rs_result) {
?>
     <tr>
          <td><?=$row['name'];?></td>
          <td><?=$row['age'];?></td>
        <td><?=$row['country'];?></td>

        <td><a href="edit_profile.php?id=<?=$id?>">Edit</a></td>
         <td><a href="profileview.php?id=<?=$id?>">View</a>
         <td><a href="delete_profile.php?id=<?=$id?>">Delete</a>
          </tr>
```

```php
<?php
}
```

There's one thing that we haven't yet created: A `delete_profile.php` page. The view and edit pages have been discussed already.

Here's how the `delete_profile.php` page would look:

```php
<?php

//delete_profile.php
$connection = mysqli_connect('localhost','<username>','<password>',
'<databasename>');

$id = $_GET['id'] ?? 'No ID';

if(is_numeric($id)) {
mysqli_query( $connection, "DELETE FROM userprofiles WHERE id = '" .$id .
"'");
} else {
 echo $id;
}
i(!is_numeric($id)) {
exit('Error: non numeric \$id');
  } else {
echo "Profile #" . $id . " has been deleted";

?>
```

Of course, since we might have a lot of user profiles in our database, we have to create a simple pagination. In any pagination system, you just need to figure out the total number of rows and how many rows you want displayed per page. We can create a function that will be able to return a URL that contains the page number and how many to view per page.

From our queries database, we first create a new function for us to select only up to the total number of items in our database:

```php
class UserProfile{
 // .... Etc ...
function count_rows($table) {
     $dbconn = new mysqli('localhost', 'root', 'somepass',
'databasename');
  $query = $dbconn->query("select COUNT(*) as num from '". $table . "'");

  $total_pages = mysqli_fetch_array($query);

  return $total_pages['num']; //fetching by array, so element 'num' =
```

```
count
}
```

For our pagination, we can create a simple `paginate` function which accepts the `base_url`
of the page where we have pagination, the rows per page – also known as the number of
records we want each page to have – and the total number of records found:

```
require('definitions.php');
require('db.php'); //our database class

Function paginate ($base_url, $rows_per_page, $total_rows) {
   $pagination_links = array(); //instantiate an array to hold our html page
links

   //we can use null coalesce to check if the inputs are  null
   ( $total_rows || $rows_per_page) ?? exit('Error: no rows per page and
total rows);
     //we exit with an error message if this function is called incorrectly
     $pages =  $total_rows % $rows_per_page;
     $i= 0;
        $pagination_links[$i] =  "<a href="http://". $base_url  .
"?pagenum=". $pagenum."&rpp=".$rows_per_page. ">"  . $pagenum . "</a>";
        }
     return $pagination_links;

}
```

This function will help display the above page links in a table:

```
function display_pagination($links) {
      $display = '<div class="pagination">
                  <table><tr>';
      foreach ($links as $link) {
             echo "<td>" . $link . "</td>";
      }

      $display .= '</tr></table></div>';

      return $display;
   }
```

Notice that we're following the principle that there should rarely be any `echo` statements
inside a function. This is because we want to make sure that other users of these functions
are not confused when they debug some mysterious output on their page.

By requiring the programmer to echo out whatever the functions return, it becomes easier to debug our program. Also, we're following the Separation of Concerns, our code doesn't output the display, it just formats the display.

So any future programmer can just update the function's internal code and return something else. It also makes our function reusable; imagine that in the future someone uses our function, this way, they won't have to double check that there's some misplaced echo statement within our functions.

A note on alternative short tags
As you know, another way to echo is to use the <?= tag. You can use it like so: <?="helloworld"?>.These are known as short tags. In PHP 7, alternative PHP tags have been removed. The RFC states that <%, <%=, %> and <script language=php> have been deprecated. The RFC at https://wiki.php.net/rfc/remove_alternative_php_tags says that the RFC does not remove short opening tags (<?) or short opening tags with echo (<?=).

Since we have laid out the groundwork of creating paginate links, we now just have to invoke our functions. The following script is all that is needed to create a paginated page using the preceding function:

```
$mysqli = mysqli_connect('localhost','<username>','<password>',
'<dbname>');

    $limit = $_GET['rpp'] ?? 10;     //how many items to show per page
default 10;

    $pagenum = $_GET['pagenum'];   //what page we are on

    if($pagenum)
      $start = ($pagenum - 1) * $limit; //first item to display on this page
    else
      $start = 0;                       //if no page var is given, set start
to 0
/*Display records here*/
$sql = "SELECT * FROM userprofiles LIMIT $start, $limit ";
$rs_result = mysqli_query ($sql); //run the query

while($row = mysqli_fetch_assoc($rs_result) {
?>
    <tr>
        <td><?php echo $row['name']; ?></td>
        <td><?php echo $row['age']; ?></td>
      <td><?php echo $row['country']; ?></td>
```

```
        </tr>

<?php
}

/* Let's show our page */
/* get number of records through  */
   $record_count = $db->count_rows('userprofiles');

$pagination_links =  paginate('listprofiles.php' , $limit, $rec_count);
 echo display_pagination($paginaiton_links);
```

The HTML output of our page links in `listprofiles.php` will look something like this:

```
<div class="pagination"><table>
 <tr>
       <td> <a href="listprofiles.php?pagenum=1&rpp=10">1</a> </td>
        <td><a href="listprofiles.php?pagenum=2&rpp=10">2</a>  </td>
       <td><a href="listprofiles.php?pagenum=3&rpp=10">2</a>  </td>
    </tr>
</table></div>
```

Summary

As you can see, we have a lot of use cases for the null coalesce.

We learned how to make a simple user profile system, and how to use PHP 7's null coalesce feature when fetching data from the database, which returns null if there are no records. We also learned that the null coalesce operator is similar to a ternary operator, except this returns null by default if there is no data.

In the next chapter, we'll have more use cases for other PHP 7 features, especially when creating the database abstraction layer for use in our projects.

2
Build a Database Class and Simple Shopping Cart

For our previous app, which was just user profiles, we only created a simple **Create-Read-Update-Delete (CRUD)** database abstraction layer – basic stuff. In this chapter, we will create a better database abstraction layer that will allow us to do more than just basic database functions.

Aside from the simple CRUD features, we will add result manipulation into the mix. We'll build the following features into our database abstraction class:

- Conversion of integers to other, more accurate numeric types
- Array to object conversion
- `firstOf()` method: Allows us to select the first of the results of a database query
- `lastOf()` method: Allows us to select the last of the results of a database query
- `iterate()` method: Will allow us to iterate over the results and return it in a format we will send to this function
- `searchString()` method: looks for a string in a list of results

We may add more functions as and when we might need them. Towards the end of the chapter, we will apply the database abstraction layer to build a simple **Shopping Cart** system.

The Shopping Cart is simple: a user who is already logged in should be able to click on some items for sale, click on **add to shopping cart**, and get the user's details. After the user has verified their items, they then click the button to purchase and we'll transfer their Shopping Cart items into a purchase order where they will fill in the delivery address, and then save this into the database.

Building the database abstraction class

In PHP, when creating a class, there is a way to call a certain method every time that class is initialized. This is called the constructor of the class. Most classes have a constructor, and so we shall have our own. The constructor function is named with two underscores with the `construct()` keyword, like this: `function __construct()`. Functions with two underscores are also known as magic methods.

In our database abstraction class we need to create a constructor to be able to return the `link` object generated by `mysqli`:

```
Class DB {
 public $db;
 //constructor
 function __construct($server, $dbname,$user,$pass) {
   //returns mysqli $link $link = mysqli_connect('');
   return $this->db = mysqli_connect($server, $dbname, $user, $pass);
 }
}
```

Raw query method

The `query` method will just execute the query of anything passed to it. We will just call MySQLi's `db->query` method in the `query` method.

Here is what it looks like:

```
public function query($sql) {
 $results =    $this->db->query($sql);
 return $results;
}
```

Create method

For our database layer, let's create the`create` method. With this, we will insert items into a database using SQL syntax. In MySQL, the syntax is as follows:

```
INSERT INTO [TABLE] VALUES ([val1], [val2], [val3]);
```

We need a way to convert array values into a string with each value separated by commas:

```
function create ($table, $arrayValues) {
  $query = "INSERT INTO  `" . $table . " ($arrayVal);   //TODO: setup
arrayVal
  $results = $this->db->query($link, $query);
}
```

Read method

For our db layer, let's create the read method. With this, we will just query our database using SQL syntax.

The syntax in MySQL is as follows:

```
SELECT * FROM [table] WHERE [key] = [value]
```

We'll need to create a function which is able to accept the preceding parameters in brackets:

```
public function read($table, $key, $value){
        $query  = SELECT * FROM $table WHERE `". $key . "` =  " . $value;
      return $this->db->query($query);
}
```

Select all method

Our read method accepts a key and value pair. However, there may be cases where we just need to select everything in a table. In this case, we should create a simple method to select all the rows in a table, which only accepts the table to select as the parameter.

In MySQL, you just select all the rows using the following command:

```
SELECT * FROM [table];
```

We'll need to create a function which is able to accept the preceding parameters in brackets:

```
public function select_all($table){
        $query  = "SELECT * FROM " . $table;
      return $this ->query($query);
}
```

Delete method

For our db layer, let's create the delete method. With this, we will delete some items in a database using SQL syntax.

The MySQL syntax is simple:

```
DELETE FROM [table] WHERE [key] = [val];
```

We'll also need to create a function which is able to accept the preceding parameters in brackets:

```
public function delete($table, $key, $value){
        $query  = DELETE FROM $table WHERE `". $key . "` = " . $value;
    return $this->query($query);
}
```

Update method

For our database layer, let's create an update method. With this, we will be able to update items in a database using SQL syntax.

The MySQL syntax looks like this:

```
UPDATE [table] SET [key1] = [val1], [key2] => [val2]  WHERE [key] = [value]
```

 Note that the WHERE clause can be longer than just one key value pair, meaning you can add AND and OR to the statement. This means that, aside from making the first keys dynamic, the WHERE clause needs to be able to accept AND/OR to its parameter.

For example, you could write the following for the $where parameter to select the person whose firstname is John and lastname is Doe:

```
firstname='John' AND lastname='Doe'
```

This is the reason why we made the condition just a string parameter in our function. The update method in our database class would finally look like this:

```
public function update($table, $updateSetArray, $where){
    Foreach($updateSetArray as $key => $value) {
        $update_fields .= $key . "=" . $value . ",";
    }
     //remove last comma from the foreach loop above
    $update_fields = substr($update_fields,0, str_len($update_fields)-1);
```

```
    $query  = "UPDATE " . $table. " SET " . $updateFields . " WHERE "
$where; //the where
    return $this->query($query);
}
```

first_of method

In our database we will create a `first_of` method which will filter out the rest of the results and just get the very first one. We will use PHP's `reset` function, which just gets the very first element in an array:

```
//inside DB class
public function first_of($results) {
  return reset($results);
}
```

last_of method

The `last_of` method is similar; we can use PHP's `end` function:

```
//inside DB class
public function last_of($results) {
  Return end($results);
}
```

iterate_over method

The `iterate_over` method will be a function which simply adds formatting – before and after HTML code – to a string – for example, for every result we get from the database:

```
public function iterate_over($prefix, $postfix, $items) {
    $ret_val = '';
    foreach($items as $item) {
        $ret_val .= $prefix. $item . $postfix;
    }
    return $ret_val;
}
```

searchString method

Given an array of results, we will look through a certain field for something to search. The way to do this is to generate the SQL code that looks like this:

```
SELECT * FROM {table} WHERE {field} LIKE '%{searchString}%';
```

The function would accept the table, and the field to check the search string `needle` in the table:

```
public function search_string($table, $column, $needle) {
  $results = $this->query("SELECT * FROM `".$table."` WHERE " .    $column .
" LIKE '%" . $needle. "%'");
    return $results;
}
```

Using the convert_to_json method to implement a simple API

Sometimes we want the results of a database to be in a specific format. An example is when we work with the results as JSON objects instead of arrays. This is useful when you are building a simple API to be consumed by a mobile application.

This could be possible, for example, in the case of another system that needs it in a certain format, for example, a JSON format, and we can feed it using the JSON format by converting objects to JSON and sending it off.

In PHP, there is the `json_encode` method, which converts any array or object into a JSON notation. Our class' method will just return the value passed into it as `json`:

```
function convertToJSON($object) {
    return json_encode($object);
    }
```

Shopping Cart

Now we will be building a simplified Shopping Cart module which will take advantage of our newly built database abstraction class.

Let's map out the features of the Shopping Cart:

- **Shopping List page**:
  - The shopper should see several items with their names and prices
  - The shopper should be able to click on a checkbox beside each item which adds it to the cart
- **Checkout page**:
  - List of items and their prices
  - Total
- **Confirmation page**:
  - Input the details such as the bill-to address, bill-to credit card number, and, of course, the name
  - The shopper should also be able to specify which address to send the goods to

Building the shopping items list

In this page, we will create basic HTML blocks to show the list of items that a shopper may wish to buy.

We will use the same template system which we had earlier, but instead of having the entire code in one page, we'll separate out the header and the footer and simply include them in our files using include(). We'll also use the same Bootstrap framework to make our frontend look nice.

Item template rendering function

We'll be creating the item render function which will render all our shopping items in div. The function will simply return the HTML markup of an item with the price, name, and picture image of the item:

```
//accepts the database results as an array and calls db functions
render_shopping_items($items)
{
$db->iterate_over("<td>", "</td>", $item_name);
    foreach($items as $item) {
      $item->name.  ' ' .$item->price . ' ' . $item->pic;


    }
$resultTable .= "</table>";
```

```
}
```

In the preceding code, we used our freshly created `iterate_over` function, which formats each value of the database. The end result is we have a table of the items we want to buy.

Let's create a simple layout structure which simply gets the header and footer in each page we build, and from now on, simply includes them:

In `header.php`:

```
<html>
<!doctype html>
<head>
<link rel="stylesheet"
href="https://maxcdn.bootstrapcdn.com/bootstrap/3.3.6/css/bootstrap.min.css
">
</head>
<body>
```

In `footer.php`:

```
<div class="footer">Copyright 2016</div></body>
</html>
```

In `index.php`:

```
<?php
require('header.php');
//render item_list code goes here
require('itemslist.php'); //to be coded
require('footer.php');
?>
```

Now let's create the `itemslist.php` page which will be included in the `index.php`:

```
<?php
include('DB.php');
$db = new DB();
$table = 'shopping_items';
$results = $db->select_all($table);
//calling the render function created earlier:
foreach(as $item) {
   echo render_shopping_items($results);
}

?>
//shopping items list goes here.
```

Our functions are ready but our database does not exist yet. We also need to populate our database.

Let's create some shopping items by creating the `shopping_items` table in our MySQL database:

```
CREATE TABLE shopping_items (
    id INT(11) NOT NULL AUTO_INCREMENT,
    name VARCHAR(255) NOT NULL,
    price DECIMAL(6,2) NOT NULL,
    image VARCHAR(255) NOT NULL,
PRIMARY KEY  (id)
);
```

Let's run MySQL and insert the following items into our database:

```
INSERT INTO `shopping_items` VALUES (NULL,'Tablet', '199.99',
'tablet.png');
INSERT INTO `shopping_items` VALUES (NULL, 'Cellphone', '199.99',
'cellphone.png');
INSERT INTO `shopping_items` (NULL,'Laptop', '599.99', 'Laptop.png');
INSERT INTO `shopping_items` (NULL,'Cable', '14.99', 'Cable.png');
INSERT INTO `shopping_items` (NULL, 'Watch', '100.99', 'Watch.png');
```

Let's save it in a file `insert_shopping_items.sql`. Then, in the same directory as the `insert_shopping_items.sql` file:

1. Log on to MySQL client and follow the procedure:

   mysql -u root -p

2. Then type `use <name of database>`:

   mysql> use <database>;

3. Import the script by using the `source` command:

   mysql> source insert_shopping_items.sql

When we run SELECT * FROM shopping_items, we should see the following:

```
mysql> SELECT * FROM shopping_items;
+----+-----------+--------+---------------+
| id | name      | price  | image         |
+----+-----------+--------+---------------+
|  1 | Tablet    | 199.99 | tablet.png    |
|  2 | Cellphone | 199.99 | cellphone.png |
|  3 | Laptop    | 599.99 | laptop.png    |
|  4 | Cable     |  14.99 | cable.png     |
|  5 | Watch     |  99.99 | watch.png     |
+----+-----------+--------+---------------+
5 rows in set (0.00 sec)
```

Adding checkboxes to the Shopping List page

Now let's create the HTML checkboxes for a user to be able to select a shopping item. We'll create the form to insert the data as follows:

```
//items.php

<html>
<body>

<form action="post_profile.php" method="POST">
<table>
  <input type="checkbox" value="<item_id>"> <td><item_image></td>
  <td><item_name></td><td>
 </table>
</form>
</body>
</html>
```

To do this, we'll need to modify our render_items method to add a checkbox:

```
public function render_items($itemsArray) {

foreach($itemsArray as $item) {
  return '<tr>
          <td><input type="checkbox" name="item[]" value="' . $item->id.
'">' .  . '</td><td>' . $item->image .'</td>
<td>'. $item->name . '</td>
'<td>'.$item->price . '</td>
'</tr>';
  }
 }
```

On the next page, when the user clicks on **submit**, we'll have to get all the IDs in an array.

Since we named our checkbox `item[]`, we should be able to get the values via `$_POST['item']` as an array. Basically, all the items that were checked will go into PHP's `$_POST` variable as an array, which will allow us to get all the values for saving our data into our database. Let's loop through the results' IDs and get the price for each in our database and save each item in an array called `itemsArray`, with the key as the name of the item and its price as the value of the item:

```
$db = new DB();
$itemsArray= []; //to contain our items - since PHP 5.4, an array can be
defined with [];
foreach($_POST['item'] as $itemId) {

    $item = $db->read('shopping_items', 'id', $itemId);
    //this produces the equivalent SQL code: SELECT * FROM shopping_items
WHERE id = '$itemId';
    $itemsArray[$item->name] = $item-price;

}
```

We are going to first confirm with the user about the items that were purchased. We will just save the items and the total amount into a cookie for now. We will access the values of the cookie on our checkout page, which will accept the user's details and save them to our database on submission of the checkout page.

> PHP session versus cookies: For data which is not very sensitive, such as the list of items a user has purchased, we can use cookies, which actually store the data (in plain text!) in the browser. If you are building this application and using it in production, it is recommended to use sessions. To learn more about sessions, go to `http://php.net/manual/en/feature s.sessions.php`.

Cookies in PHP

In PHP, to start a cookie, you just call the `setcookie` function. To save our items purchased into a cookie, we must serialize the array, the reason being, the cookies only store values as strings.

Here, we save the items into the cookie:

```
setcookie('purchased_items', serialize($itemsArray), time() + 900);
```

The preceding cookie will store the items as an array in the `purchased_items` cookie. It will expire in 15 minutes (900 seconds). However, notice the call to the `time()` function, which returns the Unix timestamp of the current time. Cookies in PHP will expire when the time set in the last parameter has been reached.

 Debugging your cookie-based application is sometimes frustrating. Make sure that the timestamp generated by `time()` is really showing the current time.

For example, it could happen that you have recently reformatted your computer and for some reason was not able to set the time correctly. To test the `time()`, simply run a PHP script with the `time()` call and check h `ttp://www.unixtimestamp.com/` if they are almost the same.

Building the Checkout page

Finally, we'll create a form where the user can input their details after checking out.

We first need to build the database table for the customer. Let's call this table `purchases`. We'll need to store the customer's name, address, e-mail, credit card, items purchased, and the total. We should also store the time of the purchase transaction and use a unique primary key to index each row.

The following is our table's schema to be imported into our MySQL database:

```
CREATE TABLE purchases (
    id INT(11) NOT NULL AUTO_INCREMENT,
    customer_name VARCHAR(255) NOT NULL,
    address DECIMAL(6,2) NOT NULL,
    email DECIMAL(6,2) NOT NULL,
    credit_card VARCHAR(255) NOT NULL,
    items TEXT NOT NULL,
    total DECIMAL(6,2) NOT NULL,
    created DATETIME NOT NULL,
    PRIMARY KEY (id)
);
```

One way to import this is by creating a file `purchases.sql`, then logging in to your MySQL command-line tool.

Then, you can select the database you want to use with:

```
USE <databasename>
```

Finally, assuming you are on the same directory as `purchases.sql`, you can run:

```
SOURCE purchases.sql
```

Let's finish off by creating a simple form with input fields for details such as the address, credit card, and name of the buyer:

```
<form action="save_checkout.php" method="post">
<table>
  <tr>
   <td>Name</td><td><input type="text" name="fullname"></td>
  </tr>
 <tr>
<td>Address</td><td><input type="text" name="address"></td>
</tr>
<tr>
<td>Email</td><td><input type="text" name="email"></td>
</tr>

<tr>
  <td>Credit Card</td><td><input type="text" name="credit_card"></td>
 </tr>
<tr>
  <td colspan="2"><input type="submit" name="submit" value="Purchase"></td>
 </tr>

</table>
</form>
```

Here is how it looks:

Finally, we'll save everything into another table in our database by using our DB class as usual. To calculate the total amount, we will query the database for the prices and use the `array_sum` of PHP to get the total:

```
$db = new DB($server,$dbname,$name,$password);


//let's get the other details of the customer
$customer_name = $_POST['fullname'];
$address = $_POST['address'];
$email = $_POST['email'];
$credit_card = $_POST['credit_card];
$time_now = date('Y-m-d H:i:s');

foreach($purchased_items as $item) {
  $prices[] = $item->price;
}


//get total using array_sum
$total = array_sum($prices);

$db->insert('purchases', [
    'address' => $address,
  'email' => $email,
  'credit_card' => $credit_card,
    'items' => //<all the items and prices>//,
    'total' => $total,
     'purchase_date' => $timenow
   ]);
?>
```

To keep things simple, as you can see in the highlighted code, we need to collect all the items that were bought into one long string, for saving in our database. Here's how you can concatenate each item and their prices:

```
foreach($purchased_items as $item) {
    $items_text .= $item->name ":" . $item->price .  ","
}
```

Then we can save this data into the variable `$items_text`. We will update the preceding highlighted code and change the text `<all the items and prices>` into it with `$items_text`:

```
...
  'items' => $items_text
  ...
```

The preceding `foreach` loop should be placed before the call to the `$db->insert` method in our code.

Thank you page

Finally, we've saved the data into our `purchased_items` table. It's time to say thank you to our customer and send an e-mail. In our HTML code of `thankyou.php`, we will just write a thank you note and let the user know that an e-mail is on its way regarding their purchases.

Here's a screenshot:

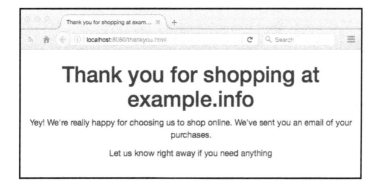

We'll name the file `thankyou.php`, and its HTML code is pretty simple:

```html
<!DOCTYPE html>
<html>
<head>
    <!-- Latest compiled and minified CSS -->
    <link rel="stylesheet"
href="https://maxcdn.bootstrapcdn.com/bootstrap/3.3.6/css/bootstrap.min.css
"
integrity="sha384-1q8mTJOASx8j1Au+a5WDVnPi2lkFfwwEAa8hDDdjZlpLegxhjVME1fgjW
PGmkzs7" crossorigin="anonymous">
    <title>Thank you for shopping at example.info</title>
</head>
<body>
 <div class="container">
        <div class="row">
            <div class="col-lg-12 text-center">
                <h1>Thank you for shopping at example.info</h1>
                    <p>Yey! We're really happy for choosing us to shop
online. We've sent you an email of your purchases. </p>
```

```
              <p>Let us know right away if you need anything</p>
        </div>
      </div>
    </div>
  </body>
</html>
```

Sending an e-mail using PHP is done using the `mail()` function:

```
mail("<to address>", "Your purchase at example.com","Thank you for
purchasing...", "From: <from address>");
```

The third parameter is the message of our e-mail. In the code, we still need to add the details of the purchase. We shall loop through the cookie we made earlier and the prices, then just output the total amount, and send the message:

```
$mail_message = 'Thank you for purchasing the following items';
$prices = [];
$purchased_items = unserialize($_COOKIE['purchased_items']);
foreach($purchased_items as $itemName => $itemPrice) {
  $mail_message .= $itemName . ": " .$itemPrice . "\r\n \r\n";
  //since this is a plain text email, we will use \r\n – which are escape
strings for us to add a new line after each price.
  $prices[] = $itemPrice;
}

$mail_message .= "The billing total of your purchases is " .
array_sum($prices);

mail($_POST['email'], "Thank you for shopping at example.info here is your
bill", $mail_message, "From: billing@example.info");
```

We can add the preceding bit of code at the very end of our `thankyou.php` file.

Installing TCPDF

You can download the TCPDF library from sourceforge, `https://sourceforge.net/proje cts/tcpdf/`

TCPDF is a PHP class for writing PDF documents.

A sample code with a PHP example of TCPDF's, looks as follows:

```
//Taken from http://www.tcpdf.org/examples/example_001.phps

// Include the main TCPDF library (search for installation path).
```

```php
require_once('tcpdf_include.php');

// create new PDF document
$pdf = new TCPDF(PDF_PAGE_ORIENTATION, PDF_UNIT, PDF_PAGE_FORMAT, true,
'UTF-8', false);

// set document information
$pdf->SetCreator(PDF_CREATOR);
$pdf->SetAuthor('Nicola Asuni');
$pdf->SetTitle('TCPDF Example 001');
$pdf->SetSubject('TCPDF Tutorial');
$pdf->SetKeywords('TCPDF, PDF, example, test, guide');

// set default header data
$pdf->SetHeaderData(PDF_HEADER_LOGO, PDF_HEADER_LOGO_WIDTH,
PDF_HEADER_TITLE.' 001', PDF_HEADER_STRING, array(0,64,255),
array(0,64,128));
$pdf->setFooterData(array(0,64,0), array(0,64,128));

// set header and footer fonts
$pdf->setHeaderFont(Array(PDF_FONT_NAME_MAIN, '', PDF_FONT_SIZE_MAIN));
$pdf->setFooterFont(Array(PDF_FONT_NAME_DATA, '', PDF_FONT_SIZE_DATA));

// set default monospaced font
$pdf->SetDefaultMonospacedFont(PDF_FONT_MONOSPACED);

// set margins
$pdf->SetMargins(PDF_MARGIN_LEFT, PDF_MARGIN_TOP, PDF_MARGIN_RIGHT);
$pdf->SetHeaderMargin(PDF_MARGIN_HEADER);
$pdf->SetFooterMargin(PDF_MARGIN_FOOTER);

// set auto page breaks
$pdf->SetAutoPageBreak(TRUE, PDF_MARGIN_BOTTOM);

// set image scale factor
$pdf->setImageScale(PDF_IMAGE_SCALE_RATIO);

// set some language-dependent strings (optional)
if (@file_exists(dirname(__FILE__).'/lang/eng.php')) {
    require_once(dirname(__FILE__).'/lang/eng.php');
    $pdf->setLanguageArray($l);
}

// ---------------------------------------------------------

// set default font subsetting mode
$pdf->setFontSubsetting(true);
```

```php
// Set font
// dejavusans is a UTF-8 Unicode font, if you only need to
// print standard ASCII chars, you can use core fonts like
// helvetica or times to reduce file size.
$pdf->SetFont('dejavusans', '', 14, '', true);

// Add a page
// This method has several options, check the source code documentation for
more information.
$pdf->AddPage();

// set text shadow effect
$pdf->setTextShadow(array('enabled'=>true, 'depth_w'=>0.2, 'depth_h'=>0.2,
'color'=>array(196,196,196), 'opacity'=>1, 'blend_mode'=>'Normal'));

// Set some content to print
$html = <<<EOD
<h1>Welcome to <a href="http://www.tcpdf.org" style="text-
decoration:none;background-color:#CC0000;color:black;"> <span
style="color:black;">TC</span><span
style="color:white;">PDF</span> </a>!</h1>
<i>This is the first example of TCPDF library.</i>
<p>This text is printed using the <i>writeHTMLCell()</i> method but you can
also use: <i>Multicell(), writeHTML(), Write(), Cell() and Text()</i>.</p>
<p>Please check the source code documentation and other examples for
further information.</p>
<p style="color:#CC0000;">TO IMPROVE AND EXPAND TCPDF I NEED YOUR SUPPORT,
PLEASE <a
href="http://sourceforge.net/donate/index.php?group_id=128076">MAKE A
DONATION!</a></p>
EOD;

// Print text using writeHTMLCell()
$pdf->writeHTMLCell(0, 0, '', '', $html, 0, 1, 0, true, '', true);

// ---------------------------------------------------------

// Close and output PDF document
// This method has several options, check the source code documentation for
more information.
$pdf->Output('example_001.pdf', 'I');
```

With this example, we can now use the preceding code and modify it a bit in order same in order to create our own invoice. All we need is the same HTML styling and the values generated by our total. Let's use the same code and update the values to the ones we need.

In this case, we will set the Author to be the site's name, `example.info`. And set our subject to `Invoice`.

First, we need to acquire the main TCPDF library. If you installed it on a different folder, we may need to provide a relative path which points to the `tcpdf_include.php` file:

```
require_once('tcpdf_include.php');
```

This instantiates a new TCPDF object with the default orientations and default page formats from the class:

```
$pdf = new TCPDF(PDF_PAGE_ORIENTATION, PDF_UNIT, PDF_PAGE_FORMAT, true,
'UTF-8', false);

$pdf = new TCPDF(PDF_PAGE_ORIENTATION, PDF_UNIT, PDF_PAGE_FORMAT, true,
'UTF-8', false);

// set document information
$pdf->SetCreator(PDF_CREATOR);
$pdf->SetAuthor('Example.Info');
$pdf->SetTitle('Invoice Purchases');
$pdf->SetSubject('Invoice');
$pdf->SetKeywords('Purchases, Invoice, Shopping');
s

$html = <<<EOD
<h1>Example.info Invoice </h1>
<i>Invoice #0001.</i>
EOD;
```

Now, let's use HTML to create an HTML table of the purchases of a customer:

```
$html .= <<<EOD
<table>
  <tr>
    <td>Item Purchases</td>
    <td>Price</td>
  </tr>
EOD;
```

 This style of writing out multi-line strings is known as the heredoc syntax.

Let's create a connection to the database by instantiating our DB class:

```
$db = new DBClass('localhost','root','password', 'databasename');
We shall now query our database with our database class:


$table = 'purchases';
$column = 'id';
$findVal = $_GET['purchase_id'];

    $result = $db->read ($table, $column, $findVal);

foreach($item = $result->fetch_assoc()) {
$html .=    "<tr>
            <td>". $item['customer_name']. "</td>
            <td>" . $item['items'] . "
</tr>";

$total = $items['total']; //let's save the total in a variable for printing
in a new row


}

$html .= '<tr><td colspan="2" align="right">TOTAL: ' ".$total. " '
</td></tr>';

$html .= <<<EOD
</table>
EOD;

$pdf->writeHTML($html, true, false, true, false, '');

$pdf->Output('customer_invoice.pdf', 'I');
```

In creating PDFs, it's important to note that most HTML to PDF converters are created simple and can interpret simple-inline CSS layouts. We used tables to print out each item, which is okay for table data. It provides a structure to the layout and makes sure that things are properly aligned.

Admin for managing purchases

We'll be building the admin system for handling all our purchases. This is in order to keep track of each customer that bought something from our site. It will consist of two pages:

- An overview of all customers who purchased something
- Being able to view the items purchased by a customer

We will also be adding some features to these pages in order to make it easier for an admin to make changes to a customer's information.

We'll also create a simple **htaccess apache rule** in order to block other people from accessing our admin site, because it contains highly sensitive data.

Let's first start selecting all the data inside our purchases table:

```php
<?php
//create an html variable for printing the html of our page:
$html = '<!DOCTYPE html><html><body>';

$table = 'purchases';
$results = $db->select_all($table);

//start a new table structure and set the headings of our table:
$html .= '<table><tr>
    <th>Customer name</th>
    <th>Email</th>
    <th>Address</th>
    <th>Total Purchase</th>
</tr>';

//loop through the results of our query:
while($row = $results->fetch_assoc()){
    $html .= '<tr><td>'$row['customer_name'] . '</td>';
    $html .= '<td>'$row['email'] . '</td>';
    $html .= '<td>'$row['address'] . '</td>';
    $html .= '<td>'$row['purchase_date'] . '</td>';
    $html .= '</tr>';
}

$html .= '</table>';
$html .= '</body></html>';

//print out the html
echo $html;
```

We shall now add a link to another view of our customer data. This view will enable the admin to see all their purchases. We can link the first page to the detailed view of the customer's purchase by adding a link on the customer's name, by changing the line where we've added the customer's name to the $html variable to this:

```
$html .= '<tr><td><a href="view_purchases.php?pid='.$row['id']
.'">'.$row['customer_name'] . '</a></td>';
```

Notice that we've made the $row['id'] be part of the URL. We can now access the ID number of the data we will be getting through the $_GET['pid'] value.

Let's create the code for viewing a customer's purchased items in a new file – view_purchases.php:

```php
<?php
//create an html variable for printing the html of our page:
$html = '<!DOCTYPE html><html><body>';

$table = 'purchases;
$column = 'id';
$purchase_id = $_GET['pid'];
$results = $db->read($table, $column, $purchase_id);
//outputs:
// SELECT * FROM purchases WHERE id = '$purchase_id';

//start a new table structure and set the headings of our table:
$html .= '<table><tr><th>Customer name</thth>Total Purchased</th></tr>';
//loop through the results of our query:
while($row = $results->fetch_assoc()){
    $html .= '<tr><td>'$row['customer_name'] . '</td>';
    $html .= '<tr><td>'$row['email'] . '</td>';
    $html .= '<tr><td>'$row['address'] . '</td>';
    $html .= '<tr><td>'$row['purchase_date'] . '</td>';
    $html .= '</tr>';
}
$html .= '</table>';
echo $html;
```

In the preceding code, we've used the $_GET['id'] variable for us to look up the table for the exact purchases of the customer. While we could have just used the customer name to look up the customer's purchases from the table purchases, that would assume that the customer only purchased once through our system. Also, we didn't use the customer name to determine if we sometimes have customers that have the same name.

By using the primary ID of the table `purchases`, in our case, selecting by the `id` field ensures that we are selecting that particular unique purchase. Note that because our database is simple, we are able to just query one table in our database – the `purchases` table – in our case.

Perhaps a better implementation might be to separate the `purchases` table into two tables – one containing the customer's details, and another containing the purchased items details. This way, if the same customer returns, their details can be automatically filled in next time, and we just need to link the new items purchased to their account.

The `purchases` table, in this case, would simply be called `purchased_items` table, and each item would be linked to a customer ID. The customer details would be stored in a `customers` table, containing their unique address, e-mail and credit card details.

You would then be able to show a customer their purchase history. Each time the customer buys from the store, the transaction date would be recorded and you would have to sort the history by date and time of each entry.

Summary

Great, we're done!

We just learned how to build a simple database abstraction layer, and how to use it for a Shopping Cart. We also learned about cookies and building an invoice using the TCPDF library.

In the next chapter, we'll build a completely different thing and use sessions to save the current user information of a user in building a PHP-based chat system.

3
Building a Social Newsletter Service

According to a reliable dictionary, a newsletter is a bulletin issued periodically to the members of a society, business, or organization.

In this chapter, we will be building an e-mail newsletter, that allows members to subscribe and unsubscribe, receive updates on certain categories, and also allows a marketer to check how many people visited a certain link.

We'll be building an authentication system for our users to log in and log out of the newsletter management system, which is a social login system for subscribed members to easily check their subscriptions, and simple dashboards for subscribers and administrators.

Authentication system

In this chapter, we will implement a new authentication system in order to allow administrators of the newsletter to be authenticated. Since PHP5, PHP has improved and added a feature that object-oriented developers have used to separate namespaces.

Let's start by defining a namespace named Newsletter as follows:

```php
<?php
namespace Newsletter;
//this must always be in every class that will use namespaces
class Authentication {
}
?>
```

In the preceding example, our `Newsletter` namespace will have an `Authentication` class. When other classes or PHP scripts need to use `Newsletter`'s `Authentication` class, they can simple declare it using the following code:

```
Use Newsletter\Authentication;
```

Inside our `Newsletter` class, let's create a simple check for the user using **bcrypt**, which is a popular and secure way of creating and storing hashed passwords.

 Since PHP 5.5, bcrypt is built into the `password_hash()` PHP function. PHP's `password_hash()` function allows a password to become a hash. In reverse, when you need to verify that hash matches the original password, you can use the `password_verify()` function.

Our class will be fairly simple-it will have one function used to verify if an e-mail address, and the hashed password that was entered is the same as the one in the database. We have to create a simple class that has only one method, `verify()`, which accepts the e-mail and the password of the user. We will use `bcrypt` to verify that the hashed password is the same as the one in our database:

```
Class Authorization {
    public function verify($email, $password) {
        //check for the $email and password encrypted with bcrypt
        $bcrypt_options = [
            'cost' => 12,
            'salt' => 'secret'
        ];
        $password_hash = password_hash($password, PASSWORD_BCRYPT,
$bcrypt_options);
        $q= "SELECT * FROM users WHERE email = '". $email. "' AND password
= '".$password_hash. "'";
        if($result = $this->db->query($q)) {
                while ($obj = results->fetch_object()) {
                        $user_id = $obj->id;
}
        } else {
    $user_id = null;
}
        $result->close();
        $this->db->close();
        return $user_id;
    }
}
```

We, however, need to get the DB class to be able to do a simple query with our database. For this simple one-off project, we can simply use the concept of dependency injection in our Authentication class.

We should create a fairly trivial IOC container class, which allows us to instantiate the database along with it.

Let's call it DbContainer, which allows us to connect a class, such as Authentication, to the DB class:

```
Namespace Newsletter;
use DB;
Class DbContainer {
    Public function getDBConnection($dbConnDetails) {
    //connect to database here:
     $DB = new \DB($server, $username, $password, $dbname);
        return $DB;
    }
}
```

However, if you use this function right away, an error will state that the file could not find and will load the DB class.

Previously, we used the use system of requiring classes. In order for this to work, we need to create an autoloader function to load our DB class without having to use require statements.

In PHP, there is the spl_autoload_register function we can create, which will take care of requiring the files needed automatically.

Following is the example implementation based on the example that can be found in the PHP manual:

```
<?php
/**
 * After registering this autoload function with SPL, the following line
 * would cause the function to attempt to load the \Newsletter\Qux class
 * from /path/to/project/src/Newsletter/Qux.php:
 *
 *      new \Newsletter\Qux;
 *
 * @param string $class The fully-qualified class name.
 * @return void
 */
spl_autoload_register(function ($class) {
    // project-specific namespace prefix
```

```
    $prefix = 'Newsletter';
    // base directory for the namespace prefix
    $base_dir = __DIR__ . '/src/';
    // does the class use the namespace prefix?
    $len = strlen($prefix);
    if (strncmp($prefix, $class, $len) !== 0) {
        // no, move to the next registered autoloader
        return;
    }
    // get the relative class name
    $relative_class = substr($class, $len);
    // replace the namespace prefix with the base directory,
//replace namespace
    // separators with directory separators in the relative class
//name, append
    // with .php
    $file = $base_dir . str_replace('', '/', $relative_class) . '.php';
    // if the file exists, require it
    if (file_exists($file)) {
        require $file;
    }
});
```

With the preceding code, we would now need to create a src directory and use this separator \\ convention in separating the folder structure within your application.

Using this example means we'll need to put the database class file DB.class.php inside the src folder and rename the filename to just DB.php.

This was done so that when you specify that you want to use DB class in another PHP script, PHP will simply perform a require src/DB.php behind the scenes automatically.

Continuing with our example DbContainer, we'll need to somehow pass all our configuration information (that is, name of the database, username, and password to the MySQL database) inside the DbContainer.

Let's simply create a file dbconfig.php that has the database details and returns it as an object, and require it:

```
//sample dbconfig.php
return array('server' => 'localhost',
    'username' => 'root',
    'password => '',
    'dbname' => 'newsletterdb'
);
```

In our `DbContainer` class, let's create a `loadConfig()` function that reads from the `dbconfig.php` file and instantiates a database connection:

```
Class DbContainer {
public function  loadConfig ($filePath) {
   if($filePath) {
     $config = require($filePath);
     return $config; //contains the array
   }

}
```

Now we need to create a `connect()` method, which will enable us to simply connect to a MySQL database and only return the connection:

```
Class DB {
//...
public function connect($server, $username, $password, $dbname) {
   $this->connection = new MySQLI($server, $username, $password, $dbname);
      return $this->connection;
}
}
```

We made our function flexible by not hard-coding the filename into our function. When calling `loadConfig()`, we need to put the path to the `config` file to load.

We also use the `$this` keyword so that any time we need to refer to other functions within the `DB` class, we just have to call `$DB->nameOfMethod(someParams)` after the autoloader loads and instantiates the `DB` class automatically when you call `$DB = new \DB()`.

With this, we now have the flexibility to easily change the `config` file's path in case we move the `config` file to other paths, for example, to a folder that is not directly accessible through the Web.

Then, we can easily use this function and generate a database instance in a separate class, for example, in our `Newsletter` class, we can now make a reference to an instance of the `DB` class connection and instantiate it within the `Newsletter` class.

Now that we're done with this, we should simply create a Bootstrap file that loads the `spl_autoload_register` function and the connection to the database using the `dbContainer` all together. Let's name the file `bootstrap.php`, and it should contain the following:

```
require('spl_autoloader_function.php');

$dbContainer = new \DBContainer; //loads our DB from src folder, using the
spl_autoload_functionabove.

$dbConfig = $db->getConfig('dbconfig.php');

$dbContainer = getDB($dbConfig); //now contains the array of database
configuration details
```

The next step is to connect to the database with the following code:

```
$DB = new \DB;
$DBConn =
$DB->connect($dbContainer['server'],$dbContainer['username'],$dbContainer['
password'],$dbContainer['dbname']);
```

After we've all connected to the database, we need to rewrite our authorization query to use the new initialized classes.

Let's create a simple `select_where` method in our DB class and then call it from the `Authorization` class:

```
public function select_where($table, $where_clause) {
    return $this->db->query("SELECT * FROM ". $table." WHERE " .
$where_clause);
}
```

The `Authorization` class now looks as follows:

```
Class Authorization {
    //this is used to get the database class into Authorization
    Public function instantiateDB($dbInstance){
        $this->db = $dbInstance;
    }

    public function verify($email, $password) {
        //check for the $email and password encrypted with bcrypt
        $bcrypt_options = [
            'cost' => 12,
            'salt' => 'secret'
        ];
```

```
        $password_hash = password_hash($password, PASSWORD_BCRYPT,
$bcrypt_options);
        //select with condition
        $this->db->select_where('users', "email = '$email' AND password =
'$password_hash'");
        if($result = $this->db->query($q)) {
                while ($obj = results->fetch_object()) {
                        $user_id = $obj->id;
}
        } else {
    $user_id = null;
}
        $result->close();
        $this->db->close();
        return $user_id;
    }
}
```

Creating a social login for members

For us to have more people subscribing easily, we will implement a way for Facebook users to simply log in and subscribe to our newsletter without having to type their e-mail address.

Login via Facebook works through **Oauth**. The first step is to generate app authentication tokens by going to `https://developers.facebook.com/`.

You should see your list of apps or click on the apps to create. You should see something similar to the following screenshot:

You should create an app first and be able to obtain your app ID and app secret by visiting the app creation page, similar to the following screenshot:

When creating the new app, Facebook now includes a way for you to test that app ID.

This is what it looks like:

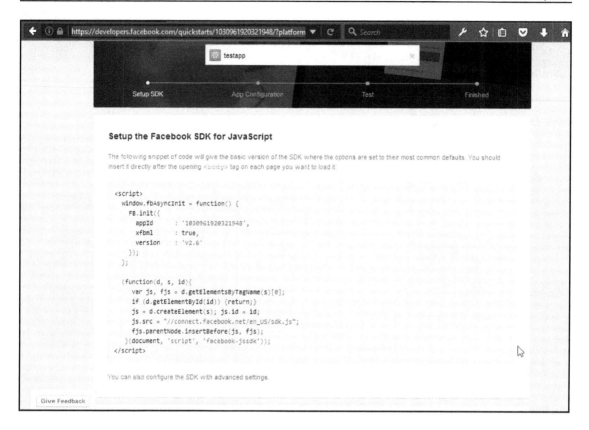

This is for you to test that the app ID actually works. It is optional and you may skip that step and just plug in the values for your app ID and app secret into the code shown in the preceding screenshot.

Now let's create the `fbconfig.php` file, which will contain a way for us to use the Facebook SDK library to enable the session.

The `fbconfig.php` script will contain the following:

```php
<?php
session_start();
$domain = 'http://www.socialexample.info';
require_once 'autoload.php';

use FacebookFacebookSession;
use FacebookFacebookRedirectLoginHelper;
use FacebookFacebookRequest;
use FacebookFacebookResponse;
use FacebookFacebookSDKException;
```

```
use FacebookFacebookRequestException;
use FacebookFacebookAuthorizationException;
use FacebookGraphObject;
use FacebookEntitiesAccessToken;
use FacebookHttpClientsFacebookCurlHttpClient;
use FacebookHttpClientsFacebookHttpable;

// init app with app id and secret (get from creating an app)
$fbAppId = '123456382121312313'; //change this.
$fbAppSecret = '8563798aasdasdasdweqwe84';
FacebookSession::setDefaultApplication($fbAppId, $fbAppSecret);
// login helper with redirect_uri
    $helper = new FacebookRedirectLoginHelper($domain . '/fbconfig.php' );
try {
  $session = $helper->getSessionFromRedirect();
} catch( FacebookRequestException $ex ) {
echo "Hello, sorry but we've encountered an exception and could not log you
in right now";
} catch( Exception $ex ) {
  // Tell user something has happened
  echo "Hello, sorry but we could not log you in right now";
}
// see if we have a session
if ( isset( $session ) ) {
  // graph api request for user data
  $request = new FacebookRequest( $session, 'GET', '/me' );
  $response = $request->execute();
  // get response
//start a graph object with the user email
  $graphObject = $response->getGraphObject();
  $id = $graphObject->getProperty('id');
  $fullname = $graphObject->getProperty('name');
  $email = $graphObject->getProperty('email');

    $_SESSION['FB_id'] = $id;
    $_SESSION['FB_fullname'] = $fullname;
    $_SESSION['FB_email'] =  $email;
//save user to session
    $_SESSION['UserName'] = $email; //just for demonstration purposes
//redirect user to index page
    header("Location: index.php");
} else {
  $loginUrl = $helper->getLoginUrl();
 header("Location: ".$loginUrl);
}
?>
```

Here, we basically start a session with `session_start()` and set up the domain of our website by saving it into a variable. We then autoload the FB SDK, which will require the files and classes needed by Facebook to access its API for logging in.

We then set up several dependencies on other Facebook SDK classes by using the `use` keyword. We set up the `facebookSession` class with our app ID and app secret and then attempt to get a session started by calling the `getSessionfromRedirect()` method.

If there are any errors that get caught from trying to start the session, we simply let the user know that we could not log him in, but if everything proceeds successfully, we start a graph object with the e-mail of the user.

For our demonstration purposes, we save a username that is actually the e-mail address of the user once we get the e-mail by using the Facebook graph.

We will authenticate everyone by checking their e-mail addresses anyway, and to make it easier for a user to login, let's just store their e-mail as the username.

We'll need to finish up our site with `index.php` that shows the user what's inside our site. We get there after the login from Facebook page redirects the user to the `index.php` page.

We'll keep it simple for now and display the full name from the Facebook profile of the user who logged in. We'll add a logout link to give the user an option to logout:

```php
<?php
session_start();
?>
<!doctype html>
<html xmlns:fb="http://www.facebook.com/2008/fbml">
  <head>
    <title>Login to SocialNewsletter.com</title>
<link href="
https://maxcdn.bootstrapcdn.com/bootstrap/3.3.6/css/bootstrap.min.css"
rel="stylesheet">
  </head>
  <body>
  <?php if ($_SESSION['FB_id']): ?>        <!-- After user login  -->
<div class="container">
<div class="hero-unit">
  <h1>Hello <?php echo $_SESSION['UserName']; ?></h1>
  <p>How to login with PHP</p>
  </div>
<div class="span4">
 <ul class="nav nav-list">
<li class="nav-header">FB ID: <?php echo $_SESSION['FB_id']; ?></li>
<li> Welcome <?php echo $_SESSION['FB_fullName']; ?></li>
```

```
<div><a href="logout.php">Logout</a></div>
</ul></div></div>
    <?php else: ?>      <!-- Before login -->
<div class="container">
<h1>Login with Facebook</h1>
         Not Connected with Facebook.
<div>
      <a href="fbconfig.php">Login with Facebook</a></div>
      </div>
    <?php endif ?>
  </body>
</html>
```

After logging in, we just have to display the dashboard for the user. We will discuss how to create a basic dashboard for the user in the next section.

Member dashboard

Finally, when the member has logged in our app, they can now subscribe to newsletters using the member subscription page. Let's first build out the databases that will be used to store member details and their subscriptions. The `member_details` table will include the following:

- `firstname` and `lastname`: The real name of the user
- `email`: To be able to e-mail the user
- `canNotify`: Boolean (true or false), if they accept being e-mailed notifications about other offers

 Here's something that's interesting about the boolean type in MySQL. When you create a field that uses boolean (true or false), MySQL actually just aliases it to `TINYINT(1)`. Boolean is basically 0 for false and 1 for true. For more info, refer to http://dev.mysql.com/doc/refman/5.7/en/numeric-type-overview.html.

The `member_details` table will handle this and it will be created using the following SQL code:

```sql
CREATE TABLE member_details(
  id INT(11) PRIMARY KEY AUTO_INCREMENT,
  firstname VARCHAR(255),
  lastname VARCHAR(255),
  email VARCHAR(255),
  canNotify TINYINT(1),
```

```
    member_id INT(11)
);
```

When logging in, our members will be stored in the `users` table. Let's create that with the following SQL code:

```
CREATE TABLE users (
    id INT(11) PRIMARY KEY AUTO_INCREMENT
    username VARCHAR(255),
    password VARCHAR(255),
);
```

Now, build the view that shows our members all the different subscriptions we have. We do this by checking the table `subscriptions`. The `subscriptions` table schema is defined as follows:

- `` `id` `` `Int(11)`: This is the primary key for the `subscriptions` table and is set with `AUTO_INCREMENT`
- `newsletter_id Int(11)`: This is the `newsletter_id` that they are subscribed to
- `active BOOLEAN`: This indicates whether the user is currently subscribed (default 1)

Using SQL, it will look like the following:

```
CREATE TABLE subscriptions (
    `id` INT(11) PRIMARY KEY AUTO_INCREMENT,
    `newsletter_id` INT(11) NOT NULL,
    `member_id` INT(11) NOT NULL,
    `active` BOOLEAN DEFAULT true
);
```

We will also have to create the `newsletters` table, which will hold all the newsletters, their template, and their content in JSON format. By using JSON as a storage format in our database, it should now make it simple to fetch data from the database and parse JSON into the proper values to insert into our template.

Since our newsletters will be stored in the database, we need to create the proper SQL schema for it. This is how it will be designed:

- `Id INT(11)`: To index our newsletters in the database
- `newsletter_name (Text)`: The title of our newsletter
- `newsletter_count INT(11)`: To record the edition of our particular newsletter

- `Status (String)`: To record the status of our newsletter, if it's been published, unpublished, or pending publication
- `Slug (String)`: To be able to view the newsletter with the browser on our social newsletter's website
- `Template (Text)`: To store the HTML template
- `Content (Text)`: To store the data that will go into our HTML template
- `Published_at (Date)`: To record the date of publication
- `Created_at (Date)`: To record the time that the newsletter was first created
- `Updated_at (Date)`: To record when the last time that someone updated the newsletter

The SQL for this is as follows:

```
CREATE TABLE newsletters (
id INT(11) PRIMARY KEY AUTO_INCREMENT,
newsletter_name (TEXT),
newsletter_count INT(11) NOT NULL DEFAULT '0',
marketer_id INT(11) NOT NULL,
is_active TINYINT(1),
created_at DATETIME,

);
```

When user unsubscribes, this will help indicate that they were previously subscribed to this newsletter. This is why we'll store an `active` field so that when they unsubscribe, instead of deleting the record, we just set this to 0.

The `marketer_id` is going to be used in the future admin portion where we mention the person who will be in charge of the management of the newsletter subscriptions.

Newsletters may also have many publications, which will be the actual newsletters that get sent to each subscription. The following SQL code is to create publications:

```
CREATE TABLE publications (
    newsleterId INT(11) PRIMARY KEY AUTO_INCREMENT,
    status VARCHAR(25),
    content TEXT,
    template TEXT,
    sent_at DATETIME,
    created_at DATETIME,
);
```

Now let's build the methods in our `Newsletter` class to select logged-in members subscriptions for displaying into our dashboard:

```
Class Dashboard {
  public function getSubscriptions($member_id) {
    $query = $db->query("SELECT * FROM subscriptions, newsletters WHERE
subscriptions.member_id ='". $member_id."'");
    if($query->num_rows() > 0) {
        while ($row = $result->fetch_assoc()) {
            $data  = array(
                'name' => $row->newsletter_name,
                'count' => $row->newsletter_count,
                'mem_id' => $row->member_id,
                'active' => $row->active
            );
        }
        return $data;
    }
  }
}
```

From the preceding code, we simply created a function that would get the subscriptions for a given member ID. First, we create the `"SELECT * FROM subscriptions,` `newsletters WHERE subscriptions.member_id ='". $member_id." query`. After this, we loop through the query results using the `fetch_assoc()` method of the MySQLi result object. Now that we've stored it in the `$data` variable, we return the variable, and in the following code, we display the data in a table by invoking the following function:

```
$member_id = $_SESSION['member_id'];
$dashboard = new Dashboard;
$member_subscriptions = $dashboard->getSubscriptions($member_id);
?>
  <table>
    <tr>
      <td>Member Id</td><td>Newsletter Name</td><td>Newsletter
count</td><td>Active</td>
    </tr>
<?php
  foreach($member_subscriptions as $subs) {
    echo '<tr>
    <td>'. $subs['mem_id'] . '</td>' .
    '<td>' . $subs['name'].'</td>' .
    '<td>' . $subs['count'] . '</td>'.
    '<td>' . $subs['active'] . '</td>
    </tr>';
  }
  echo '</table>';
```

Marketers dashboard

Our marketers, who administer each newsletter that they own, will be able log in to our system and be able to see how many members are subscribed and their e-mail addresses.

It is going to be an admin system that enables a marketer to update a member's record, view recent subscriptions, and allow a marketer to send custom e-mails to any member of their newsletter.

We'll have a table called `marketers`, which will have the following fields:

- `id`: To store the index
- Marketer's name: To store the name of the marketer
- Marketer's e-mail: To store the e-mail address of the marketer
- Marketer's password: To store the marketer's login password

Our SQL for creating the preceding fields is simple:

```
CREATE TABLE marketers (
id INT(11) AUTO_INCREMENT,
marketer_name VARCHAR(255) NOT NULL,
marketer_email VARCHAR(255) NOT NULL,
marketer_password VARCHAR(255) NOT NULL,

PRIMARY KEY `id`
);
```

In another table, we'll define the many-to-many relationship of marketers and their newsletters that they manage.

We'll need an `id` to be the index, the ID of the marketer who owns the newsletter, and the newsletter's ID, which is owned by the marketer.

The SQL to create this table is as follows:

```
CREATE TABLE newsletter_admins (
  Id INT(11) AUTO_INCREMENT,
  marketer_id INT(11) ,
  newsletter_id INT(11),
  PRIMARY KEY `id`,
);
```

Now let's build a query for fetching the admins of a newsletter that they own. This is going to be a simple class where we will reference all our database functions:

```php
<?php
class NewsletterDb {
public $db;

function __construct($dbinstance) {
$this->db = $dbinstance;
}

//get admins = marketers
public function get_admins ($newsletter_id) {
$query = "SELECT * FROM newsletter_admins LEFT JOIN marketers ON
marketers.id = newsletter_admins.admin_id.WHERE
newsletters_admins.newsletter_id = '".$newsletter_id."'";
  $this->db->query($query);
}
}
```

Administration system for managing marketers

We need a way for the marketers to log in and be authenticated with a password. We need a way for an admin to create the account and register a marketer and their newsletter.

Let's build that part first.

In our admin view, we'll need to set a default and ask for an authenticated password for every action that is performed. This is something we don't need to store in the database since there will be only one administrator.

In our `config/admin.php` file, we will define the username and the password as follows:

```php
<?php
$admin_username = 'admin';
$password = 'test1234';
?>
```

We then just include the file in our login page, `login.php`.We will simply check for it. The code for the login page is as follows:

```php
<html>
<?php
if(isset($_POST['username']) && isset($_POST['password'])) {
  //check if they match then login
```

```
    if($_POST['username'] == $admin_username
      && $_POST['password'] == $password) {
    //create session and login
    $ SESSION['logged_in'] = true;
    $_SESSION['logged_in_user'] = $admin_username;
        header('http://ourwebsite.com/admin/welcome_dashboard.php');
  }
  ?>
}
</html>
```

Notice that we have to set our website URL correctly, depending on where we're developing it. In the preceding example, the page will redirect to `http://ourwebsite.com/admin/welcome_dashboard.php` after logging in. We can create variables to store the domain and the URL fragment to redirect to so that this can be dynamic; see the following example:

```
$domain = 'http://ourwebsite.com';
$redirect_url = '/admin/welcome_dashboard.php';
header($domain . $redirect_url);
```

Once logged in, we'll need to build a simple CRUD (Create, Read, Update, Delete) system to manage the marketers who will be administering their newsletters.

The following is the code to be able to get the list of marketers and the newsletters they manage:

```
Function get_neewsletter_marketers() {
    $q = "SELECT * FROM marketers LEFT JOIN newsletters ';
    $q .= "WHERE marketers.id = newsletters.marketer_id";

    $res = $db->query($q);

    while ($row = $res->fetch_assoc()) {
     $marketers = array(
       'name' => $row['marketer_name'],
       'email' => $row['marketer_email'],
       'id' => $row['marketer_id']
     );
    }
    return $marketers;
}
```

We'll need to add a way to edit, create, and delete marketers. Let's create a `dashboard/table_header.php` to include at the top of our script.

The following is what the `table_header.php` code looks like:

```
<table>
<tr>
 <th>Marketer Email</th>
  <th>Edit</th>
 <th>Delete</th>
</tr>
```

We will now create a `for()` loop to loop through each of the marketer. Let's create a way to select through all the marketers in our database. First, let's call our function to get data:

```
$marketrs = get_newsletter_marketers();
```

Then let's use a `foreach()` loop to loop through all the marketers:

```
foreach($marketers as $marketer) {
  echo '<tr><td>'. $marketer['email'] .'</td>
   <td><a href="edit_marketer.php?id='. $marketer['id'].'">Edit</a></td>
   <td><a href="delete_marketer.php">delete</td>
   </tr>';
}
echo '</table>';
```

Then we end the code with a closing element for the table with `</table>`.

Let's create the `delete_marketer.php` script and the `edit_marketer.php` scripts. The following will be the delete script:

```
function delete_marketer($marketer_id) {
  $q = "DELETE FROM marketers WHERE marketers.id = '" .    $marketer_id .
"'";
    $this->db->query($q);
}
$marketer_id = $_GET['id'];
delete_marketer($marketer_id);
```

Here is the edit script composed of a form that will update the data once submitted:

```
if(empty($_POST['submit'])) {
  $marketer_id = $_GET['id'];
  $q = "SELECT * FROM marketers WHERE id = '" . $marketer_id."'";
 $res = $db->query($q);

  while ($row = $res->fetch_assoc()) {
   $marketer = array(
     'name' => $row['marketer_name'],
```

```php
      'email' => $row['marketer_email'],
      'id' => $row['id']
    );
  }

  ?>
  <form action="update_marketer.php" method="post">
    <input type="hidden" name="marketer_id" value="<?php echo
$marketer['id'] ?>">
    <input type="text" name="marketer_name" value="<?php echo
$marketer['name'] ?>">
    <input type="text" name="marketer_email" value="<?php echo
$marketer['email'] ?>">
    <input type="submit" name="submit" />
</form>
  <?php
  } else {
    $q = "UPDATE marketers SET marketer_name='" . $_POST['marketer_name']
. ", marketer_email = '". $_POST['marketer_email']."' WHERE id =
'".$_POST['marketer_id']."'";
    $this->db->query($q);
    echo "Marketer's details has been updated";
  }
?>
```

Custom template for our newsletter

Every marketer needs to lay out their newsletter. In our case, we can allow them to create a simple sidebar newsletter and a simple top-down newsletter. To build a simple sidebar, we can create an HTML template that looks like the following:

```html
<html>
<!doctype html>

<sidebar style="text-align:left">
{{MENU}}
</sidebar>

<main style="text-align:right">
    {{CONTENT}}
</main>
</html>
```

In the preceding code, we style the HTML e-mail using in-line tags simply because some e-mail clients do not render stylesheets referenced from outside our HTML.

We can use **regex** to substitute the `{{MENU}}` and `{{CONTENT}}` patterns with the data to populate them.

Our database will store the content as JSON, and once we parse the JSON, we'll have the content and menu data to insert into their respective places.

In our database, we need to add the `newsletter_templates` table. Here is how we will create it:

```
CREATE TABLE newsletter_templates (
  Id INT(11) PRIMARY KEY AUTO_INCREMENT,
Newsletter_id INT(11) NOT NULL,
    Template TEXT NOT NULL,
    Created_by INT(11) NOT NULL
) ENGINE=InnoDB;
```

With the template in place, we need a way for marketers to update the template.

From the dashboard, we display a list of templates for the newsletter.

Let's create the form as follows:

```
$cleanhtml = htmlentities('<html>
<!doctype html>

<sidebar style="text-align:left">
{{MENU}}
</sidebar>

<main style="text-align:right">
    {{CONTENT}}
</main>
</html>
');
<form>
    <h2>Newsletter Custom Template</h2>
    <textarea name="customtemplate">
<?php echo $cleanhtml; ?>
</textarea>
    <input type="submit" value="Save Template" name="submit">
    </form>
```

We also populated the `textarea` by adding values to it. Note that in the preceding code, we needed to clean the HTML code for the template using `htmlentities` first. This is because our HTML might be interpreted as part of the web page and cause problems when rendered by a browser.

We now have everything in place in order for our newsletter to send an actual newsletter. To do the sending, we'll need to create a script that will loop through all the members in a newsletter and then simply use the PHP mail function to send them.

Using the PHP mail function, we just have to loop through all the newsletter members in our database.

This is what that script looks like:

```
$template = require('template.class.php');
$q = "SELECT * FROM newsletter_members WHERE newsletter_id = 1"; //if we're
going to mail newsletter #1
$results = $db->query($q);
While ($rows =$results->fetch_assoc() ) {
  //gather data
  $newsletter_title = $row['title'];
  $member_email = $row['template'];
  $menu = $row['menu']; //this is a new field to contain any menu html
  $content = $row['content'];
  $content_with_menu = $template->replace_menu($menu, $content);
  $emailcontent = $template->
replace_contents($content,$content_with_menu);
  //mail away!
  mail($member_email, 'info@maillist.com', $newsletter_title
,$email_content);
}
```

We need to complete the `replace_menu` and `replace_contents` functions. Let's simply build the text replace function that will replace the content we have already fetched in the preceding code. The data comes from the newsletter table in the database:

```
class Template {
    public function replace_menu($menu, $content) {
      return  str_replace('{{MENU}}', $menu, $content);
    }
    public function replace_contents ($actualcontent, $content) {
      return str_replace('{{CONTENT}}', $actualcontent,  $content);
    }
}
```

Note that we modified our table to have a menu in the newsletter. This menu must be created by the user and with HTML markup. It will basically be an HTML list of links. The proper markup for the menu should be like the following:

```
<ul>
  <li><a href="http://someUrl.com">some URL</a></li>
<li><a href="http://someNewUrl.com">some new URL</a></li>
<li><a href="http://someOtherUrl.com">some other URL</a></li>
</ul>
```

Link tracking

For our link tracking system, we will need to allow a marketer to embed links, which actually pass through our system for us to keep track of the number of clicks on the link.

What we will do is actually create a service that will automatically shorten the links we enter to a random hash. The URL will look like `http://example.com/link/xyz123`, and the hash `xyz123` will be stored in our database. When a user accesses the link, we'll match the link.

Let's create the links table and create a function that will help us generate the shortened links. At the bare minimum, we need to be able to store the title of the link, the actual link, the shortened link, as well as who created the link so that we can put it on the marketer's dashboard.

The SQL for the links table looks like the following:

```
CREATE TABLE links (
    id INT(11) PRIMARY KEY AUTO_INCREMENT,
    link_title TEXT NOT NULL,
    actual_link TEXT,
    shortened_link VARCHAR(255),
    created DATETIME,
    created_by INT(11)
);
```

Now let's create the following function, which will generate a random hash:

```
public function createShortLink($site_url,$title, $actual_url,$created_by)
{
    $created_date = date('Y-m-d H:i:s');
  $new_url = $site_url . "h?=" . md5($actual_url);
  $res = $this->db->query("INSERT INTO links VALUES (null, $title ,'".
$actual_url. "', '". $new_url.", '". $created_date."','".$created_by."'"),;
  ));
    return $res;
}
```

We also need to store the number of hits or clicks to the link. We will use another table that will link `link_id` to the number of hits, and we'll just update that table every time someone has used a shortened link:

```
CREATE TABLE link_hits (
    link_id INT(11),
    num_hits INT(11)
);
```

We won't need to index the preceding SQL table because we won't really need to do fast searches on it. Every time we generate a new URL, we should populate the table already with the num hits defaulting to 0:

Add the following function in the `createShortLink` function:

```
$res = $this->db->query("INSERT INTO links VALUES (null,
'$actual_url',$title, '$new_url', '$created_date', '$created_by'");
$new_insert_id = $this->db->insert_id;

$dbquery = INSERT INTO link_hits VALUES($new_insert_id,0);

$this->db->query($dbquery);
```

The `insert_id` is the ID of the last inserted record of MySQL. It's a function that returns the new ID generated every time a new row is added.

Let's generate the link hit class that contains two functions, one to initialize the database and another that will update the `link_hits` table every time a user clicks on a link:

```
Class LinkHit {

    Public function __construct($mysqli) {
        $this->db = $mysqli;
    }

    public function  hitUpdate ($link_id) {

    $query = "UPDATE link_hits SET num_hits++ WHERE link_id='".    $link_id.
"'";
      //able to update
        $this->db->query($query)
    }

    Public function checkHit ($shorturl) {
        $arrayUrl = parse_url($shortUrl);
parse_str($parts['query'],$query);
$hash = $query['h'];
```

```
    $testQuery = $this->db->query("SELECT id FROM links WHERE shortened_link
LIKE '%$hash%'");
    if($this->db->num_rows > 0) {
        while($row = $testQuery->fetch_array() ) {
    return $row['id'];
        }
    } else {
      echo "Could not find shorted link";
      return null;
    }
}


//instantiating the function:
$mysqli = new
mysqli('localhost','test_user','test_password','your_database');
$Link = new LinkHit($mysqli);
$short_link_id =
$Link->checkHit("http://$_SERVER[HTTP_HOST]$_SERVER[REQUEST_URI]");

if($short_link_id !== null) {
  $link->hitUpdate($isShort);
}
```

For our marketers to view the links, we will need to display their links on a `links` page in our portal.

We create the function for checking the links and their hits that is attributed to the admin user who is logged in:

```
$user_id = $_SESSION['user_id'];
$sql = "SELECT * FROM links LEFT JOIN link_hits ON links.id =
link_hits.link_id WHERE links.created_by='" . $user_id. "'";
$query = $mysqli->query($sql);
?>
<table>
<tr>
<td>Link id</td><td>Link hits</td></tr>
<?php
while($obj = $query->fetch_object()) {
  echo '<tr><td>'.$obj->link.'</td>
<td>' . $obj->link_hits.'</td></tr></tr>';
}
?>
</table>
```

In the preceding code, we just got the logged-in user's ID by checking the variable `$_SESSION['user_id']`. Then we performed an SQL query by executing the string variable `$SQL`. After this, we loop through the results and show the results into an HTML table. Note that we exit the PHP code when we display a permanent HTML markup such as start of the table and the headers and the ending of the `</table>` tag.

PHP performs slightly better without using echo statements, and this is the beauty of PHP scripting, you are really allowed to go into the PHP sections and then into the HTML sections in your code. Your opinion may differ on the beauty of this idea, but we just want to show what PHP can do in this exercise.

AJAX socket chat for support

This system allows the subscribers to contact the administrator of a particular newsletter group. It will just contain a contact form. Also, we shall need to implement a way to send a notification to the administrator in real time.

We will basically add a socket connection to the administrator so that when ever someone sends an inquiry, it will flash a notification on the marketer's dashboard.

This is pretty simple with **socket.io** and a browser technology called WebSockets.

Introduction to socket.io

With socket.io, we don't need to create the code for checking the server periodically for an event. We'll just pass through the data the user entered by using AJAX and trigger the listeners to the sockets by emitting the events. It offers long polling and communication through WebSockets and is supported by modern web browsers.

 WebSockets extends the concept of having socket connections through a browser. To read more on WebSockets, please visit `http://www.html5roc ks.com/en/tutorials/websockets/basics/`.

A sample code on the socket.io site just includes the `socket.io.js` script:

```
<script src="socket.io/socket.io.js"></script>
```

Our PHP webserver will be using something called **Ratchet**, which has a website at `http://socketo.me`. It basically allows us to use WebSockets for PHP.

Here is their website:

Ratchet is just a tool to allow PHP developers "*to create real time, bi-directional applications between clients over WebSockets*". By creating a bi-directional flow of data, it allows developers to create things such as real-time chat and other real-time applications.

Let's get started by following their tutorial at `http://socketo.me/docs/hello-world`.

With Ratchet, we have to install **Composer** and add the following to our `composer.json` file in our project directory:

```
{
    "autoload": {
        "psr-0": {
            "MyApp": "src"
        }
    },
    "require": {
        "cboden/ratchet": "0.3.*"
    }
}
```

If you've had prior experience with Composer, basically what it does is use the `psr-0` standard in writing the path to a script that needs autoloading. Then we run `composer install` in the same directory. After having Ratchet set up, we need to set up the proper components for handling certain events.

We need to create a folder labeled `SupportChat` and put `Chat.php` inside. This is because using psr-0 in the preceding `composer.json` file, it expects a directory structure inside the `src` directory.

Let's create a class with the stubbed functions that we need to implement:

```
namespace SupportChat;
use Ratchet\MessageComponentInterface;
use Ratchet\ConnectionInterface;

class SupportChat implements MessageComponentInterface {
  Protected $clients;
  Public function __construct() {
    $this->clients = new \SplObjectStorage;
  }
}
```

We need to declare the `$clients` variable to store the clients that will connect to our chat app.

Let's implement the interface for when the client opens a connection:

```
Public function onOpen(ConnectionInterface $conn) {
  $this->clients->attach($conn);
  echo "A connection has been established";
}
```

Now let's create the `onMessage` and `onClose` methods as follows:

```
Public function onMessage (ConnectionInterface $from, $msg) {
  foreach ($this->clients as $client) {
        if ($from !== $client) {
            $client->send($msg);
        }
    }
}


public function onClose(ConnectionInterface $conn) {
$this->clients->detach($conn);
}
```

Let's also create an `onError` method for handling errors as follows:

```
public function onError (ConnectionInterface $conn) {
$this->clients->detach($conn);
}
```

Now we need to implement the client (browser) side of the application.

Create a file called `app.js` in your `htdocs` or `public` folder with the following code:

```
var messages = [];
// connect to the socket server
var conn = new WebSocket('ws://localhost:8088');
conn.onopen = function(e) {
    console.log('Connected to server:', conn);
}
conn.onerror = function(e) {
    console.log('Error: Could not connect to server.');
}
conn.onclose = function(e) {
    console.log('Connection closed');
}
// handle new message received from the socket server
conn.onmessage = function(e) {
    // message is data property of event object
    var message = JSON.parse(e.data);
    console.log('message', message);
    // add to message list
    var li = '<li>' + message.text + '</li>';
    $('.message-list').append(li);
}
// attach onSubmit handler to the form
$(function() {
    $('.message-form').on('submit', function(e) {
        // prevent form submission which causes page reload
        e.preventDefault();
        // get the input
        var input = $(this).find('input');
        // get message text from the input
        var message = {
                type: 'message',
                text: input.val()
        };
        // clear the input
        input.val('');
        // send message to server
        conn.send(JSON.stringify(message));
    });
});
```

We need to create the HTML for the preceding code to be used. We should name the file `app.js`. Now, let's implement a simple input text for the user to enter their messages:

```
<!DOCTYPE html>
<html>
<head>
```

```
    <title>Chat with Support</title>
    <script
src="https://cdnjs.cloudflare.com/ajax/libs/jquery/2.2.3/jquery.js"></scrip
t>
    <script src="app.js"></script>
</head>
<body>
    <h1>Chat with Support</h1>
    <h2>Messages</h2>
    <ul class="message-list"></ul>
    <form class="message-form">
        <input type="text" size="40" placeholder="Type your message here"
/>
        <button>Send message</button>
    </form>
</body>
</html>
```

App.js is where the JavaScript code we wrote earlier should go. We also need to create a WebSocket server to handle the WebSocket on port 8088:

```php
<?php
// import namespaces
use Ratchet\Server\IoServer;
use Ratchet\WebSocket\WsServer;
use SupportChat\Chat;
// use the autoloader provided by Composer
require dirname(__DIR__) . '/vendor/autoload.php';
// create a websocket server
$server = IoServer::factory(
    new WsServer(
        new Chat()
    )
    , 8088
);
$server->run();
```

Our chat app is now ready for public use. However, we need to start our chat server, which will handle WebSockets by starting it with php bin/server.php.

Note that on Windows, it will prompt about the network being used:

Simply click on **Allow access** and then click on **OK**.

Now when we visit http://localhost/client.html, we should see the following:

However, we need to spiff up the contact form by adding the username and e-mail for support to get back to him via e-mail in case no one from support is available to reply to the user.

Our form now looks as follows:

```
<form class="message-form" id="chatform">
        <input type="text" name="firstname" size="25" placeholder="Your
Name">
        <input type="text" name="email" size="25" placeholder="Email">

        <input type="text" name="message" size="40" placeholder="Type your
message here" />
        <button>Send message</button>
    </form>
```

Since we've added those details, we need to store them in our database. We can do this by having all the data forwarded to another PHP script to do the sending. In JavaScript, the code would add to the handler a way to send to the sendsupportmessage.php the values from the form.

Here is how that JavaScript code, with jQuery, will look:

```
<script>
$(document).ready(function() {
    $('submit').on('click', function() {
      $.post('sendsupportmessage.php', $("#chatform").serialize())
        .done(function(data) {
          alert('Your message has been sent');
      });
    });
});
</script>
```

In the script that will receive the messages, sendsupportmessage.php, we'll need to parse the information and create an e-mail to send to the support e-mail, contact@yoursite.com; see the following example:

```
<?php
  if( !empty($_POST['message'])) {
    $message = htmlentities($_POST['message']);
  }

  if( !empty($_POST['email'])) {
    $email = htmlentities($_POST['email']);
  }
  if( !empty($_POST['firstname']) ) {
    $firstname = htmlentities($_POST['firstname']);
  }

  $emailmessage = 'A support message from ' . $firstname . ';
```

```
$emailmessage .=  ' with email address: ' . $email . ';
$emailmessage .= ' has been received. The message is '. $message;
 mail('contact@yoursite.com', 'Support message', $emailmessage);

 echo "success!";
?>
```

The script just checks if the submitted values are not blank. By experience, using !empty () instead of checking for a set value with the isset() function is better because an empty string (' ') may be evaluated by PHP to still be set:

```
$foo = '';
if(isset($foo)) { print 'But no its empty'; }
else { print 'PHP7 rocks!'; }
```

We now need to display to the user, as we sent the message to the server using AJAX, and update the AJAX box. In the JavaScript code, we should change the .done() callback code to the following:

```
.done(function(data) {
   if(data === 'succccess!') {
     var successHtml = '<li>Your message was sent</li>';
     $('.message-list').append(successHtml);
   }
     }
```

Fantastic! Notice that we changed the alert box call and instead appended the message Your message was sent back into the message list. Our support form now sends who the message is from and our support team can receive the message in their e-mails.

Summary

You learned a lot in this chapter. To summarize, we built a simple admin system to manage our marketers. After this, we also created a way for members of the newsletter to log in which leads the user to a home page.

Then we reviewed how to send an e-mail with a simple template system, which allowed a user to add his/her own menu and the content to the layout. We were also able to add Facebook social login by using the Facebook PHP SDK and its authentication process.

In the latter part of the chapter, we built a simple chat system that will send an e-mail immediately to the support e-mail address of our website. We checked out Ratchet, a PHP library to help us work with real-time messaging in PHP, and used AJAX to asynchronously send the data to another script that will do the e-mailing to the support e-mail.

We've now created an impressive newsletter app that is more than the regular, with social login features and a support chat box, and allows other newsletter marketers to manage their content through a website.

4
Build a Simple Blog with Search Capability using Elasticsearch

In this chapter, we will create a simple blog that can create and delete posts. Then we will work on adding some features to our blog such as the following:

- Implement a very simple blog with CRUD and admin features
- Work and install Elasticsearch and Logstash
- Try out the PHP client of Elasticsearch
- Learn to build a tool for working with Elasticsearch
- Build a cache for searches to our database
- Build a chart based on our Elasticsearch information

Creating the CRUD and admin system

First, let's build the SQL of our posts. The database table should contain at the very least the post title, post content, post date, and modified and published dates.

This is what the SQL should look like:

```
CREATE TABLE posts(
id INT(11) PRIMARY KEY AUTO INCREMENT,
post_title TEXT,
post_content TEXT,
post_date DATETIME,
modified DATETIME,
published DATETIME
);
```

Now let's create a function to read the data. A typical blog site has comments and some additional metadata for SEO related to the blog post. But in this chapter, we won't be creating this part. Anyway, it should be fairly trivial to add a table relating to comments data and to have data about SEO metadata about each post in another table.

Let's start by creating the admin system. We need to log in, so we'll have to create a simple login-logout script:

```php
//admin.php
<form action="admin.php" method="post">
Username: <input type="text" name="username"><br />
Password: <input type="text" name="username"><br />
<input type="submit" name="submit">
</form>
<?php
$db = new mysqli(); //etc


Function checkPassword($username, $password) {
//generate hash
    $bpassword = password_hash($password);

//clean up username for sanitization
$username = $db->real_escape_string($username);

    $query = mysqli_query("SELECT * FROM users WHERE
password='".$bpassword."' AND username = '". $username. "'");
if($query->num_rows() > 0) {
return true;
      }
return false;
}

if(isset$_POST[' assword']) && isset ($_POST['username']) ) {
If(checkPassword($_POST['username'], $_POST['password'])) {
$_SESSION['admin'] = true;
$_SESSION['logged_in'] = true;
$_SESSION['expires'] = 3600; //1 hour
    $_SESSION['signin_time'] = time(); //unix time
    header('Location: admin_crud_posts.php');
}
else {
    //lead the user out
header('Location: logout.php');
  }
  }
}
```

When you log in to admin.php, you set the sessions and are then redirected to the CRUD page.

The script for the admin CRUD page is as follows:

```php
<?php
$db = new mysqli(); //etc
function delete($post_id) {
    $sql_query = "DELETE FROM posts WHERE id= '". $post_id."'";
  $db->query($sql_query);

}

function update($postTitle, $postContent, $postAuthor, $postId) {
$sql_query = "UPDATE posts
    SET  title = '".$postTitle. "',
    post_content = '". $postContent. "',
    post_author='". $postAuthor."'
    WHERE id = '".$postId."'";
    $db->query($sql_query);
}

function create($postTitle, $postContent, $postAuthor) {

$insert_query = "INSERT INTO posts (null ,
    '" . $postTitle."',
    '". $postContent."',
   '" $postAuthor."')";
$db->query($insert_query);

}

$query = "SELECT * FROM posts";
$result = $db->query($query);

//display
?>
<table>
<tr>
<td>Title</td>
<td>Content</td>
<td>Author</td>
<td>Administer</td>
</tr>
while($row = $db->fetch_array($query,MYSQLI_ASSOC)) {
  $id = $row['id'];
echo '<tr>';
```

```php
echo '<td>' .$row['title'] . '</td>';

echo '<td>' . $row['content'] . '</td>';

echo '<td>' . $row['author'] . '</td>';

echo '<td><a href="edit.php?postid='.$id.'">Edit</a>';
echo '<a href="delete.php?postid='.$id.'">Delete</a>'.'</td>';'
echo '</tr>';
}
echo "</table>";

?>
```

In the preceding script, we simply defined some functions that will handle the CRUD operations for us. To display the data, we just simply loop through the database and output it in a table.

The edit and delete pages, which are the scripts needed for a user interface and functions to edit or delete the posts, are as follows:

`edit.php`:

```php
<?php
function redirect($home) {
header('Location: '. $home);
}
if(!empty($_POST)) {
    $query = 'UPDATE posts SET title='" . $_POST['title']. "', content='".
$_POST['content']."' WHERE id = ".$_POST['id'];
    $db->query($query);
    redirect('index.php');
} else {
  $id = $_GET['id'];
  $q = "SELECT * FROM posts WHERE id= '".$_GET['id'] . "'"
?>
<form action="edit.php" method="post">

<input name="post_title type="text" value=" ="<?php echo  $_POST[
title'] ?>">

<input type="text" value="<?php echo $_POST['content'] ?>">

<input type="hidden" value="<?php echo $_GET['id'] ?>">

</form>
<?php
}
```

```
?>
```

Let's create the actual functionality for deleting the post. Following is how `delete.php` would look like:

```php
<?php

function redirect($home) {
    header('Location: '. $home);
}
if(isset ($_GET['postid'])) {
    $query = "DELETE FROM  posts WHERE id = '".$_GET['post_id']."'";
$db->query($query);
redirect('index.php');
}
```

Our logger for PHP, Monolog, will add the posts to the Elasticsearch using the Logstash plugin for Elasticsearch.

We'll set up a Logstash plugin, which first checks if the document exists and, if not, then inserts it.

To update Elasticsearch, we'll need to perform an **upsert**, which will update the same record if it exists, and if it does not exist, it will create a new one.

Also, we've implemented a way to delete the post from being visible in our CRUD, but not actually delete it from the database, as we'll need it for retrieval purposes.

For every action that needs to be done, we simply use the `$_GET['id']` to determine what we are going to do when that is clicked.

Like any blog, we need a front page for the user to display the posts that are available to read:

`index.php`:

```php
<html>
<?php
$res = $db->query("SELECT * FROM posts LIMIT 10");
foreach$posts as $post {
<h1><?phpecho $post[]?>
?>
}
?>
```

In the preceding code, we make extensive use of shorthand opening php tags so that we can focus on the page layout. Notice how it weaves in and out of PHP mode, but it looks like we are just using a template, meaning we can see the general outline of the HTML markup without getting too much into the details of the PHP code.

Seeding the post table

Without any data, our blog is useless. Therefore, for demonstration purposes, we'll just use a seeder script to automatically populate our table with data.

Let's use a popular library for generating fake content, **Faker**, which is available at https://github.com/fzaninotto/Faker.

With Faker, all you have to do is load it by providing the required path to its autoload.php file and load it using composer (composer require fzaninotto/faker).

The complete script for generating fake content is as follows:

```php
<?php
require "vendor/autoload";
$faker = FakerFactory::create();
for($i=0; $i < 10; $i++) {
  $id = $i;
  $post = $faker->paragraph(3, true);
  $title  = $faker->text(150);
  $query = "INSERT INTO posts VALUES (".$id.",'".$title."','".$post .
"','1')"
}

?>
```

Now let's move on to getting acquainted with Elasticsearch, the database search engine for our blog posts.

What is Elasticsearch?

Elasticsearch is a search server. It's a full-text search engine that comes with an HTTP web interface and schema-free JSON documents. What this means is that we store new searchable data by using JSON. The API to enter these documents uses the HTTP protocol. In this chapter, we will learn how to use PHP and build a rich search engine that can do the following:

- Set up the Elasticsearch PHP client
- Add search data to Elasticsearch for indexing
- Learn how to use keywords for relevance
- Cache our search results
- Use Elasticsearch with Logstash to store apache logs
- Parse XML for storage into Elasticsearch

Installing Elasticsearch and the PHP client

Creating the web interface for consumption of Elasticsearch.

As far as you need to know, Elasticsearch just needs to be installed by simply using the latest source code of Elasticsearch.

The installation instructions are as follows:

1. Go to `https://www.elastic.co/` and download the source file that's related to your computer system, whether it's a Mac OSX, a Linux, or a Windows machine.
2. After downloading the file to your computer, you should run the setup installation notes.
3. For example, for Mac OSX and Linux operating systems, you can do the following:

- Install Java 1.8.
- Download Elasticsearch through curl (in the command line):

```
curl -L -O
https://download.elastic.co/elasticsearch/release/org/elasticsearch
/distribution/tar/elasticsearch/2.1.0/elasticsearch-2.1.0.tar.gz
```

- Extract the archive and change directory into it:

```
tar -zxvf elasticsearch-2.1.0.tar.gz
cd /path/to/elasticsearch/archive
```

- Start it up:

```
cd bin
./elasticsearch
```

An alternative way to install Elasticsearch for Mac OSX is using homebrew, which is available at `http://brew.sh/`. Then, install it by using brew with the following command:

```
brew install elasticsearch
```

1. For Windows operating systems, you just need to click through the wizard installation program, as shown in the following screenshot:

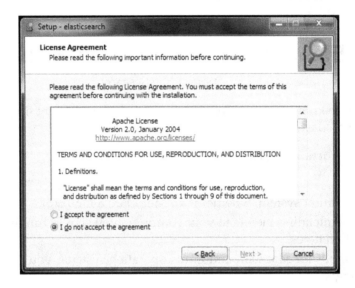

2. Once that is installed, you also need to install the **Logstash agent**. The Logstash agent is in charge of sending data to Elasticsearch from various input sources.
3. You can download it from the Elasticsearch website and follow the installation instructions for your computer system.
4. For Linux, you can download a `tar` file and then you just have the other way for Linux, that is to use the package manager, which is either `apt-get` or `yum`, depending on your flavor of Linux.

You can test Elasticsearch by installing **Postman** and doing a `GET request` to `http://localhost:9200`:

1. Install Postman by opening Google Chrome and visiting `https://www.getpostm an.com/`. You can install it on Chrome by going to add-ons and searching for Postman.
2. Once Postman is installed, you can register or skip registration:

3. Now try doing a GET request to http://localhost:9200:

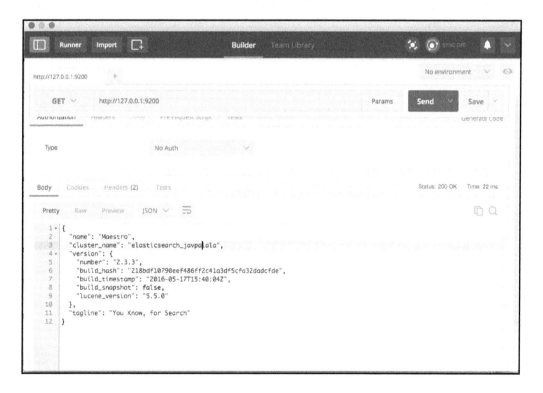

4. The next step is to try out the PHP client library for Elasticsearch in your composer. Following is how to do that:

5. First, include Elasticsearch in your `composer.json` file:

```
{
"require":{
"elasticsearch/elasticsearch":"~2.0"
}
}
```

6. Get composer:

```
curl-s http://getcomposer.org/installer | php
phpcomposer.phar install --no-dev
```

7. Instantiate a new client by including it in your project:

```
require'vendor/autoload.php';

$client =Elasticsearch\ClientBuilder::create()->build();
```

Now let's try indexing a document. To do so, let's create a PHP file to use the PHP client as follows:

```
$params=[
    'index'=> 'my_index',
    'type'=> 'my_type',
    'id'=> 'my_id',
    'body'=>['testField'=> 'abc']
];

$response = $client->index($params);
print_r($response);
```

We can also retrieve that document by creating a script with the following code:

```
$params=[
    'index'=> 'my_index',
    'type'=> 'my_type',
    'id'=> 'my_id'
];

$response = $client->get($params);
print_r($response);
```

If we're performing a search, the code is as follows:

```
$params=[
    'index'=> 'my_index',
    'type'=> 'my_type',
    'body'=>[
        'query'=>[
            'match'=>[
                'testField'=> 'abc'
]
]
]
];

$response = $client->search($params);
print_r($response);
```

In a nutshell, the Elasticsearch PHP client makes it easier to insert, search, and get a document from Elasticsearch.

Building a PHP Elasticsearch tool

The aforementioned functionality can be used to create a PHP-backed user interface to insert, query, and search for documents using the Elasticsearch PHP client.

Here is a simple bootstrap (an HTML CSS framework) form:

```
<div class="col-md-6">
<div class="panel panel-info">
<div class="panel-heading">Create Document for indexing</div>
<div class="panel-body">
<form method="post" action="new_document" role="form">
<div class="form-group">
<label class="control-label" for="Title">Title</label>
<input type="text" class="form-control" id="newTitle" placeholder="Title">
</div>
<div class="form-group">
<label class="control-label" for="exampleInputFile">Post Content</label>
<textarea class="form-control" rows="5" name="post_body"></textarea>
<p class="help-block">Add some Content</p>
</div>
<div class="form-group">
<label class="control-label">Keywords/Tags</label>
<div class="col-sm-10">
<input type="text" class="form-control" placeholder="keywords, tags, more keywords" name="keywords">
</div>
```

```
<p class="help-block">You know, #tags</p>
</div>
<button type="submit" class="btnbtn-default">Create New Document</button>
</form>
</div>
</div>
</div>
```

This is what the form should look like:

When the user submits the details of the content, we'll need to catch the content, keywords, or tags that the user has inputted. The PHP script that will enter the inputs into MySQL and then into our script, which will push it onto our Elasticsearch:

```
public function insertData($data) {
    $sql = "INSERT INTO posts ('title', 'tags', 'content') VALUES('" .
$data['title] . "','" . $data['tags'] . "','" .$data['content'] . ")";
mysql_query($sql);
}

insertData($_POST);
```

Now let's try to post this document to Elasticsearch as well:

```
$params=[
    'index'=> 'my_posts',
    'type'=>'posts',
    'id'=>'posts',
    'body'=>[
        'title'=>$_POST['title'],
        'tags' => $_POST['tags'],
```

```
          'content' => $_POST['content']
    ]
];

$response = $client->index($params);
print_r($response);
```

Adding documents to our Elasticsearch

Elasticsearch uses indexes to store each data point into its database. From our MySQL database, we need to post the data into Elasticsearch.

Let's discuss how indexing in Elasticsearch actually works. What makes it faster than conventional search by MySQL is that it searches the index instead.

How does indexing work in Elasticsearch? It uses the**Apache Lucene** to create something called an **inverted index**. An inverted index means that it looks up the search terms without having to scan every single entry. It basically means that it has a lookup table that lists all the words ever entered the system.

Here is an overview of the architecture of the ELK stack:

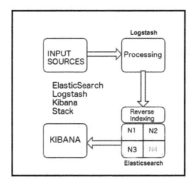

In the preceding diagram, we can see that **INPUT SOURCES**, usually the logs or some other data source, goes into **Logstash**. From **Logstash**, it then goes into **Elasticsearch**.

Once the data reaches **Elasticsearch**, it goes through some tokenizing and filtering. **Tokenizing** is the process of dissecting strings into different parts. **Filtering** is when some terms are sorted into separate indexes. For example, we may have an Apache log index, and then also have another input source, such as **Redis**, pushing into another searchable index.

The searchable index is the reversed index we mentioned previously. A searchable index is basically made searchable by storing each term and referring to their original content into an index. It's similar to what is done in an indexed database. It is the same process when we create primary keys and use it as the index to search entire records.

You can have many nodes performing this indexing in a cluster, all handled by the Elasticsearch engine. In the preceding diagram, the nodes are labeled **N1** to **N4**.

Querying Elasticsearch

We now understand each part, so how do we query Elasticsearch? First, let's get introduced to Elasticsearch. When you start running Elasticsearch, you should send an HTTP request to `http://localhost:9200`.

We can do this using the Elasticsearch web API, which allows us to use RESTful HTTP requests to the Elasticsearch server. This RESTful API is the only way to insert records into Elasticsearch.

Installing Logstash

Logstash is simply the central logging system where all the messages going to Elasticsearch will pass through.

To set up Logstash, follow the guide that's available on the Elasticsearch website:

`https://www.elastic.co/guide/en/logstash/current/getting-started-with-logstash.html`.

Elasticsearch and Logstash work together to get different types of indexed logs into Elasticsearch.

We need to create something called a **transport** or middleware between the two data points. To do so, we need to set up Logstash. It is known as the **ingestion workhorse** for Elasticsearch and much more. It is a data collection engine that pipelines data from data source to the destination, which is Elasticsearch. Logstash is basically like a simple data pipeline.

We will create a cronjob, which is basically a background task, that will add new entries from our post table and put them into Elasticsearch.

Unix and Linux users who are familiar with the concept of a pipe, | , will be familiar with what a pipeline does.

Logstash simply transforms our raw log messages into a format called **JSON**.

> **JSON**, also known as **JavaScript Object Notation**, is a popular format for transferring data between web services. It is lightweight, and many programming languages, including PHP, have a way to encode and decode JSON-formatted messages.

Setting up the Logstash configuration

The input part of a Logstash configuration is concerned with reading and parsing log data correctly. It consists of the input data source and the parser to use. Here is a sample configuration where we will read from a `redis` input source:

```
input {
redis {
key =>phplogs
data_type => ['list']
  }
}
```

But first, to be able to push to `redis`, we should install and use `phpredis`, an extension library that allows PHP to insert data into `redis`.

Installing PHP Redis

Installing PHP Redis should be simple. It's available in most package repositories for Linux platforms. You can read the documentation on how to install it at `https://github.com/ph predis/phpredis`.

Once you have it installed, you can test that your PHP Redis installation is working by creating the following script and running it:

```
<?php
$redis = new Redis() or die("Cannot load Redis module.");
$redis->connect('localhost');
$redis->set('random', rand(5000,6000));
echo $redis->get('random');
```

In the preceding example, we're able to start a new Redis connection and from there set a key called `random` to a number between 5000 and 6000. Finally, we echo out the data that we've just entered by calling `echo $redis->get('random')`.

With that in place, let's create the real PHP code using the logging library for PHP, called **Monolog**, to store our logs in Redis.

Let's create a `composer.json` that the logging project will use.

In the terminal, let's run the initialize composer:

```
composer init
```

It will interactively ask some questions after which it should create a `composer.json` file.

Now install Monolog by typing the following:

```
composer require monolog/monolog
```

Let's set up the PHP code that will read from our MySQL database and then push it over to Elasticsearch:

```php
<?php
require'vendor/autoload.php'

useMonolog\Logger;
useMonolog\Handler\RedisHandler;
useMonolog\Formatter\LogstashFormatter;
usePredis\Client;

$redisHandler=newRedisHandler(newClient(),'phplogs');
$formatter =newLogstashFormatter('my_app');
$redisHandler->setFormatter($formatter);

// Create a Logger instance
$logger =newLogger('logstash_test', array($redisHandler));
$logger->info('Logging some infos to logstash.');
```

In the preceding code, we've created a `redisHandler` with the name of the logs to be called `phplogs`. We then set the `LogstashFormatter` instance to use the application name `my_app`.

At the end of the script, we create a new `logger` instance, connect it to the `redisHandler`, and call the `info()` method of the `logger` to log the data.

Monolog separates the responsibilities of the formatter from the actual logging. The `logger` is responsible for creating the messages, and the Formatter formats the messages into the appropriate format so that Logstash can understand it. Logstash, in turn, pipes it to Elasticsearch, where the data about the log is indexed and is stored in the Elasticsearch index for querying later.

That's the wonderful thing about Elasticsearch. As long as you have Logstash, you can choose from different input sources for Logstash to process and Elasticsearch will do its job of saving the data when Logstash pushes to it.

Encoding and decoding JSON messages

Now that we know how to work with the Monolog library, we need to integrate it into our blog application. We'll do so by creating a cronjob that will check for new blog posts for that day and store them in Elasticsearch through the use of a PHP script.

First, let's create a folder called `server_scripts` where we put all our cronjobs:

```
$ mkdir ~/server_scripts
$ cd ~/server_scripts
```

Now, here is our code:

```php
<?php
$db_name = 'test';
$db_pass = 'test123';
$db_username = 'testuser'
$host = 'localhost';
$dbconn = mysqli_connect();
$date_now = date('Y-m-d 00:00:00');
$date_now_end = date('Y-m-d 00:00:00',mktime() + 86400);
$res = $dbcon->query("SELECT * FROM posts WHERE created >= '". $date_now."'
AND created < '". $date_now_end. "'");

while($row = $dbconn->fetch_object($res)) {
   /* do redis queries here */

}
```

Using Logstash, we can read from our `redis` data and let it do its work, which would then process it and output it with the following output plugin code for Logstash:

```
output{
elasticsearch_http{
host=> localhost
}
}
```

Storing Apache logs in Elasticsearch

Monitoring logs is an important aspect of any web application. Most critical systems have what is known as a dashboard, and that is exactly we will build in this segment with PHP.

As a bonus to this chapter, let's talk about another logging topic, server logs. Sometimes we want to be able to determine the performance of the server at a certain time.

Another thing you can do with Elasticsearch is to store Apache logs. For our application, we can add this so that we know about our users a little bit more.

This could be useful, for example, if we're interested in monitoring the browser a user is using and where users are coming from when they access our site.

To do so, we just have to set up some configuration using the Apache input plugin as follows:

```
input {
file {
path => "/var/log/apache/access.log"
start_position => beginning
ignore_older => 0
    }
}

filter {
grok {
match => { "message" => "%{COMBINEDAPACHELOG}" }
    }
geoip {
source => "clientip"
    }
}

output {
elasticsearch {}
stdout {}
}
```

A **Kibana** dashboard may be created when you install Kibana from Elasticsearch; however, it requires end users to already know how to use the tool to create various queries.

However, there is a need to make it simpler for upper management to view the data without having to know how to create Kibana dashboards.

For our end users to not have to learn how to use Kibana and create dashboards, we will simply query the **ILog** information when the dashboard page is requested. For the charting library, we will use a popular library known as **Highcharts**. To get the information, however, we will need to create a simple query that will return some information to us in JSON format.

Handle the Apache logs, we can create it using PHP Elasticsearch client library. It's a simple client library that allows us to query Elasticsearch for information that we need, including the number of hits.

We will create a simple histogram for our website to show the number of accesses that are logged in our database.

For example, we'll use the PHP Elasticsearch SDK to query Elasticsearch and display the Elasticsearch results.

We also have to make the histogram dynamic. Basically, when the user wants to select between certain dates, we should be able to set up Highcharts to just get the data points and create a graph. If you haven't checked out Highcharts, please refer to `http://www.highchar ts.com/`.

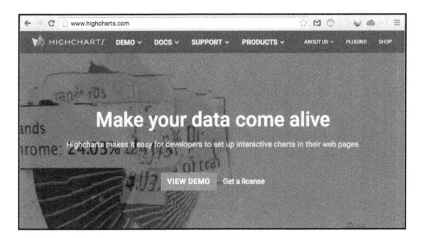

Getting filtered data to display with Highcharts

Like any chart user, we sometimes require the ability to filter down whatever we see in our graph. Instead of relying on Highcharts to give us controls to filter down our data, we should be able to do the filtering by changing the data that Highcharts will render.

In the following Highcharts code, we are adding the following container divider for our page; first, we get the data from our Elasticsearch engine using JavaScript:

```
<script>

$(function () {
client.search({
index: 'apachelogs',
type: 'logs',
body: {
query: {
        "match_all": {
        },
        {
          "range": {
              "epoch_date": {
                "lt": <?php echo mktime(0,0,0, date('n'), date('j'),
date('Y') ) ?>,

                "gte": <?php echo mktime(0,0,0, date('n'), date('j'),
date('Y')+1 ) ?>
            }
          }
        }
        }
      }
}).then(function (resp) {
var hits = resp.hits.hits;
varlogCounts = new Array();
    _.map(resp.hits.hits, function(count)
    {logCounts.push(count.count)});

  $('#container').highcharts({
chart: {
type: 'bar'
        },
title: {
text: 'Apache Logs'
        },
xAxis: {
categories: logDates
        },
yAxis: {
title: {
text: 'Log Volume'
            }
        },
    plotLines: [{
```

```
                value: 0,
                width: 1,
                color: '#87D82F'
                }]
        },
        tooltip: {
        valueSuffix: ' logs'
          },
        plotOptions: {
        series: {
                cursor: 'pointer',
                point: {
        },
        marker: {
        lineWidth: 1
            }
          }
        },
        legend: {
                layout: 'vertical',
                align: 'right',
                verticalAlign: 'middle',
                borderWidth: 0
            },
        series: [{
        name: 'Volumes',
        data: logCounts
            }]
            });

}, function (err) {
console.trace(err.message);
    $('#container').html('We did not get any data');
});


});
    </script>

    <div id="container" style="width:100%; height:400px;"></div>
```

This is done is using the filter command of JavaScript and then parsing that data into our Highcharts graph. You'll also need to use underscore for the filtering function, which will help sort out which data we want to present to the user.

Let's first build the form to filter our Highcharts histogram.

This is what the HTML code for the search filter in the CRUD view will look like:

```
<form>
<select name="date_start" id="dateStart">
<?php
$aWeekAgo = date('Y-m-d H:i:s', mktime( 7 days))
    $aMonthAgo = date(Y-m-d H:i:s', mktime( -30));
//a month to a week
<option value="time">Time start</option>
</select>
<select name="date_end" id="dateEnd">
<?php
    $currentDate= date('Y-m-d H:i:s');
$nextWeek = date('', mktime(+7 d));
    $nextMonth = date( ,mktime (+30));
?>
<option value=""><?php echo substr($currentData,10);?>
</option>
<button id="filter" name="Filter">Filter</button>
</form>
```

To enable quick re-rendering of our graph, we have to attach a listener using plain old JavaScript every time the filter button is clicked and then simply erase the information of the `div` element that contains our Highcharts graph.

The following JavaScript code will update the filter using jQuery and underscore and the same code in the first bar chart:

```
<script src="https://code.jquery.com/jquery-2.2.4.min.js"
integrity="sha256-BbhdlvQf/xTY9gja0Dq3HiwQF8LaCRTXxZKRutelT44="
crossorigin="anonymous"></script>

<script src="txet/javascript">
$("button#filter").click {
dateStart = $('input#dateStart').val().split("/");
dateEnd = $('input#dateEnd').val().split("/");
epochDateStart = Math.round(new Date(parseInt(dateStart[])]),
parseInt(dateStart[1]), parseInt(dateStart[2])).getTime()/1000);
epochDateEnd = Math.round(new Date(parseInt(dateEnd [])]), parseInt(dateEnd
[1]), parseInt(dateEnd[2])).getTime()/1000);

        };

client.search({
index: 'apachelogs',
type: 'logs',
body: {
```

```
query: {
        "match_all": {
        },
        {
          "range": {
              "epoch_date": {
                "lt": epochDateStart,

                "gte": epochDateEnd
            }
          }
        }
          }
        }
}).then(function (resp) {
var hits = resp.hits.hits; //look for hits per day fromelasticsearch apache
logs
varlogCounts = new Array();
    _.map(resp.hits.hits, function(count)
    {logCounts.push(count.count)});

$('#container').highcharts({
chart: {
type: 'bar'
        },
title: {
text: 'Apache Logs'
        },
xAxis: {
categories: logDates
        },
yAxis: {
title: {
text: 'Log Volume'
          }
      }

    });
});
</script>
```

In the preceding code, we've included `jquery` and underscore libraries. When the button is clicked to focus on some dates, we set `$_GET['date']` through the form and then PHP gets the information using a simple trick where we re-render the `div` containing the graph by simply flushing the `ihtml` elements inside it, and then asking Highcharts to re-render the data.

To make this a little cooler, we can use a CSS animation effect so it looks like we're focusing a camera.

This can be done using the jQuery CSS transform techniques, and then resizing it back to normal and reloading a new graph:

```
$("button#filter").click( function() {
    //..other code
    $("#container").animate ({
width: [ "toggle", "swing" ],
height: [ "toggle", "swing" ]
});
});
```

Now we've learned how to filter using JavaScript and allow filtering of the JSON data using the filter style. Take note that filter is a relatively new JavaScript function; it only got introduced with **ECMAScript 6**. We've used it to create the dashboard that upper management needs to be able to generate reports for their own purposes.

We can use the underscore library, which has the filter function.

We'll just load the latest logs that are in Elasticsearch, and then, if we want to perform a search, we'll create a way to filter and specify what data to search in the logs.

Let's create the Logstash configuration for Apache's logs to be grokked by Elasticsearch.

All we need to do is point the input Logstash configuration to our Apache logs location (usually a file in the /var/log/apache2 directory).

This is the basic Logstash configuration for Apache, which reads the Apache access log file at /var/log/apache2/access.log:

```
input {    file {
path => '/var/log/apache2/access.log'
            }
}

filter {
grok {
    match =>{ "message" => "%{COMBINEDAPACHELOG}" }
    }
date {
match => [ "timestamp" , "dd/MMM/yyyy:HH:mm:ss Z" ]
    }
}
```

It uses something called a grok filter that matches anything that resembles an Apache log format and matches the timestamp to the dd/MMM/yyyy:HH:mm:ss Z date format.

If you think of Elasticsearch as the end of the rainbow and Apache logs as the start of the rainbow, then Logstash is like the rainbow that transports the logs from both ends into a format that Elasticsearch can understand.

Grokking is the term used to describe reformatting a message format into something that Elasticsearch can interpret. This just means that it will search for a pattern and filter match for that pattern in particular, it will look up the log's timestamp and message and other attributes in JSON, which is what Elasticsearch then stores in its database.

Dashboard app for viewing Elasticsearch logs

Let's now create a dashboard for our blog that will allow us to see the data that we have in Elasticsearch, both posts and Apache logs. We'll use the PHP Elasticsearch SDK to query Elasticsearch and display the Elasticsearch results.

We'll just load the latest logs that are in Elasticsearch, and then, if we want to perform a search, we'll create a way to filter and specify what data to search in the logs.

This is what the search filter form will look like:

In search.php, we'll create a simple form for searching values in Elasticsearch:

```
<form action="search_elasticsearch.php" method="post">
<table>
   <tr>
<td>Select time or query search term
<tr><td>Time or search</td>
<td><select>
    <option value="time">Time</option>
     <option value="query">Query Term</option>
<select>
</td>
</tr>
```

```
<tr>
<td>Time Start/End</td>
  <td><input type="text" name="searchTimestart" placeholder="YYYY-MM-DD
HH:MM:SS" > /
  <input type="text" name="searchTimeEnd" placeholder="YYYY-MM-DD HH:MM:SS"
>
</td>
</tr>
<tr>
<td>Search Term:</td><td><input name="searchTerm"></td>
</tr>
<tr><td colspan="2">
<input type="submit" name="search">
</td></tr>
</table>
</form>
```

When the user clicks on **Submit**, we will then show the results to the user.

Our form should simply show us what records we have for that day for both the Apache logs and the blog posts.

This is how we query `ElasticSearch` for that information in the command line using curl:

$ curl http://localhost:9200/_search?q=post_date>2016-11-15

Now we'll get a JSON response from Elasticsearch:

```
{"took":403,"timed_out":false,"_shards":{"total":5,"successful":5,"failed":
0},"hits":{"total":1,"max_score":0.01989093,"hits":[{"_index":"posts","_typ
e":"post","_id":"1","_score":0.01989093,"_source":{
   body: {
     "user" : "kimchy",
     "post_date" : "2016-11-15T14:12:12",
     "post_body" : "trying out Elasticsearch"
   }
}}]}}
```

We can use a REST client (a way to query RESTful API's in Firefox) as well to query the database just specify the GET method and the path and set the q variable in the URL to the parameters you want to search:

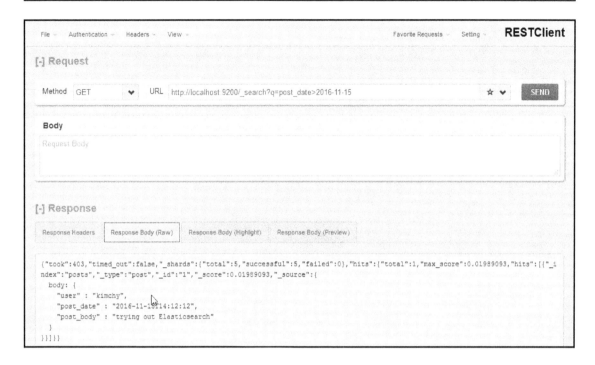

Simple search engine with result caching

To install the PHP Redis, visit https://github.com/phpredis/phpredis.

Every time the user searches, we can save their recent searches in Redis and just present those results if they already exist. The implementation might looks as follows:

```php
<?php
$db = new mysqli(HOST, DB_USER, DB_PASSWORD, DB_NAME); //define the
connection details
if(isset($_POST['search'])) {

$hashSearchTerm = md5($_POST['search']);
    //get from redis and check if key exist,
    //if it does, return search result
    $rKeys = $redis->keys(*);
    if(in_array($rKeys, $hashSearchTerm){
        $searchResults =  $redis->get($hashSearchTerm);
        echo "<ul>";
        foreach($searchResults as $result) {
                echo "<li>
    <a href="readpost.php?id=" . $result ['postId'].
```

```php
"">".$result['postTitle'] . "</a>
        </li>" ;
         echo "</ul>";
      }
    } else {
      $query = "SELECT * from posts WHERE post_title LIKE
'%".$_POST['search']."%' OR post_content LIKE '%".$_POST['search']."%'";

      $result = $db->query($query);
      if($result->num_rows() > 0) {
      echo "<ul>;"
      while ($row = $result->fetch_array(MYSQL_BOTH))
        {
        $queryResults = [
        'postId' => $row['id'],
        'postTitle' => $row['post_title'];
        ];

        echo "<li>
      <a href="readpost.php?id=" . $row['id']. "">".$row['post_title'] .
"</a>
        </li>" ;
        }
      echo "</ul>";
      $redis->setEx($hashSearchTerm, 3600, $queryResults);

      }
    }
} //end if $_POST
else {
  echo "No search term in input";
}
?>
```

Redis is a simple dictionary. It stores a key and the value of that key in its database. In the preceding code, we use it to store a reference to the user's search results so that next time the same search is performed, we can just pull what we have from the Redis data.

In the preceding code, we converted the search term into a hash so that it can be easily identified as the same query that came through and it can be stored easily as the key (which should be one string only, no spaces allowed). If after hashing we find the key in Redis, then we get it from Redis instead of fetching it from the database.

Redis can expire keys by saving the key using the $redis->setEx method, which allows us to store the key and expire it after X number of seconds. In this case, we're storing it for 3,600 seconds, which is equivalent to an hour.

Cache basics

The concept of a cache is to return the already searched items back to the user so that for other users who are searching for the same exact search results, the application should no longer need to do a full database fetch from the MySQL database.

The bad thing with having a cache is that you have to perform cache invalidation.

Cache invalidation of Redis data

Cache invalidation is when you need to expire and delete the cache data. This is because your cache may no longer be real time after a while. Of course, after invalidation, you need to renew the data in the cache, which happens when there is a new request to the data. The cache invalidation process can take one of the following three methods:

- **Purge** is when we remove content from the cache data right away.
- **Refresh** just means get new data and overwrite the already existing data. This means that even though there is a match in the cache, we will refresh that match with the new information fresh from wherever it comes from.
- **Ban** is basically adding previously cached content to a ban list. When another client fetches the same information and, upon checking the blacklist, if it already exists, the cached content just gets updated.

We can run a cronjob continuously in the background that will update every cache result with new results for that search.

This is what the background PHP script that runs every 15 minute might look like in crontab:

```
0,15,30,45 * * * * php /path/to/phpfile
```

To get Logstash to put data in Redis, we just need to do the following:

```
# shipper from apache logs to redis data
output {
redis { host => "127.0.0.1" data_type => "channel" key => "logstash-
%{@type}-%{+yyyy.MM.dd.HH}" }
}
```

This is how the PHP script that deletes data from the cache would work:

```
functiongetPreviousSearches() {
return   $redis->get('searches'); //an array of previously searched
searchDates
}

$prevSearches = getPreviousSearches();

$prevResults = $redis->get('prev_results');

if($_POST['search']) {

   if(in_array($prevSEarches)&&in_array($prevResults[$_POST['search']])) {
if($prevSEarches[$_POST['search']])] {
            $redis->expire($prevSearches($_POST['searchDate'])) {
         Return $prevResults[$_POST['search']];
} else {
         $values =$redis->get('logstash-'.$_POST['search']);
            $previousResults[] = $values;
         $redis->set('prev_results', $previousResults);
          }
}
      }
   }
```

In the preceding script, we basically check the searchDate searched earlier, and if we have it, we set it to expire.

If it also appears in the previousResults array, we give that to the user; otherwise, we do a new redis->get command to get the results for that searched date.

Using browser localStorage as cache

Another option for cache storage is to save it in the client browser itself. The technology is known as **localStorage**.

We can use it as a simple cache for the user and store the search results, and if the user wants to search for the same thing, we just check the localStorage cache.

> localStorage can only store 5 MB of data. But this is quite a lot considering that a regular text file is just a few kilobytes.

We can make use of the `elasticsearch.js` client instead of the PHP client to make requests to our Elasticsearch. The browser-compatible version can be downloaded from htt ps://www.elastic.co/guide/en/elasticsearch/client/javascript-api/current/bro wser-builds.html.

We can also use Bower to install the `elasticsearch.js` client:

```
bower install elasticsearch
```

For our purpose, we can take advantage of the jQuery Build by creating a client using jQuery:

```
var client = new $.es.Client({
hosts: 'localhost:9200'
});
```

We should now be able to use JavaScript to populate the `localStorage`.

Since we are just querying and displaying on the client side, it's a perfect match!

Take note that we might not be able to log the data that was searched for by using a client-side script. However, we could save the search query history as a model containing the items keys that were searched for.

The basic JavaScript `searchQuery` object would look like the following:

```
varsearchQuery = {
search: {queryItems: [ {
'title: 'someName',
  'author': 'Joe',
    'tags': 'some tags'}
] };
};
```

We can test whether the client works by running the following JavaScript file:

```
client.ping({
requestTimeout: 30000,

    // undocumented params are appended to the query string
hello: "elasticsearch"
}, function (error) {
if (error) {
console.error('elasticsearch cluster is down!');
    } else {
console.log('All is well');
    }
```

```
});
```

The results could be cached into `localStorage` by doing the following:

```
localStorage.setItem('results',JSON.stringify(results));
```

We'll populate the results with data we find from `elasticsearch` and then just check if the same query was done earlier.

We also need to keep the data fresh. Let's hypothesize that it takes about 15 minutes before a user gets bored and would refresh the page to try to see new information.

In the same manner, we check whether the search result have been displayed in the past:

```
var searches = localStorage.get('searches');
if(searches != mktime( date('H'), date('i')-15) ) {
  //fetch again
varsearchParams = {
index: 'logdates',
body:
query: {
match: {
date: $('#search_date').value;

}
client.search();
} else {
  //output results from previous search;
prevResults[$("#search_date").val()];
}
```

Now, whenever we expire the search criteria, say after about 15 minutes, we will simply clear the cache and put in the new search results that Elasticsearch finds.

Working with streams

Here, we will take advantage of PHP's Monolog library and then stream the data instead of pushing complete strings. The nice thing about working with streams is that they can easily pipe into Logstash and, in turn, store it into Elasticsearch as indexed data. Logstash also has features for creating data streams and streaming the data.

We can directly input our data without even using Logstash, using something that is known as streams. For more information on streams, refer to `http://php.net/manual/en/book.stream.php`.

Here, for example, is a way to push some data to Elasticsearch:
`http://localhost/dev/streams/php_input.php`:

```
curl -d "Hello World" -d "foo=bar&name=John"
http://localhost/dev/streams/php_input.php
```

In `php_input`, we can put the following code:

```
readfile('php://input')
```

We'll be getting `Hello World&foo=bar&name=John`, which means that PHP was able to get the very first string as a stream using the PHP input stream.

To play around with PHP streams, let's create a stream using PHP manually. PHP developers usually have some experience working with stream data already when working with output buffering.

The idea with output buffering is to collect the stream until it's complete and then show it to the user.

This is especially useful when the stream isn't finished yet and we need to wait for the ending character for the data to be completely transferred.

We can push streams into Elasticsearch! This can be done using the Logstash input plugin to handle streams. This is how PHP can output to a stream:

```php
<?php
require 'vendor/autoload.php';
$client = new Elasticsearch\Client();
ob_start();
$log['body'] = array('hello' => 'world', 'message' => 'some test');
$log['index'] = 'test';
$log['type'] = 'log';
echo json_encode($log);
//flush output of echo into $data
$data = ob_get_flush();
$newData = json_decode($data); //turn back to array
$client->index($newData);
```

Storing and searching XML documents using PHP

We can also work with XML documents and insert them into Elasticsearch. To do so, we can transform the data into JSON and then push the JSON into Elasticsearch.

First, you can check out the following XML to JSON converter:

If you want to check that the XML has been converted correctly to JSON, check out the **XML TO JSON Converter** tool at `http://codebeautify.org/xmltojson`; from there, you can easily check out how to export an XML to JSON:

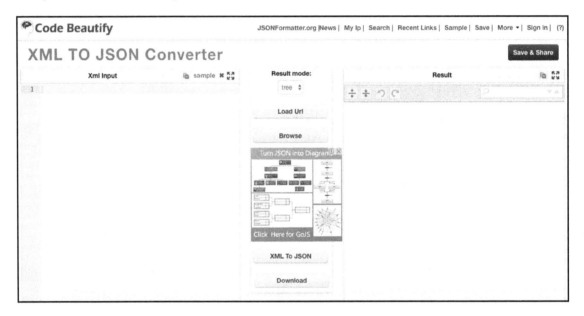

Using Elasticsearch to search a social network database

In this section, we'll simply use our knowledge to apply it to an existing social network built with PHP.

Let's pretend we have users who want to be able to search their social feed. Here's where we build a full-blown auto-dropdown search system.

Every time the user posts, we need to be able to store all the data in Elasticsearch.

However, in our search queries, we will match search results to the actual word that the user fetched. If it doesn't match the query in each, character-by-character, we won't display it.

We first need to build the feed. The SQL schema will look as follows:

```
CREATE TABLE feed (
Id INT(11) PRIMARY KEY,
Post_title TEXT,
post_content TEXT,
post_topics TEXT,
post_time DATETIME,
post_type VARCHAR(255),
posted_by INT (11) DEFAULT '1'
) ;
```

Post_type would handle the type of post—photo, video, link, or just plain text.

So, if the user added a type of picture, it would be saved as an image type. And when a person searches for a post, they can filter by the type.

Every time users save a new photo, or a new post, we will also store the data into Elasticsearch, which will look as follows:

```
INSERT INTO feed (`post_title`, `post_content`, `post_time`, `post_type`)
VALUES ('some title', 'some content', '2015-03-20 00:00:00', 'image', 1);
```

Now we need to make an input form when the user inserts the preceding new posting. We'll just build the one that can upload a photo with a title or just add text:

```
<h2>Post something</h2>

<form type="post" action="submit_status.php" enctype="multipart/form-data">
Title:<input name="title" type="text" />
Details: <input name="content" type="text">
Select photo:
<input type="file" name="fileToUpload" id="fileToUpload">
<input type="hidden" value="<?php echo $_SESSION['user_id'] ?>"
name="user_id">
<input name="submit" type="submit">

</form>
```

The `submit_status.php` script will have the following code to save into the database:

```php
<?php
use Elasticsearch\ClientBuilder;

    require 'vendor/autoload.php';

$db = new mysqli(HOST, DB_USER, DB_PASSWORD, DATABASE);

 $client = ClientBuilder::create()->build();
if(isset($_POST['submit'])) {
   $contentType = (!empty($_FILES['fileToUpload'])) ? 'image' : '

$db->query("INSERT INTO feed (`post_title`, `post_content`, `post_time`,
`post_type`, `posted_by`)
VALUES ('". $_POST['title'] ."','" . $_POST['content'] . "','" . date('Y-m-
d H:i:s'). "','" . $contentType . "','" . $_POST['user_id']);

//save into elasticsearch
$params = [
    'index' => 'my_feed',
    'type' => 'posts',
    'body' => [
      'contenttype' => $contentType,
      'title'  => $_POST['title'],
      'content' => $_POST['content'],
      'author' => $_POST['user_id']
    ]
];
      $client->index($params);
  }

  ?>
```

Displaying randomized search engine results

The preceding feed database table is the table that everyone will post to. We need to enable randomly showing what's on the feed. We can insert posts into feeds instead of storing.

By searching from Elasticsearch and randomly rearranging the data, we can make our searches more fun. In a way, this makes sure that people using our social network will be able to see random posts in their feed.

To search from the posts, instead of doing a direct query to SQL, we will search the Elasticsearch database for the data.

First, let's figure out how to insert the data into an Elasticsearch index called `posts`. With Elasticsearch open, we simply do the following:

```
$ curl-XPUT 'http://localhost:9200/friends/'-d '{
"settings":{
"number_of_shards":3,
"number_of_replicas":2
}
}'
```

We will probably also want to search our friends, and if we have a ton of friends, they won't all be on the feed. So, we just need another index to search called the `friends` index.

The following code, when run in the Linux command line, will allow us to create a new `friends` index:

```
$ curl-XPUT 'http://localhost:9200/friends/'-d '{
"settings":{
"number_of_shards":3,
"number_of_replicas":2
}
}'
```

So, we can now store data about our friends using the `friends` index:

```
$ curl-XPUT 'http://localhost:9200/friends/posts/1'-d '{
"user":"kimchy",
"post_date":"2016-06-15T14:12:12",
"message":"fred the friend"
}'
```

We'll usually look for friends of friends and we'll, of course, show that to our user if there are any friends with the search query.

Summary

In this chapter, we discussed how to create a blog system, experimented with Elasticsearch, and were able to do the following:

- Create a simple blog application and store data in MySQL
- Install Logstash and Elasticsearch
- Practice working with Elasticsearch using curl
- Get data into Elasticsearch using the PHP Client
- Chart information (hits) from Elasticsearch using Highcharts
- Use the `elasticsearch.js` client to query Elasticsearch for information
- Use Redis and localStorage in the browser to work with caching

5
Creating a RESTful Web Service

The goal of this chapter is to implement a RESTful Web Service that can be used to manage user profiles. Each user will have some basic contact information (such as a username, a given name, and a family name), a password for authentication, and a profile image.

This service will be implemented using the Slim micro framework, a small and lightweight framework that is available as an open-source library (MIT licensed) for PHP 5.5 and newer (we'll be using PHP 7, of course). For persistence, a MongoDB database will be used. This offers the perfect chance to explore PHP's MongoDB extension, which replaces the old (similarly named, but completely different) Mongo extension that was removed with PHP 7.

In this chapter, we will cover the following:

- The basics of RESTful Web Services, most importantly the common HTTP request and response methods
- Installing and using the Slim framework, and also the basics of the PSR-7 standard
- Designing and implementing the actual example RESTful Web Service using the Slim framework and MongoDB storage
- How to work with PSR-7 streams and store large files in a MongoDB database with GridFS

RESTful basics

In this section, we will recapitulate the basics of RESTful Web Services. You will learn about the basic architectural goals of REST Web Services and the most common protocol semantics of the **Hypertext Transfer Protocol (HTTP)**, which is commonly used to implement such services.

REST architectures

The term **Representational State Transfer** was coined by Roy Fielding in 2000 and describes an architectural style for distributed systems that is, in principle, independent of any concrete communication protocol. In practice, most REST architectures are implemented using the **Hypertext Transfer Protocol** – in short, HTTP.

The key component of each RESTful Web Service is the resource. Each resource should meet the following requirements:

- **Addressability**: Each resource must be identifiable by a **Uniform Resource Identifier (URI)**, which is standardized in RFC 3986. For instance, a user with the username johndoe might have the URI
  `http://example.com/api/users/johndoe`.
- **Statelessness**: The participants' communication between each other is stateless; this means that REST applications typically do not use user sessions. Instead, each request needs to contain all information that the server will need to fulfill the request.
- **Uniform interface**: Each resource must be accessible by a set of standard methods. When using HTTP as a transfer protocol, you will typically use the HTTP methods for querying or modifying the state of resources. The next section of this chapter contains a short overview of the most common HTTP standard methods and response codes.
- **Decoupling of resources and representation**: Each resource can have multiple representations. For example, a REST service might serve both a JSON and an XML representation of a user profile. Typically, the client specifies in which format the server should respond, and the server will choose a representation that best fits the requirements specified by the client. This process is called **Content Negotiation**.

In this chapter, you will learn to implement all these architectural principles in a small RESTful Web Service. You will implement several different resource types with different representations and learn how to use different HTTP methods and response codes to query and modify these resources. Additionally, you will learn how you can use advanced HTTP features to your advantage (such as the rich set of cache-control headers).

Common HTTP methods and response codes

HTTP defines a set of standard methods (or *verbs*) that clients can use in requests, and status codes that servers can use in responses to said requests. In REST architectures, the different request methods are used to either query or modify the server-side state of the resource that is identified by the request URI. These request methods and response status codes are standardized in RFC 7231. **Table 1** and **Table 2** show an overview of the most common request methods and status codes.

The request methods GET, HEAD, and OPTIONS are defined as *safe*. Servers should not modify their own state when processing these kinds of requests. Furthermore, both the safe methods and PUT and DELETE methods are defined as *idempotent*. Idempotency means that repeated identical requests should have the same effect as a single request – for instance, multiple DELETE requests to the /api/users/12345 URI should still result in that one resource being deleted.

Table 1, Common HTTP request methods:

HTTP method	Description
GET	Used for querying the state of the resource identified by the URI. The server responds with a representation of the queried resource.
HEAD	Just like GET, except the server returns only the response headers and not the actual resource representation.
POST	POST requests can contain a resource representation in their request body. The server should store this object as a new sub-resource of the resource identified by the request URI.
PUT	Just like POST, PUT requests also contain a resource representation in their request body. The server should ensure that a resource with the given URI and representation exists and should create one if necessary.
DELETE	Deletes the resource with the specified URI.
OPTIONS	Can be used by clients to query which operations are allowed for a given resource.

Table 2: Common HTTP response status codes:

Status code	Description
200 OK	The request was successfully processed; the response message typically contains a representation of the requested resource.
201 Created	Like 200 OK, but in addition, explicitly states that a new resource was created by the request.
202 Accepted	The request was accepted for processing, but has not yet been processed. This is useful when a server processes time-consuming requests asynchronously.
400 Bad Request	The server was unable to interpret the client's request. This might be the case when a request contains invalid JSON or XML data.
401 Unauthorized	The client needs to authenticate before accessing this resource. The response can contain more information on the required authentication and the request can be repeated with appropriate credentials.
403 Forbidden	Can be used when the client was authenticated, but is not authorized to access a given resource.
404 Not Found	Used when the resource specified by the URI does not exist.
405 Method Not Allowed	The request method is not allowed for the specified resource.
500 Internal Server Error	An error occurred on the server while processing the request.

First steps with the Slim framework

In this section, you will take you first steps with the Slim framework. For this, you will first use Composer to install the framework and then build a small sample application that will show you the basic principles of the framework.

Installing Slim

The Slim framework can be easily installed using Composer. It requires PHP in at least version 5.5, but also works well with PHP 7. Start by initializing a new project with Composer:

```
$ composer init .
```

This will create a new project-level `composer.json` file for our project. Now you can add the slim/slim package as a dependency:

```
$ composer require slim/slim
```

A small sample application

You can now start using the Slim framework in your PHP application. For this, create an `index.php` file in your web server's document root with the following content:

```php
<?php
use \Slim\App;
use \Slim\Http\Request;
use \Slim\Http\Response;

require "vendor/autoload.php";

$app = new App();
$app->get("/", function(Request $req, Response $res): Response {
    return $res->withJson(["message" => "Hello World!"]);
});
$app->run();
```

Let's have a look at how the Slim framework works here. The central object here is the `$app` variable, an instance of the `Slim\App` class. You can then use this application instance to register routes. Each route is a mapping of an HTTP request path to a simple callback function that handles an HTTP request. These handler functions need to accept a request and a response object and need to return a new response object.

Before you can test this application, you may need to configure your web server to rewrite all requests to your `index.php` file. If you are using Apache as a web server, this can be done with a simple `.htaccess` file in your document root:

```
RewriteEngine on
RewriteCond %{REQUEST_FILENAME} !-f
RewriteCond %{REQUEST_FILENAME} !-d
RewriteRule ^([^?]*)$ /index.php [NC,L,QSA]
```

This configuration will rewrite requests for all URLs to your `index.php` file.

You can test your (admittedly still very simple) API with your browser. If you prefer the command line, I can recommend the**HTTPie** command-line tool. HTTPie is Python-based and you can easily install it using your operating system's package manager or Python's own package manager, **pip**:

```
apt-get install httpie
# Alternatively:
pip install --upgrade httpie
```

You can then use `HTTPie` on the command-line to perform RESTful HTTP requests easily and also get syntax-highlighted output. See the following figure for an example output of HTTPie when used with the example application:

Example output of HTTPie with the Slim example application

Accepting URL parameters

Slim routes can also contain parameters in their path. In your `index.php`, add the following route before the last `$app->run()` statement:

```
$app->get(
    '/users/{username}',
    function(Request $req, Response $res, array $args): Response {
        return $res->withJson([
            'message' => 'Hello ' . $args['username'
        ]);
    }
);
```

As you can see, any route specification can contain arbitrary parameters in curly brackets. The route handler function can then accept a third parameter that contains all path parameters from the URL as an associative array (such as the username parameter in the preceding example).

Accepting HTTP requests with a message body

So far, you have only worked with HTTP GET requests. Of course, the Slim framework also supports any other kind of request method that is defined by the HTTP protocol. One interesting difference between a GET and – for example – a POST request, however, is that some requests (such as POST, PUT, and others) can contain a request body.

The request body consists of structured data that is serialized as a string according to some pre-defined encoding. When sending a request to a server, the client uses the **Content-Type** HTTP header to tell the server which encoding is used for the request body. Common encodings include the following:

- application/x-www-form-urlencoded is typically used by browsers when submitting an HTML form
- application/json for JSON encoding
- application/xml or text/xml for XML encoding

Luckily, the Slim framework supports all these encodings and determines the correct method to parse a request body automatically. You can test this with the following simple route handler:

```
$app->post('/users', function(Request $req, Response $res): Response {
    $body = $req->getParsedBody();
    return $response->withJson([
        'message' => 'creating user ' . $body['username']
    ]);
});
```

Note the use of the getParsedBody() method that is offered by the Request class. This method will use the request body and automatically use the correct decoding method depending on the Content-Type header that was present in the request.

You can now use any of the preceding content encodings presented to POST data to this route. This can be easily tested using the following curl commands:

```
$ curl -d '&username=martin&firstname=Martin&lastname=Helmich'
http://localhost/users
$ curl -d
```

```
'{"username":"martin","firstname":"Martin","lastname":"Helmich"}' -
H'Content-Type: application/json' http://localhost/users
    $ curl -d
'<user><username>martin</username><firstname>Martin</firstname><lastname>He
lmich</lastname></user>' -H'Content-Type: application/xml'
```

All of these requests will yield the same response from your Slim application, as they're containing the exact same data, just using a different content encoding.

The PSR-7 standard

One of the Slim framework's main features is the PSR-7 compliance. PSR-7 is a **PHP Standard Recommendation** (**PSR**) defined by the **PHP Framework Interoperability Group** (**FIG**) and describes a set of standard interfaces that can be implemented by HTTP servers and client libraries written in PHP to increase operability between those products (or in plain English, to enable these libraries to be used with each other).

PSR-7 defines a set of PHP interfaces that the framework can implement. The following figure illustrates the interfaces that are defined by the PSR-7 standard. You can even install these interfaces in your project by acquiring the `psr/http-messages` package using Composer:

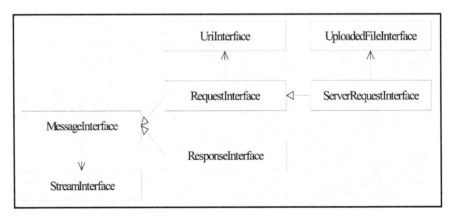

The interfaces defined by the PSR-7 standard

The `Slim\Http\Request` and `Slim\Http\Response` classes that you have worked with in the previous examples already implement these PSR-7 interfaces (the `Slim\Http\Request` class implements the `ServerRequestInterface` and `Slim\Http\Response` implements `ResponseInterface`).

These standardized interfaces become especially useful when you want to use two different HTTP libraries together. As an interesting example, consider a PSR-7 compliant HTTP server framework like Slim used together with a PSR-7 compliant client library, for example **Guzzle** (use the package key `guzzlehttp/guzzle` if you want to install it with Composer). You can use these two libraries and easily wire them together for a dead-simple reverse proxy:

```
$httpClient = new \GuzzleHttp\Client();

$app = new \Slim\App();
$app->any('{path:.*}',
    function(
        ServerRequestInterface $req,
        ResponseInterface $response
    ) use ($client): ResponseInterface {
        return $client->send(
            $request->withUri(
                $request->getUrl()->withHost('your-upstream-server.local')
            )
        );
    }
);
```

What exactly happens here? The Slim request handler gets an implementation of the `ServerRequestInterface` passed as a first parameter (remember; this interface inherits the regular `RequestInterface`) and needs to return a `ResponseInterface` implementation. Conveniently, the `send()` method of `GuzzleHttp\Client` also accepts a `RequestInterface` and returns a `ResponseInterface`. Because of this, you can simply re-use the request object that you received in your handler and pipe it into the Guzzle client and also re-use the response object returned by the Guzzle client. Guzzle's `send()` method actually returns an instance of the `GuzzleHttp\Psr7\Response` class (and not `Slim\Http\Response`). That is completely acceptable, as both of these classes implement the same interface. In addition, the preceding example uses the method defined by the PSR-7 interfaces to modify the host part of the request URI.

Immutable Objects

You may have wondered about the `withUri` and `withHost` methods in the preceding code example. Why do the PSR-7 interfaces not imply declare methods such as `setUri` or `setHost`? The answer is that all PSR-7 implementations are designed to be immutable. This means that objects are not intended to be modified after they are created. All the methods starting with `with` (and PSR-7 actually defines a lot of them) are designed to return a copy of the original object with one modified property.

So basically, instead of modifying objects with setter methods, you'll be passing around clones of an original object:

```
// using mutable objects (not supported by PSR-7)
$uri->setHost('foobar.com');
// using immutable objects
$uri = $uri->withHOst('foobar.com');
```

Middleware

Middleware is one of the most important features of the Slim framework and similar libraries. It allows you to modify an HTTP request before it is passed to the actual request handler, modify an HTTP response after being returned from the request handler, or bypass a request handler entirely. There are quite a number of possible use cases for this:

- You can handle authentication and authorization in middleware. Authentication encompasses identifying a user from given request parameters (maybe the HTTP request contains an authorization header or a cookie with a session ID) and authorization involves checking if the authenticated user is actually allowed to access a particular resource.
- You can implement a rate limiting for your API by counting requests by a particular user and returning with an error response code early before hitting the actual request handler.
- In general, all kinds of operations that enrich a request with additional data before being processed by the request handler.

Middleware is also chainable. The framework can manage any number of middleware components, and an incoming request will be piped through all registered middleware. Each item of middleware must be callable as a function and accept a `RequestInterface`, a `ResponseInterface`, and a function that represents the next instance of middleware (or the request handler itself).

The following code example shows middleware that adds an (admittedly extremely simple) HTTP authentication to an application:

```php
$app->add(function (Request $req, Response $res, callable $next): Response
{
    $auth = $req->getHeader('Authorization');
    if (!$auth) {
        return $res->withStatus(401);
    }

    if (substr($auth, 0, 6) !== 'Basic ' ||
        base64_decode(substr($auth, 6)) !== 'admin:secret') {
        return $res->withStatus(401);
    }

    return $next($req, $res);
}

$app->get('/users/{username}', function(Request $req, Response $res):
Response {
    // Handle the request
});

$app->get('/users/{username}', function(Request $req, Response $res):
Response {
    // Handle the request
});
```

The `$app->add()` function can be used to register middleware that will be invoked on any request. As you can see, the middleware function itself looks similar to a regular request handler, with the only difference being the third parameter, `$next`. Each request can be passed through a potentially indeterminate amount of middleware. The `$next` function gives a component of middleware control over whether a request should be passed to the next component of middleware in the chain (or the registered request handler itself). It is important to note, however, that the middleware does not have to call the `$next` function at any time. In the preceding example, an unauthorized HTTP request will never even get through to the actual request handler, because the middleware that handles authentication does not invoke `$next` at all when there is no valid authentication.

This is where PSR-7 comes into play. Because of PSR-7, you can develop and distribute middleware and they will work with all frameworks and libraries that also implement PSR-7. This guarantees interoperability between libraries and also ensures that there is a shared ecosystem of libraries that can be widely re-used. A simple Internet search for `PSR-7 middlewares` yields a plethora of libraries that you can use nearly out-of-the box.

Implementing the REST service

In this chapter, you will begin implementing the actual user profile service. As a first step, we will design the RESTful API of the service and then continue by implementing the designed API endpoints.

Designing the service

Now it is time to get to the actual task that we want to implement in this chapter. In this chapter, you will develop a RESTful Web Service using the Slim framework and MongoDB to access and read user profiles. In short, one of the first steps that you should take when designing a REST Web Service is to think about the resources that you want to offer to your users.

Keeping RESTful

Be sure to design around resources whose state you modify with HTTP verbs such as POST, PUT, and DELETE. I've often seen HTTP APIs being developed around procedures, not resources, that end up in URLs such as POST /users/create or POST /users/update that resemble more of an RPC-based API design.

The table that follows shows the resources and operations that we'll be working with in this chapter. There are a few central resources:

- /profiles is a collection of all known profiles. It is read-only – meaning that only GET (and HEAD) operations will be allowed – and contains a collection of all user profiles. Users of your API should be able to filter the set by a set of constraints or limit the returned collection to a given length. Both filtering and limitations can be implemented as optional query parameters:

  ```
  GET /profiles?firstName=Martin&limit=10
  ```

- /profiles/{username} is a resource that represents a single user. A GET request on this resource will return this user's profile, while a PUT request will create the profile or update it if it already exists and a DELETE request will delete the profile.
- /profiles/{username}/image represents a user's profile image. It can be set using a PUT operation, read with a GET operation, and removed with a DELETE operation.

Route	Purpose
`GET /profiles`	Lists all users, optionally filtered by search parameters
`GET /profiles/{username}`	Returns a single user
`PUT /profiles/{username}`	Creates a new user with a given username or updates an already existing one with that username
`DELETE /profiles/{username}`	Deletes a user
`PUT /profiles/{username}/image`	Stores a new profile image for a user
`GET /profiles/{username}/image`	Retrieves the user's profile image
`DELETE /profiles/{username}/image`	Deletes a profile image

One question that might arise is why this example uses a `PUT` request to create new profiles, and not `POST`. I've often seen `POST` being associated with *creating objects* and `PUT` with *updating objects* – this is an incorrect interpretation of the HTTP standards. Note that we're using the username as part of the profile's URI. This means that when creating a profile for a new user with a given user name, you already know which URI the resource will have after it's created.

And that is exactly what the `PUT` resource is for – ensuring that a resource with a given representation exists with the given URI. The advantage is that you can rely on `PUT` requests being idempotent. This means that a dozen identical `PUT` requests to `/profiles/martin-helmich` will not do any harm, while a dozen identical `POST` requests to `/profiles/` might very well create a dozen different user profiles.

Bootstrapping the project

Before beginning to implement your REST service, you will probably need to take care of some system requirements. For the sake of simplicity, we'll be working with a set of linked Docker containers in this example. Start by creating a new container running a MongoDB instance using the official MongoDB image:

```
$ docker run --name profiles-db -d mongodb
```

For the application container, you can use the official PHP image. However, as the MongoDB PHP driver is not part of the standard PHP distribution, you will need to install it via **PECL**. For this, you can create a custom **Dockerfile** to build your application container:

```
FROM php:7-apache

RUN apt-get update && \
    apt-get install -y libssl-dev && \
    pecl install mongodb && \
    docker-php-ext-enable mongodb
RUN a2enmod rewrite
```

Next, build your container and run it. Link it to the already running MongoDB container:

```
$ docker build -t packt-chp5 .
$ docker run --name profiles-web --link profiles-db:db \
-v $PWD:/var/www/html -p 80:80 packt-chp5
```

This will create a new Apache container running PHP 7 with the current working directory mapped to the web server's document root. The -p 80:80 flag allows the Apache container to be accessed using http://localhost from your browser or a command-line client.

Just like in the first examples in this chapter, we will be using Composer to manage the project's dependencies and for automatic class loading. You can start with the following composer.json file:

```
{
    "name": "packt-php7/chp5-rest-example",
    "type": "project",
    "authors": [{
        "name": "Martin Helmich",
        "email": "php7-book@martin-helmich.de"
    }],
    "require": {
        "php": ">=7.0",
        "slim/slim": "^3.1",
        "mongodb/mongodb": "^1.0",
        "phpunit/phpunit": "^5.1",
        "ext-mongodb": "*"
    },
    "autoload": {
        "psr-4": {
            "Packt\\Chp5": "src/"
        }
    }
}
```

After creating the `composer.json` file, install the project's dependencies with `composer install`. If you are not running Composer in an environment that matches all specified constraints, you can add the `--ignore-platform-reqs` flag to the Composer command.

In this example, we will be using Composer's PSR-4 autoloader with `Packt\Chp5` as a base namespace and all classes located in the `src/` directory. That means that a class such as `Packt\Chp5\Foo\Bar` needs to be defined in the file `src/Foo/Bar.php`.

Building the persistence layer with MongoDB

The first step we'll take in this example is to build an object-oriented model of the application's domain – the user profile. In the first step, this will not be overly complicated. Let's start by defining a `Profile` class with the following properties:

- A username that uniquely identifies the user and can serve as a login username
- A given name and a family name
- A list of interests and hobbies that the user cares about
- The user's birthday
- The hash value of the user's password, which will come in handy later when you want users to authenticate before editing their own profile (and keeping them from editing other people's profiles)

This can be implemented as a simple PHP class. Note that the class is currently completely immutable, as its properties can only be set using the constructor. Also, this class does not contain any kind of persistence logic (meaning getting data from the database or putting it back). Following *Separation of Concerns*, modeling data and persisting it from and into a database are two different concerns that should be handled in different classes.

```
declare(strict_types = 1);
namespace Packt\Chp5\Model;

class Profile
{
    private $username;
    private $givenName;
    private $familyName;
    private $passwordHash;
    private $interests;
    private $birthday;

    public function __construct(
        string $username,
```

```
        string $givenName,
        string $familyName,
        string $passwordHash,
        array $interests = [],
        DateTime $birthday = null
    ) {
        $this->username     = $username;
        $this->givenName    = $givenName;
        $this->familyName   = $familyName;
        $this->passwordHash = $passwordHash;
        $this->interests    = $interests;
        $this->birthday     = $birthday;
    }

    // getter methods omitted for brevity
}
```

Now you can model user profiles within your application – but you cannot do anything with them yet. Our first goal will be to store instances of the `Profile` class in the MongoDB database backend. This will be done in the `Packt\Chp5\Service\ProfileService` class:

```
declare(strict_types = 1);
namespace Packt\Chp5\Service;

use MongoDB\Collection;
use Packt\Chp5\Model\Profile;

class ProfileService
{
    private $profileCollection;

    public function __construct(Collection $profileCollection)
    {
        $this->profileCollection = $profileCollection;
    }
}
```

The `ProfileService` gets an instance of the `MongoDB\Collection` class passed as a dependency into its constructor. This class is provided by the `mongodb/mongodb` Composer package and models one single MongoDB collection (although not exactly true, a collection is MongoDB's equivalent to a MySQL table). Again, we follow Separation of Concerns: establishing the connection to the database is not the `ProfileService`'s concern and will be handled at a different place.

Let's start by implementing a method in this service that can add new user profiles to the database. A fitting name for such a method is `insertProfile`:

```
public function insertProfile(Profile $profile): Profile
{
    $record = $this->profileToRecord($profile);
    $this->profileCollection->insertOne($profile);
    return $profile;
}

private function profileToRecord(Profile $profile): array
{
    return [
        'username'     => $profile->getUsername(),
        'passwordHash' => $profile->getPasswordHash(),
        'familyName'   => $profile->getFamilyName(),
        'givenName'    => $profile->getGivenName(),
        'interests'    => $profile->getInterests(),
        'birthday'     => $profile->getBirthDay()->format('Y-m-d')
    ];
}
}
```

Note that this code example contains a private method, `profileToRecord()`, that converts an instance of the `Profile` class to a plain PHP array that will be stored as a document in the collection. This code was extracted into its own method, because it will be useful to have it as a re-usable function later. The actual insertion is performed by the collection's `insertOne` method, which takes a simple PHP array as a parameter.

As the next step, let's continue by extending the profile service with another method, `updateProfile`, that can – you guessed it – update existing profiles:

```
public function updateProfile(Profile $profile): Profile
{
    $record = $this->profileToRecord($profile);
    $this->profileCollection->findOneAndUpdate(
        ['username' => $profile->getUsername()],
        ['$set' => $record]
    );
    return $profile;
}
```

The first parameter passed to the `findOneAndUpdate` method is a MongoDB query. It contains a set of constraints that a document should match (in this case, the document's `username` property being equal to whatever value `$profile->getUsername()` returns).

Just like SQL queries, these can get arbitrarily complex. For example, the following query will match all users whose given name is `Martin` and are born after January 1st, 1980 and like either open source software or science fiction literature. You can find a full reference of MongoDB query selection operators at `https://docs.mongodb.com/manual/reference/operator/query/`.

```
[
    'givenName' => 'Martin',
    'birthday' => [
      '$gte' => '1980-01-01'
    ],
    'interests' => [
      '$elemMatch' => [
        'Open Source',
        'Science Fiction'
      ]
    ]
]
```

The second parameter to `findOneAndUpdate()` contains a set of update operations which will be applied to the first document found that matches the given query. In this example, the `$set` operator contains an array of property values that will be updated on matched documents. Just like queries, these update statements can get more complex. The following will update all matched users' given names to `Max` and `add` music to their list of interests:

```
[
    '$set' => [
      'givenName' => 'Max',
    ],
    '$addToSet' => [
      'interests' => ['Music']
    ]
]
```

Using a simple test script, you can now already test this profile service. For this, you will need to establish a connection to your MongoDB database. If you used the Docker commands previously, the hostname of your MongoDB server will simply be `db`:

```
declare(strict_types = 1);
$manager = new \MongoDB\Driver\Manager('mongodb://db:27017');
$collection = new \MongoDB\Collection($manager, 'database-name',
'profiles');

$profileService = new \Packt\Chp5\Service\ProfileService($collection);
$profileService->insertProfile(new \Packt\Chp5\Model\Profile(
    'jdoe',
    'John',
```

```
        'Doe',
        password_hash('secret', PASSWORD_BCRYPT),
        ['Open Source', 'Science Fiction', 'Death Metal'],
        new \DateTime('1970-01-01')
));
```

Adding and updating user profiles is nice, but the profile service does not yet support loading those profiles back from the database. For this, you can extend your `ProfileService` with a few more methods. Start with a `hasProfile` method that simply checks if a profile for a given username exists or not:

```
public function hasProfile(string $username): bool
{
    return $this->profileCollection->count(['username' => $username]) > 0;
}
```

The `hasProfile` method simply checks if a profile for a given username is stored in the database. For this, the collection's `count` method is used. This method accepts a MongoDB query object and will return the count of all documents matching this constraint (in this case, the number of all documents with a given username). The `hasProfile` method will return true when a profile with the given username already exists.

Continue by implementing the `getProfile` method, which loads a user profile from the database and returns a respective instance of the `Profile` class:

```
public function getProfile(string $username): Profile
{
    $record = $this->profileCollection->findOne(['username' => $username]);
    if ($record) {
        return $this->recordToProfile($record);
    }
    throw new UserNotFoundException($username);
}

private function recordToProfile(BSONDocument $record): Profile
{
    return new Profile(
        $record['username'],
        $record['givenName'],
        $record['familyName'],
        $record['passwordHash'],
        $record['interests']->getArrayCopy(),
        new \DateTime($record['birthday']));
    );
}
```

The `getProfile` method uses the collection's `findOne` method (which incidentally accepts the same query object), which returns the first document that matches the constraint (or null, when no document can be found). When no profile with the given username can be found, `Packt\Chp5\Exception\UserNotFoundException` will be thrown. The implementation of this class is left as an exercise for the reader. The document – if found – is then passed into the private `recordToProfile` method, which inverts the `profileToRecord` method that you've already implemented earlier. Note that all MongoDB query method do not return plain arrays as documents, but always returns instances of the `MongoDB\Model\BSONDocument` class. You can use these exactly as you would use a regular array, but can trip over it when type-hinting function arguments or return values.

Adding and retrieving users

As you have now successfully implemented the persistence logic of the profile REST service, you can now start implementing the actual REST Web Service.

In the previous examples, we have used simple callback functions as request handlers for the Slim framework:

```
$app->get('/users', function(Request $req, Response $res): Response {
    return $response->withJson(['foo' => 'bar']);
});
```

This is perfectly fine for getting started quickly, but will get difficult to maintain as your application grows. In order to structure your application in a more scalable way, you can exploit the fact that a Slim request handler does not have to be an anonymous function, but can in fact be anything that is callable. In PHP, you can also make objects callable by implementing the __invoke method. You can use this to implement a request handler that can be a stateful class with its own properties.

Before implementing the request handler, though, let us take a look at the web service's responses. As we have chosen JSON as our primary representation format, you will frequently need to convert instances of the `Profile` class to a JSON object – and of course also the other way around. In order to keep this conversion logic reusable, it is recommended that this functionality be implemented in a separate unit. For this, you can implement a `ProfileJsonMapping` trait as, shown in the following example:

```
namespace Packt\Chp5\Mapper;

trait ProfileJsonMapping
{
```

```php
    private function profileToJson(Profile $profile): array
    {
        return [
            'username'   => $profile->getUsername(),
            'givenName'  => $profile->getGivenName(),
            'familyName' => $profile->getFamilyName(),
            'interests'  => $profile->getInterests(),
            'birthday'   => $profile->getBirthday()->format('Y-m-d')
        ];
    }

    private function profileFromJson(string $username, array $json):
Profile
    {
        return new Profile(
            $username,
            $json['givenName'],
            $json['familyName'],
            $json['passwordHash'] ?? password_hash($json['password']),
            $json['interests'] ?? [],
            new \DateTime($json['birthday'])
        );
    }
}
```

With the representation logic taken care of, you can now continue by implementing the route for getting a single user profile. In this example, we will implement this route in the Packt\Chp5\Route\ShowUserRoute class and use the ProfileJsonMapping trait shown previously:

```php
namespace Packt\Chp5\Route;
// imports omitted for brevity

class ShowProfileRoute
{
    use ProfileJsonMapping;
    private $profileService;

    public function __construct(ProfileService $profileService)
    {
        $this->profileService = $profileService;
    }

    public function __invoke(Request $req, Response $res, array $args):
Response
    {
        $username = $args['username'];
        if ($this->profileService->hasProfile($username)) {
```

```
            $profile = $this->profileService->getProfile($username);
            return $res->withJson($this->profileToJson($profile));
        } else {
            return $res
                ->withStatus(404)
                ->withJson(['msg' => 'the user ' . $username . ' does not
exist']);
        }
    }
}
```

As you can see, the __invoke method in this class has the same signature as the callback request handlers that you've seen in the previous examples. Also, this route class uses the ProfileService that you have implemented in the previous section. The actual handler first checks if a profile exists with a given username and returns a **404 Not Found** status code when the requested profile does not exist. Otherwise, the Profile instance will be converted to a plain array and returned as a JSON string.

You can now initialize your Slim application in your index.php as follows:

```
use MongoDB\Driver\Manager;
use MongoDB\Collection;
use Packt\Chp5\Service\ProfileService;
use Packt\Chp5\Route\ShowProfileRoute;
use Slim\App;

$manager        = new Manager('mongodb://db:27017');
$collection     = new Collection($manager, 'database-name', 'profiles');
$profileService = new ProfileService($collection);

$app = new App();
$app->get('/profiles/{username}', new
ShowProfileRoute($profileService));
$app->run();
```

If your database still contains some test data from the previous section, you can now already test this API, for example, by using HTTPie.

Using the REST API to access user profiles

For creating new user profiles (and updating existing ones), you can now create a new request handler class. As a PUT request to /profiles/{username} will either create a new profile or update an already existing one, the new request handler will need to do both:

```php
namespace Packt\Chp5\Route;
// Imports omitted for brevity

class PutProfileRoute
{
    use ProfileJsonMapping;
    private $profileService;

    public function __construct(ProfileService $profileService)
    {
        $this->profileService = $profileService;
    }

    public function __invoke(Request $req, Response $res, array $args):
Response
    {
        $username      = $args['username'];
        $profileJson   = $req->getParsedBody();
        $alreadyExists = $this->profileService->hasProfile($username);
```

```
        $profile = $this->profileFromJson($username, $profileJson);
        if ($alreadyExists) {
            $profile = $this->profileService->updateProfile($profile);
            return $res->withJson($this->profileToJson($profile));
        } else {
            $profile = $this->profileService->insertProfile($profile);
            return
$res->withJson($this->profileToJson($profile))->withStatus(201);
        }
    }
}
```

In this example, we are using the `Request` class' `getParsedBody` method to retrieve the parsed message body. Fortunately, this method is intelligent enough to look at the request's `Content-Type` header and automatically choose an appropriate parsing method (in the case of an `application/json` request, the `json_decode` method will be used to parse the request body).

After retrieving the parsed message body, the `profileFromJson` method defined in the `ProfileJsonMapping` trait is used to create an actual instance of the `Profile` class from this body. Depending on whether a profile with this username already exists, we can then insert or update the user profile using the methods implemented in the `ProfileService` class. Note that depending on whether a new profile is created or an existing one is updated, a different HTTP status code is returned (`201 Created` when a new profile was created, or `200 OK` otherwise).

What about validation?

You will note that currently, you can pass literally anything as a body parameter and the request handler will try to save it as a user profile, even when necessary properties are missing or the body does not contain valid JSON. PHP 7's new type safety features will give you some safety, as – thanks to strict typing, which is enabled with `declare(strict_types=1)` – they will simply throw a `TypeError` when some fields are missing in the input body. A more thorough implementation of input validation will be looked at in the *Validating input* section:

```
// As both parameters have a "string" type hint, strict typing will
// cause PHP to throw a TypeError when one of the two parameters should
// be null
$profile = new Profile(
    $jsonObject['familyName'],
    $jsonObject['givenName']
);
```

You can now connect this class with a new route in your `index.php`:

```
$app = new App();
$app->get('/profiles/{username}', new
ShowProfileRoute($profileService));
$app->put('/profiles/{username}', new
PutProfileRoute($profileService));
$app->run();
```

Afterwards, you can try to create a new user profile using HTTPie:

```
$ http PUT http://localhost/profiles/jdoe givenName=John familyName=Doe \
password=secret birthday=1970-01-01
```

You can also try to update the created profile by simply repeating the same PUT request with a different set of parameters. The HTTP response code (`201 Created` or `200 OK`) allows you to determine if a new profile was created or an existing one was updated.

Listing and searching users

The current state of your API allows users to read, create, and update specific user profiles. However, the web service is still missing functionality for searching the profile collection or listing all known user profiles. For listing profiles, you can extend the `ProfileService` class with a new function, `getProfiles`:

```
namespace Packt\Chp5\Service\ProfileService;
// ...

class ProfileService
{
    // ...

    public function getProfiles(array $filter = []): Traversable
    {
        $records = $this->profileCollection->find($filter);
        foreach ($records as $record) {
            yield $this->recordToProfile($record);
        }
    }
}
```

In case you are not familiar with this syntax: the previous function is a **generator** function. The `yield` statement will cause the function to return an instance of the `Generator` class, which itself implements the `Traversable` interface (meaning that you can iterate over it using a `foreach` loop). This construct is particularly handy when dealing with large data sets. As the `find` function itself also returns a `Traversable`, you can stream the matching profile documents from the database, lazily map them to user objects, and pass the data stream into your request handler, without the need to put the entire collection of objects into memory.

For comparison, consider the following implementation, which works with plain arrays instead of generators. You will notice that, due to usage of the `ArrayObject` class, even the method's interface stays the same (returning a `Traversable`). However, this implementation stores a list of all found profile instances within the `ArrayObject` instance, whereas the previous implementation only handled one object at a time:

```php
public function getProfiles(array $filter = []): Traversable
{
    $records  = $this->profileCollection->find($filter);
    $profiles = new ArrayObject();

    foreach ($records as $record) {
        $profiles->append($this->recordToProfile($record));
    }

    return $profiles;
}
```

As the MongoDB API directly accepts well-structured query objects for matching documents instead of a custom text-based language (yes, I'm looking at you, SQL), you will not have to worry about injection attacks that traditional SQL-based systems are (not always, but often) vulnerable to. This allows our `getProfiles` function to accept a query object in the `$filter` argument that we simply pipe into the `find` method.

In the next step, you can extend the `getProfiles` function by adding new arguments for sorting the result set:

```php
public function getProfiles(
    array  $filter       = [],
    string $sorting      = 'username',
    bool   $sortAscending = true
): Traversable {
    $records = $this->profileCollection->find($filter, ['sort' => [
        $sorting => $sortAscending ? 1 : -1
    ]]);
```

```
    // ...
}
```

Using this new function, it is easy to implement a new class,
Packt\Chp5\Route\ListProfileRoute, that you can use to query the entire user
collection:

```
namespace Packt\Chp5\Route;


class ListProfileRoute
{
    use ProfileJsonMapping;

    private $profileService;

    public function __construct(ProfileService $profileService)
    {
        $this->profileService = $profileService;
    }

    public function __invoke(Request $req, Response $res): Response
    {
        $params = $req->getQueryParams();

        $sort = $params['sort'] ?? 'username';
        $asc  = !($params['desc'] ?? false);
        $profiles      = $this->profileService->getProfiles($params, $sort,
$asc);
        $profilesJson = [];

        foreach ($profiles as $profile) {
            $profilesJson[] = $this->profileToJson($profile);
        }

        return $response->withJson($profilesJson);
    }
}
```

After that, you can register the new request handler at your Slim application in the
index.php file:

```
$app = new App();
$app->get('/profiles', new ListProfileRoute($profileService));
$app->get('/profiles/{username}', new ShowProfileRoute($profileService));
$app->put('/profiles/{username}', new PutProfileRoute($profileService));
$app->run();
```

Deleting profiles

Deleting user profiles should be an easy task by now. First, you'll need a new method in your `ProfileService` class:

```
class ProfileService
{
    // ...

    public function deleteProfile(string $username)
    {
        $this->profileCollection->findOneAndDelete(['username' =>
    $username]);
    }
}
```

The MongoDB collection's `findOneAndDelete` method does exactly what it promises. The first parameter to this function is a MongoDB query object as you have already used it in the previous sections. The first document matched by this query object will be deleted from the collection.

After that, you can implement a new request handler class that uses the profile service to delete a profile, if present. When trying to delete a non-existing user, the request handler will respond with the correct status code, **404 Not Found**:

```
namespace Packt\Chp5\Route;
// Imports omitted...

class DeleteProfileRoute
{

    /** @var ProfileService */
    private $profileService;

    public function __construct(ProfileService $profileService)
    {
        $this->profileService = $profileService;
    }

    public function __invoke(Request $req, Response $res, array $args):
Response
    {
        $username = $args['username'];
        if ($this->profileService->hasProfile($username)) {
            $this->profileService->deleteProfile($username);
            return $res->withStatus(204);
        } else {
```

```
        return $res
            ->withStatus(404)
            ->withJson(['msg' => 'user "' . $username . '" does not
exist']);
        }
    }
}
```

You will notice that there is now some duplicate code in our example codebase.
Both `ShowProfileRoute` and `DeleteProfileRoute` need to check if a user profile with a
given username exists, and if not, return a `404 Not Found` response.

This is a good use case for using middleware. As already stated in the previous section,
middleware can either send a response to an HTTP request by itself, or pass the request to
the next middleware component or the actual request handler. This allows you to
implement middleware that takes the username from the route parameters, check if a
profile exists for that user, and return an error response if that user does not exist. If that
user does in fact exist, the request can be passed to the request handler:

```
namespace Packt\Chp5\Middleware

class ProfileMiddleware
{
    private $profileService;

    public function __construct(ProfileService $profileService)
    {
        $this->profileService = $profileService;
    }

    public function __invoke(Request $req, Response $res, callable $next):
Response
    {
        $username =
$request->getAttribute('route')->getArgument('username');
        if ($this->profileService->hasProfile($username)) {
            $profile = $this->profileService->getProfile($username);
            return $next($req->withAttribute('profile', $profile));
        } else {
            return $res
                ->withStatus(404)
                ->withJson(['msg' => 'user "' . $username . '" does not
exist');
        }
    }
}
```

All PSR-7 requests can have arbitrary attributes that can be set with `$req->withAttribute($name, $value)` and retrieved with `$req->getAttribute($name)`. This allows middleware to pass any kind of value to the actual request handler – this is exactly what `ProfileMiddleware` does by attaching the `profile` attribute to the request. The actual request handler can then retrieve the user profile, which has already been loaded, by simply calling `$req->getAttribute('profile')`.

Middleware is registered in a similar fashion to regular request handlers. Each time you register a new request handler with `$app->get(...)` or `$app->post(...)`, this method will return an instance of the route configuration to which you can assign different middleware. In your `index.php` file, you can register your middleware like this:

```php
$profileMiddleware = new ProfileMiddleware($profileService);

$app = new App();
$app->get('/profiles', new ListProfileRoute($profileService));
$app->get('/profiles/{username}', new ShowProfileRoute($profileService))
    ->add($profileMiddleware);
$app->delete('/profiles/{username}', new
DeleteProfileRoute($profileService))
    ->add($profileMiddleware);
$app->put('/profiles/{username}', new PutProfileRoute($profileService));
$app->run();
```

After registering the middleware for the GET /profiles/{username} and DELETE /profiles{username} route, you can modify the respective route handlers to simply use the profile request attribute and remove the error checking:

```php
class ShowProfileRoute
{
    // ...

    public function __invoke(Request $req, Response $res): Response
    {
        $profile = $req->getAttribute('profile');
        return $res->withJson($this->profileToJson($profile));
    }
}
```

The same goes for the `DeleteProfileRoute` class:

```php
class DeleteProfileRoute
{
    // ...
```

```
public function __invoke(Request $req, Response $res): Response
{
    $profile = $req->getAttribute('profile');
    $this->profileService->deleteProfile($profile->getUsername());
    return $res->withStatus(204);
}
}
```

Validating input

When implementing the PUT /profiles/{username} route, you might have noticed that we did not pay that much attention to the validation of user inputs. To an extent, we can actually use PHP 7's new strict typing for validating user inputs. You can activate strict typing by using a declare(strict_types = 1) statement in the first line of your code. Consider the following example:

```
return new Profile(
    $username,
    $json['givenName'],
    $json['familyName'],
    $json['passwordHash'] ?? password_hash($json['password']),
    $json['interests'] ?? [],
    $json['birthday'] ? new \DateTime($json['birthday']) : NULL
);
```

Assuming, for example, that the Profile class' $givenName parameter is type-hinted with string, the previous statement will throw a TypeError when $json['givenName'] is not set. You would then be able to catch this error using a try/catch statement and return the appropriate **400 Bad Request** HTTP response:

```
try {
    $this->jsonToProfile($req->getParsedBody());
} catch (\TypeError $err) {
    return $response
        ->withStatus(400)
        ->withJson(['msg' => $err->getMessage()]);
}
```

However, this provides only rudimentary error checking, as you can only verify data types and cannot assert logical constraints. Also, this approach provides a bad user experience, as the error response will only contain the first triggered error.

For implementing a more elaborate validation, you can add another middleware to your application (using middleware is a good choice here, because it allows you to keep the concern of validation logic encapsulated in a single class). Let's call this class `Packt\Chp5\Middleware\ProfileValidationMiddleware`:

```
namespace Packt\Chp5\Middleware;

class ProfileValidationMiddleware
{
    private $profileService;

    public function __construct(ProfileService $profileService)
    {
        $this->profileService = $profileService;
    }

    public function __invoke(Request $req, Response $res, callable $next):
Response
    {
        $username       =
$request->getAttribute('route')->getArgument('username');
        $profileJson    = $req->getParsedBody();
        $alreadyExists = $this->profileService->hasProfile($username);

        $errors = [];

        if (!isset($profileJson['familyName'])) {
            $errors[] = 'missing property "familyName"';
        }

        if (!isset($profileJson['givenName'])) {
            $errors[] = 'missing property "givenName"';
        }

        if (!$alreadyExists &&
            !isset($profileJson['password']) &&
            !isset($profileJson['passwordHash'])
        ) {
            $errors[] = 'missing property "password" or "passwordHash";
        }

        if (count($errors) > 0) {
            return $res
                ->withStatus(400)
                ->withJson([
                    'msg' => 'request body does not contain a valid user
profile',
```

```
                    'errors' => $errors
                ]);
        } else {
            return $next($req, $res);
        }
    }
}
```

After declaring the validation middleware class, you can register it in your `index.php` file:

```
$profileMiddleware = new ProfileMiddleware($profileService);
$validationMiddleware = new ProfileValidationMiddleware($profileService);

$app = new App();
$app->get('/profiles', new ListProfileRoute($profileService));
$app->get('/profiles/{username}', new ShowProfileRoute($profileService))
    ->add($profileMiddleware);
$app->delete('/profiles/{username}', new
DeleteProfileRoute($profileService))
    ->add($profileMiddleware);
$app->put('/profiles/{username}', new PutProfileRoute($profileService))
    ->add($validationMiddleware);
$app->run();
```

Streams and large files

So far, our web service can perform the basic operations on a user profile. In this chapter, we will extend the user profile service to also handle a user's profile image. During the course of this chapter, you will learn how you can process even very large files using PHP streams.

Profile image upload

Basically, in a RESTful application, you can treat an image just as any other resource. You can create and update it using POST and/or PUT operations, and you can retrieve it using GET. The only difference is the chosen representation of the resource. Instead of JSON encoding using `application/json` as a Content-Type, you will now work with resources that have a JPEG or PNG representation, with their respective `image/jpeg` or `image/png` content types.

At this point, it will be useful to understand how the PSR-7 standard models HTTP requests and response bodies. Since technically, each message (both request and response) body is just a string of characters, these could be modeled as simple PHP strings. This works fine for the messages that you have been working with in the past few sections, but may present problems when working with larger messages (say, for example, images). This is why PSR-7 models all message bodies as streams that a user can read from (in case of request bodies) or write to (in case of response bodies). You can pipe data from a stream into a file or another networked stream, without ever needing to fit the entire contents into the memory of your PHP process.

In the next step, we will implement the user's profile image as a new resource. A user's profile image will have the URI, `/profiles/{username}/image`. Loading a user's image will be a simple GET request (returning a response with the appropriate `Content-Type: image/jpeg` or `image/png` header and the image's binary contents as message body). Updating an image will work the other way around, using a PUT request with a Content-Type header and the image contents as message body.

Start by implementing a new request handler class, in which you read blocks from the request streams and write them into a file:

```php
namespace Packt\Chp5\Route;

class PutImageRoute
{
    private $imageDir;

    public function __construct(string $imageDir)
    {
        $this->imageDir = $imageDir;
    }

    public function __invoke(Request $req, Response $res): Response
    {
        if (!is_dir($this->imageDir)) {
            mkdir($this->imageDir);
        }

        $profile    = $req->getAttribute('profile');
        $fileName   = $this->imageDir . '/' . $profile->getUsername();
        $fileHandle = fopen($fileName, 'w');
        while (!$req->getBody()->eof()) {
            fwrite($fileHandle, $req->getBody()->read(4096));
        }
        fclose($fileHandle);
        return $res->withJson(['msg' => 'image was saved']);
```

```
        }
    }
```

This request handler opens a file handle for writing using `fopen(...)`, then reads the request body in blocks of 4 KB and writes them into the opened file. The advantage of this solution is that it does not really matter if the file you are saving is 4 KB or 400 MB. As you are only reading 4 KB blocks of the input at any time, you will have a more-or-less constant memory usage, independent of input size.

On scalability

Storing files in the local filesystem is not very scalable and should only be considered as an example in this case. In order to keep this scalable, you could put your image directory on a network storage (for example, NFS) or use other distributed storage solutions. In the following section, *Using GridFS storage* you will also learn how to use GridFS to store files in a scalable way.

Next, register the request handler at your Slim application:

```
$profileMiddleware = new ProfileMiddleware($profileService);
$validationMiddleware = new ProfileValidationMiddleware($profileService);

$app = new App();
// ...
$app->put('/profiles/{username}/image', new PutImageRoute(__DIR__ .
'/images'))     ->add($profileMiddleware);
$app->run();
```

In order to test this route, find an arbitrary-sized image file on your computer and use the following curl command on the command line (remember; as we are using `profileMiddleware` for the new route, you will need to specify a user profile that actually exists in your database for this):

```
curl --data-binary @very-big-image.jpeg -H 'Content-Type: image/jpeg' -X
PUT
-v http://localhost/profiles/jdoe/image
```

After running this command, you should find a `jdoe` file in the `images/` directory in your project folder with the exact same contents as the original file.

Delivering profile images back to your users works in a similar way. For this, implement a new request handler called `Packt\Chp5\Route\ShowImageRoute`:

```
namespace Packt\Chp5\Route;

class ShowImageRoute
```

```
{
    /** @var string */
    private $imageDir;

    public function __construct(string $imageDir)
    {
        $this->imageDir = $imageDir;
    }

    public function __invoke(Request $req, Response $res, array $args):
Response
    {
        $profile     = $req->getAttribute('profile');
        $filename    = $this->imageDir . '/' . $profile->getUsername();
        $fileHandle  = fopen($filename, 'r');
        $contentType = mime_content_type($filename);

        return $res
            ->withStatus(200)
            ->withHeader('Content-Type', $contentType)
            ->withBody(new Body($fileHandle));
    }
}
```

Here, we are using the `mime_content_type` method to load the actual content type of the uploaded file. The content type is needed, because the HTTP response needs to contain a Content-Type header, which is in turn required by the browser to correctly display the image.

Also, we are using the `Slim\Http\Body` class, which makes the implementation even easier: this class implements the PSR-7 `StreamInterface` and can be initialized with an open stream (which might, for example, be an open file handler). The Slim framework will then take care of delivering the contents of this file to the user.

This request handler can also be registered in the `index.php`:

```
$app = new \Slim\App();
// ...
$app->get('/profiles/{username}/image', new
ShowImageRoute(__DIR__ . '/images'))
    ->add($profileMiddleware);
$app->put('/profiles/{username}/image', new PutImageRoute(__DIR__ .
'/images'))
    ->add($profileMiddleware);
$app->run();
```

If you have uploaded a test image after implementing the `PUT` route, you can now test the `GET` route with the same user profile. As a curl command will only return a large blob of binary data, it might be preferable to visit `http://localhost/profiles/jdoe/image` in a browser of your choice.

Using GridFS storage

Storing user-uploaded files in the server's local filesystem is a viable solution for small sites. However, as soon as you feel the need to horizontally scale your application, you will need to look into distributed filesystems. For example, you could replace your user images folder with a network device that is mounted via the NFS filesystem. As you have already been working with MongoDB a lot in this chapter, in this section you will learn about GridFS. GridFS is a specification for storing – potentially very large – files in a MongoDB database.

The GridFS specification is simple. You will need two collections – `fs.files` and `fs.chunks`. The former will be used to store file metadata, while the latter will store the actual content of the files. Since MongoDB documents are limited to 16 MB by default, each stored file will be split into several *chunks* of (by default) 255 KB. A file document will have the following form:

```
{
    "_id": <object ID>
    "length": <file size in bytes>,
    "chunkSize": <size of each chunk in bytes, default 261120>,
    "uploadDate": <timestamp at which the file was saved>,
    "md5": <MD5 checksum of the file, as hex string>,
    "filename": <the file's name>,
    "contentType": <MIME type of file contents>,
    "aliases": <list of alternative file names>,
    "metadata": <arbitrary metadata>
}
```

A chunk document will have the following form:

```
{
    "_id": <chunk ID>,
    "files_id": <object ID of the file this chunk belongs to>,
    "n": <index of the chunk within the file>,
    "data": <binary data, of the file's chunk length>
}
```

Note that GridFS is simply a recommendation on how you can store files in a MongoDB database, and you would be free to implement any other kind of file storage in a MongoDB store. However, GridFS is a widely accepted standard, and the chances are good that you will find GridFS implementations for nearly every language. So, if you want to write files into a GridFS storage using a PHP application, and then read them from there using a Python program, you'll find standard implementations for both runtimes that you can use out-of-the-box, without having to re-invent the wheel.

In PHP 7, you can use the `helmich/gridfs` library for GridFS access. You can acquire it using Composer:

```
composer require helmich/gridfs
```

GridFS is oriented around buckets. Each bucket can contain an arbitrary number of files, and internally stores them in two MongoDB collections, `<bucket name>.files` and `<bucket name>.chunks`.

Begin by modifying your application Bootstrap in your `index.php` by creating a new bucket for the user profile images, using the `Helmich\GridFS\Bucket` class. Each bucket can be initialized with a `BucketOptions` instance, in which you can configure several bucket options, such as the bucket name.

After creating the bucket, you can pass it as a dependency into the `ShowImageRoute` and `PutImageRoute` classes:

```php
$manager = new \MongoDB\Driver\Manager('mongodb://db:27017');
$database = new \MongoDB\Database($manager, 'database-name');

$bucketOptions = (new \Helmich\GridFS\Options\BucketOptions)
->withBucketName('profileImages');$bucket = new
\Helmich\GridFS\Bucket($database, $bucketOptions);
$profiles = $database->selectCollection('profiles');

// ...

$app->get('/profiles/{username}/image', new
ShowImageRoute($bucket))
    ->add($profileMiddleware);
$app->put('/profiles/{username}/image', new
PutImageRoute($bucket))
    ->add($profileMiddleware);
$app->run();
```

The PutImageRoute and ShowImageRoute now get a GridFS bucket passed as a dependency. You can now adjust these classes to write uploaded files into that bucket. Let's start by adjusting the PutImageRoute class:

```
use Helmich\GridFS\BucketInterface;

class PutImageRoute
{
    private $bucket;

    public function __construct(BucketInterface $bucket)
    {
        $this->bucket = $bucket
    }

    // ...
}
```

The interface of a GridFS bucket is described in the BucketInterface, which we are using in this example. You can now modify the __invoke method of PutImageRoute, to store uploaded profile images in the bucket:

```
public function __invoke(Request $req, Response $res, array $args):
Response
{
    $profile      = $req->getAttribute('profile');
    $contentType  = $req->getHeader('content-type')[0];
    $uploadOptions = (new \Helmich\GridFS\Options\UploadOptions)
      ->withMetadata(['content-type' => $contentType]);

    $stream = $req->getBody()->detach();
    $fileId = $this->bucket->uploadFromStream(
        $profile->getUsername(),
        $stream,
        $uploadOptions
    );
    fclose($stream);
    return $res->withJson(['msg' => 'image was saved']);
}
```

In this example, we are using the $req->getBody()->detach() method to get the actual underlying input stream from the request body. This stream is then passed into the bucket's uploadFromStream method, together with a filename (in this case, simply the username) and an UploadOptions object. The UploadOptions object defines configuration options for the file upload; among others, you can specify arbitrary metadata that will be stored alongside GridFS' own metadata in the <bucketname>.files collection.

Now, all that's left is to adjust the `ShowProfileRoute` to also use the GridFS bucket. First of all, modify the class' constructor to accept a `BucketInterface` as parameter, just as we did with the `PutProfileRoute`. Then, you can adjust the `__invoke` method to download the requested profile images from the GridFS bucket:

```php
public function __invoke(Request $req, Response $res, array $args):
Response
{
    $profile = $req->getAttribute('profile');
    $stream =
$this->bucket->openDownloadStreamByName($profile->getUsername());
    $file = $stream->file();

    return $res
        ->withStatus(200)
        ->withHeader('content-type', $file['metadata']['content-type'])
        ->withBody(new
\Helmich\GridFS\Stream\Psr7\DownloadStreamAdapter($stream));
}
```

In this example, we're using the Bucket's `openDownloadStreamByName` method to find a file in the bucket by its name and return a stream object from which we can download the file.

The opened download stream is an implementation of the `Helmich\GridFS\Stream\DownloadStream` interface. Unfortunately, you cannot use this interface directly in your HTTP response. However, you can use the `Helmich\GridFS\Stream\Psr7\DownloadStreamAdapter` interface to create a PSR-7 compatible stream from the GridFS stream that you can use in the HTTP response.

Summary

In this chapter, you have learned about the basic architectural principles of RESTful Web Services and also how to build one on your own using the Slim framework. We have also had a look at the PSR-7 standard that allows you to write HTTP components in PHP that are portable across frameworks and become highly re-usable. Finally, you have also learned how to use PHP's new MongoDB extension for both direct access to stored collections, and also in combination with other high-level abstractions, such as the GridFS standard.

Both your newly acquired Slim knowledge and your understanding of the PSR-7 standard will benefit you in the following chapter, in which you will build a real-time chat application using the Ratchet framework – and then use PSR-7 to integrate Ratchet with the Slim framework.

6
Building a Chat Application

In this chapter, we will build a real-time chat application using **WebSocket**. You will learn how to use the **Ratchet** framework to build standalone WebSocket and HTTP servers with PHP and how to connect to WebSocket servers in a JavaScript client application. We will also discuss how you can implement authentication for WebSocket applications and how to deploy them in a production environment.

The WebSocket protocol

In this chapter, we'll be working extensively with WebSockets. To fully understand the workings of the chat application that we're going to build, let's first have a look at how WebSockets work.

The WebSockets protocol is specified in **RFC 6455** and uses HTTP as the underlying transport protocol. In contrast to the traditional request/reply paradigm, in which the client sends a request to the server, who then replies with a response message, WebSocket connections can be kept open for a long time, and both server and client can send and receive messages (or *data frames*) on the WebSocket.

WebSocket connections are always initiated by the client (so, typically, a user's browser). The following listing shows an example request that a browser might send to a server supporting WebSockets:

```
GET /chat HTTP/1.1
Host: localhost
Upgrade: websocketConnection: upgrade
Origin: http://localhost
Sec-WebSocket-Key: de7PkO6qMKuGvUA3OQNYiw==
Sec-WebSocket-Protocol: chat
Sec-WebSocket-Version: 13
```

Just like regular HTTP requests, the request contains a request method (`GET`) and a path (`/chat`). The `Upgrade` and `Connection` headers tell the server that the client would like to *upgrade* the regular HTTP connection into a WebSocket connection.

The `Sec-WebSocket-Key` header contains a random, base64-encoded string that uniquely identifies this single WebSocket connection. The `Sec-WebSocket-Protocol` header can be used to specify a subprotocol that the client would like to use. Subprotocols can be used to further define what the communication between the server and the client should look like and are often application-specific (in our case, the `chat` protocol).

When the server accepts the upgrade request, it will respond with a `101 Switching Protocols` response, as shown in the following listing:

```
HTTP/1.1 101 Switching Protocols
Upgrade: websocket
Connection: Upgrade
Sec-WebSocket-Accept: BKb5cchTfWayrC7SKtvK5yW413s=
Sec-WebSocket-Protocol: chat
```

The `Sec-WebSocket-Accept` header contains a hash of the `Sec-WebSocket-Key` from the request (the exact hashing is specified in RFC 6455). The `Sec-WebSocket-Protocol` header in the response confirms that the server understands the protocol that the client specified in its request.

After this handshake is completed, the connection will stay open and both server and client can send and receive messages from the socket.

First steps with Ratchet

In this section, you will learn how to install and use the Ratchet framework. It's important to note that Ratchet applications work differently than regular PHP applications that are deployed in a web server and work on a per-request basis. This will require you to adopt a new way of thinking of how PHP applications are run and deployed.

Architectural considerations

Implementing a WebSocket server with PHP is not trivial. Traditionally, PHP's architecture revolves around the classical request/reply paradigm: the web server receives a request, passes it to the PHP interpreter (which is typically built into the web server or managed by a process manager such as PHP-FPM), which processes the request and returns a response to the web server who in turn responds to the client. The lifetime of data in a PHP script is limited to a single request (a principle that is called**Shared Nothing**).

This works well for classical web applications; especially the Shared Nothing principle as it is one of the reasons that PHP applications usually scale very well. However, for WebSocket support, we need a different paradigm. Client connections need to stay open for a very long time (hours, potentially days) and servers need to react to client messages at any time during the connection lifetime.

One library that implements this new paradigm is the `Ratchet` library that we'll be working with in this chapter. In contrast to regular PHP runtimes that live within a web server, Ratchet will start its own web server that can serve long-running WebSocket connections. As you'll be dealing with PHP processes with extremely long run times (a server process may run for days, weeks, or months), you will need to pay special attention to things such as memory consumption.

Getting started

Ratchet can be easily installed using**Composer**. It requires PHP in at least version 5.3.9 and also works well with PHP 7. Start by initializing a new project with the `composer init` command on a command line in your project directory:

```
$ composer init .
```

Next, add Ratchet as a dependency to your project:

```
$ composer require cboden/ratchet
```

Also, configure Composer's autoloader by adding the following section to the generated `composer.json` file:

```
'autoload': {
  'PSR-4': {
    'Packt\Chp6\Example': 'src/'
  }
}
```

As usual, PSR-4 autoloading means that the Composer class loader will look for classes of the `Packt\Chp6\Example` namespace within the `src/` folder of your project directory. A (hypothetical) `Packt\Chp6\Example\Foo\Bar` class would need to be defined in the file `src/Foo/Bar.php` file.

As Ratchet implements its own web server, you will not need a dedicated web server such as **Apache** or **Nginx** (for now). Start by creating a file called server.php, in which you initialize and run the Ratchet web server:

```
$app = new \Ratchet\App('localhost', 8080, '0.0.0.0');
$app->run()
```

You can then start your web server (it will listen on the port that you have specified as the second parameter of the Ratchet\App constructor) using the following command:

```
$ php server.php
```

If you do not have a PHP 7 installation ready on your machine, you can get started quickly with**Docker**, using the following command:

```
$ docker run --rm -v $PWD:/opt/app -p 8080:8080 php:7 php
/opt/app/server.php
```

Both of these commands will start a long-running PHP process that can directly handle HTTP requests on your command line. In a later section, you will learn how to deploy your application to production servers. Of course, this server does not really do much, yet. However, you can still test it using a CLI command or your browser, as shown in the following screenshot:

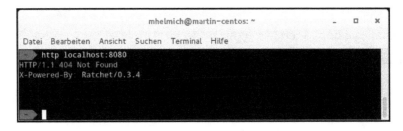

Testing the example application with HTTPie

Let's continue by adding some business logic to our server. WebSocket applications served by Ratchet need to be PHP classes that implement Ratchet\MessageComponentInterface. This interface defines the following four methods:

- onOpen(\Ratchet\ConnectionInterface $c) will be called whenever a new client connects to the WebSocket server
- onClose(\Ratchet\ConnectionInterface $c) will be called when a client disconnects from the server

- onMessage(\Ratchet\ConnectionInterface $sender, $msg) will be called when a client sends a message to the server
- onError(\Ratchet\ConnectionInterface $c, \Exception $e) will be called when an exception occurred at some point while handling a message

Let's start with a simple example: a WebSocket service that clients can send messages to, and it will respond to the same client with the same message, but reversed. Let's call this class Packt\Chp6\Example\ReverseEchoComponent; the code is as follows:

```
namespace Packt\Chp6\Example;

use Ratchet\ConnectionInterface;
use Ratchet\MessageComponentInterface;

class ReverseEchoComponent implements MessageComponentInterface
{
    public function onOpen(ConnectionInterface $conn)
    {}

    public function onClose(ConnectionInterface $conn)
    {}

    public function onMessage(ConnectionInterface $sender, $msg)
    {}

    public function onError(ConnectionInterface $conn,
                            Exception $e)
    {}
}
```

Note that although we do not need all of the methods specified by the MessageComponentInterface, we need to implement all of them nonetheless in order to satisfy the interface. For example, if you do not need anything special to happen when a client connects or disconnects, implement the onOpen and onClose methods, but just leave them empty.

In order to better understand what's happening in this application, add some simple debug messages to the onOpen and onClose methods, as follows:

```
public function onOpen(ConnectionInterface $conn)
{
    echo "new connection from " . $conn->remoteAddress . "\n";
}

public function onClose(ConnectionInterface $conn)
{
```

```
        echo "connection closed by " . $conn->remoteAddress . "\n";
    }
```

Next, implement the `onMessage` method. The `$msg` parameter will contain the message that was sent by the client as string, and you can use the `ConnectionInterface` class' `send()` method to send messages back to the client, as shown in the following code snippet:

```
public function onMessage(ConnectionInterface $sender, $msg)
{
    echo "received message '$msg' from {$conn->remoteAddress}\n";
    $response = strrev($msg);
    $sender->send($response);
}
```

You might be inclined to use PHP 7's new type hinting feature to hint the `$msg` parameter as `string`. This does not work in this case, because it would change the method's interface that is prescribed by the `Ratchet\MessageComponentInterface` and cause a fatal error.

You can then register your WebSocket application at the `Ratchet\App` instance in your `server.php` file using the following code:

```
$app = new \Ratchet\App('localhost', 8080, '0.0.0.0');
$app->route('/reverse', new Packt\Chp6\Example\ReverseEchoComponent);
$app->run();
```

Testing WebSocket applications

To test WebSocket applications, I can recommend the **wscat** tool. It is a command-line tool written in JavaScript (and thus requires Node.js to be running on your machine) and can be installed using npm, as follows:

```
$ npm install -g wscat
```

With the WebSocket server listening at port `8080`, you can use `wscat` to open a new WebSocket connection using the following CLI command:

```
$ wscat -o localhost --connect localhost:8080/reverse
```

This will open a command-line prompt in which you can enter messages that are sent to the WebSocket server. Messages received from the server will also be displayed. See the following screenshot for an example output of both the WebSocket server and wscat:

Testing WebSocket applications using wscat

Playing with the event loop

In the preceding example, you have only sent messages to clients after having received a message from the same client. This is the traditional request/reply communication pattern that works well in most scenarios. However, it is important to understand that when using WebSockets, you are not forced to follow this pattern, but can send messages to connected clients at any time you like.

In order to gain a better understanding of the possibilities you have in a Ratchet application, let's have a look at the architecture of Ratchet. Ratchet is built on ReactPHP; an event-driven framework for network applications. The central component of a React application is the **event loop**. Each event that is triggered in the application (for example, when a new user connects or sends a message to the server) is stored in a queue, and the event loop processes all events stored in this queue.

ReactPHP offers different implementations of event loops. Some of these require additional PHP extensions such as `libevent` or `ev` to be installed (and typically, the event loops based on `libevent`, `ev`, or similar extensions offer the best performance). Usually, applications like Ratchet will automatically choose which event loop implementation to use so that you do not need to concern yourself with the inner workings of ReactPHP if you do not want to.

By default, a Ratchet application creates its own event loop; however, you can also inject your own event loop into the `Ratchet\App` class that you've created yourself.

All ReactPHP event loops must implement the interface `React\EventLoop\LoopInterface`. You can use the class `React\EventLoop\Factory` to automatically create an implementation of this interface that is supported by your environment:

```
$loop = \React\EventLoop\Factory::create();
```

You can then pass this `$loop` variable into your Ratchet application:

```
$app = new \Ratchet\App('localhost', 8080, '0.0.0.0', $loop)
$app->run();
```

Having direct access to the event loop allows you to implement some interesting features. For example, you can use the event loop's `addPeriodicTimer` function to register a callback that will be executed by the event loop in a periodic interval. Let's use this feature in a short example by building a new WebSocket component called `Packt\Chp6\Example\PingComponent`:

```
namespace Packt\Chp6\Example;

use Ratchet\MessageComponentInterface;
use React\EventLoop\LoopInterface;

class PingCompoment extends MessageComponentInterface
{
    private $loop;
    private $users;

    public function __construct(LoopInterface $loop)
    {
        $this->loop  = $loop;
        $this->users = new \SplObjectStorage();
    }

    // ...
}
```

In this example, the `$users` property will help us to keep track of connected users. Each time a new client connects, we can use the `onOpen` event to store the connection in the `$users` property, and use the `onClose` event to remove the connection:

```
public function onOpen(ConnectionInterface $conn)
{
    $this->users->attach($conn);
}

public function onClose(ConnectionInterface $conn)
{
    $this->users->detach($conn);
}
```

As our WebSocket component now knows the connected users, we can use the event loop to register a timer that periodically broadcasts messages to all connected users. This can be easily done in the constructor:

```
public function __construct(LoopInterface $loop)
{
    $this->loop  = $loop;
    $this->users = new \SplObjectStorage();

    $i = 0;
    $this->loop->addPeriodicTimer(5, function() use (&$i) {
        foreach ($this->users as $user) {
            $user->send('Ping ' . $i);
        }
        $i ++;
    });
}
```

The function passed to `addPeriodicTimer` will be called every five seconds and will send a message with an incrementing counter to each connected user. Modify your `server.php` file to add this new component to your Ratchet application:

```
$loop = \React\EventLoop\Factory::create();
$app = new \Ratchet\App('localhost', 8080, '0.0.0.0', $loop);
$app->route('/ping', new PingCompoment($loop));
$app->run();
```

You can again test this WebSocket handler using wscat, as shown in the following screenshot:

Periodic messages cast by a periodic event loop timer

This is a good example of a scenario in which a WebSocket client receives updates from a server without having explicitly requested them. This offers efficient ways to push new data to connected clients in near real-time, without the need to repeatedly poll for information.

Implementing the chat application

After this short introduction in the development with WebSockets, let us now begin implementing the actual chat application. The chat application will consist of the server-side application built in PHP with Ratchet, and an HTML and JavaScript-based client that will run in the user's browser.

Bootstrapping the project server-side

As mentioned in the previous section, applications based on ReactPHP will achieve the best performance when used with an event-loop extension such as `libevent` or `ev`. Unfortunately, the `libevent` extension is not compatible with PHP 7, yet. Luckily, ReactPHP also works with the `ev` extension, whose latest version already supports PHP 7. Just like in the previous chapter, we'll be working with Docker in order to have a clean software stack to work on. Start by creating a *Dockerfile* for your application container:

```
FROM php:7
RUN pecl install ev-beta && \
    docker-php-ext-enable ev
WORKDIR /opt/app
CMD ["/usr/local/bin/php", "server.php"]
```

You will then be able to build an image from this file and start the container using the following CLI command from within your project directory:

```
$ docker build -t packt-chp6
$ docker run -d --name chat-app -v $PWD:/opt/app -p 8080:8080
  packt-chp6
```

Note that this command will not actually work as long as there is no `server.php` file in your project directory.

Just as in the previous example, we will be using Composer as well for dependency management and for autoloading. Create a new folder for your project and create a `composer.json` file with the following contents:

```
{
    "name": "packt-php7/chp6-chat",
    "type": "project",
    "authors": [{
        "name": "Martin Helmich",
        "email": "php7-book@martin-helmich.de"
    }],
    "require": {
```

```
            "php": ">= 7.0.0",
            "cboden/ratchet": "^0.3.4"
        },
        "autoload": {
            "psr-4": {
                "Packt\\Chp6": "src/"
            }
        }
    }
```

Continue by installing all required packages by running `composer install` in your project directory and create a provisional `server.php` file with the following contents:

```php
<?php
require_once 'vendor/autoload.php';

$app = new \Ratchet\App('localhost', 8080, '0.0.0.0');
$app->run();
```

You have already used the `Ratchet\App` constructor in the introductory example. A few words concerning this class' constructor parameters:

- The first parameter, `$httpHost` is the HTTP hostname at which your application will be available. This value will be used as the allowed origin host. This means that when your server is listening on `localhost`, only JavaScript running on the `localhost` domain will be allowed to connect to your WebSocket server.
- The `$port` parameter is specified at which port your WebSocket server will listen on. Port `8080` will suffice for now; in a later section, you will learn how you can safely configure your application to be available on the HTTP standard port `80`.
- The `$address` parameter describes the IP address the WebSocket server will listen on. This parameter's default value is `'127.0.0.1'`, which would allow clients running on the same machine to connect to your WebSocket server. This won't work when you are running your application in a Docker container. The string `'0.0.0.0'` will instruct the application to listen on all available IP addresses.
- The fourth parameter, `$loop`, allows you to inject a custom event loop into the Ratchet application. If you do not pass this parameter, Ratchet will construct its own event loop.

You should now be able to start your application container using the following command:

```
$ docker run --rm -v $PWD:/opt/app -p 8080:8080 packt-chp6
```

TIP

As your application is now one single, long-running PHP process, changes to your PHP code base will not become effective until you restart the server. Keep in mind that you stop the server using *Ctrl + C* and restart it using the same command (or using the `docker restart chat-app` command) when making changes to your application's PHP code.

Bootstrapping the HTML user interface

The user interface for our chat application will be based on HTML, CSS, and JavaScript. For managing frontend dependencies, we will be using **Bower** in this example. You can install Bower using `npm` with the following command (as root or with `sudo`):

```
$ npm install -g bower
```

Continue by creating a new directory `public/` in which you can place all your frontend files. In this directory, place a file `bower.json` with the following contents:

```
{
    "name": "packt-php7/chp6-chat",
    "authors": [
        "Martin Helmich <php7-book@martin-helmich.de>"
    ],
    "private": true,
    "dependencies": {
        "bootstrap": "~3.3.6"
    }
}
```

After creating the `bower.json` file, you can install the declared dependencies (in this case, the **Twitter Bootstrap** framework) using the following command:

```
$ bower install
```

This will download the Bootstrap framework and all its dependencies (actually, only the jQuery library) into the directory `bower_components/`, from which you will be able to include them in your HTML frontend files later.

It's also useful to have a web server up and running that can serve your HTML frontend files. This is especially important when your WebSocket application is restricted to a `localhost` origin, which will only allow requests from JavaScript served from the `localhost` domain (which does not include local files opened in a browser). One quick and easy way is to use the `nginx` Docker image. Be sure to run the following command from within your `public/` directory:

```
$ docker run -d --name chat-web -v $PWD:/var/www -p 80:80 nginx
```

After that, you will be able to open `http://localhost` in your browser and view the static files from your `public/` directory. If you place an empty `index.html` in that directory, Nginx will use that page as an index page that will not need to be explicitly requested by its path (meaning that `http://localhost` will serve the contents of the file `index.html` to the user).

Building a simple chat application

You can now start implementing the actual chat application. As already shown in the previous examples, you need to implement `Ratchet\MessageComponentInterface` for this. Start by creating a `Packt\Chp6\Chat\ChatComponent` class and implementing all methods that are required by the interface:

```
namespace Packt\Chp6\Chat;

use Ratchet\MessageComponentInterface;
use Ratchet\ConnectionInterface;

class ChatComponent implements MessageComponentInterface
{
    public function onOpen(ConnectionInterface $conn) {}
    public function onClose(ConnectionInterface $conn) {}
    public function onMessage(ConnectionInterface $from, $msg) {}
    public function onError(ConnectionInterface $conn, \Exception $err) {}
}
```

The first thing that the chat application needs to do is to keep track of connected users. For this, you will need to maintain a collection of all open connections, add new connections when a new user connects, and remove them when a user disconnects. For this, initialize an instance of the `SplObjectStorage` class in the constructor:

```
private $users;

public function __construct()
{
    $this->users = new \SplObjectStorage();
}
```

You can then attach new connections to this storage in the onOpen event and remove them in the onClose event:

```
public function onOpen(ConnectionInterface $conn)
{
    echo "user {$conn->remoteAddress} connected.\n";
    $this->users->attach($conn);
}

public function onClose(ConnectionInterface $conn)
{
    echo "user {$conn->remoteAddress} disconnected.\n";
    $this->users->detach($conn); }
```

Each connected user can now send messages to the server. For each received message, the component's onMessage method will be called. To implement a real chat application, each received message needs to be relayed to the other users-conveniently, you already have a list of all connected users in your $this->users collection to whom you can then send the received message:

```
public function onMessage(ConnectionInterface $from, $msg)
{
    echo "received message '$msg' from user {$from->remoteAddress}\n";
foreach($this->users as $user) {
        if ($user != $from) {
            $user->send($msg);
        }
    }}
```

You can then register your chat component at the Ratchet application in your server.php file:

```
$app = new \Ratchet\App('localhost', 8080, '0.0.0.0');
$app->route('/chat', new \Packt\Chp6\Chat\ChatComponent);
$app->run();
```

After restarting your application, test the chat functionality by opening two WebSocket connections with wscat in two separate terminals. Each message that you send in one connection should pop up in the other.

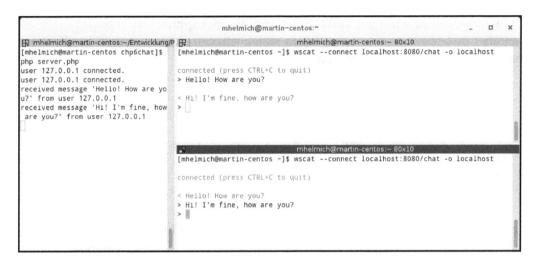

Testing the rudimentary chat application using two wscat connections

Now that you have an (admittedly, still rudimentary) chat server running, we can start building the HTML frontend for the chat application. For the beginning, a static HTML file will be completely sufficient for this. Begin by creating an empty `index.html` file in your `public/` directory:

```html
<!DOCTYPE html>
<html>
  <head>
    <title>Chat application</title>
    <script src="bower_components/jquery/dist/jquery.min.js"></script>
    <script
src="bower_components/bootstrap/dist/js/bootstrap.min.js"></script>
<link rel="stylesheet"
href="bower_components/bootstrap/dist/css/bootstrap.min.css"/>
  </head>
  <body>
  </body>
</html>
```

In this file, we are already including the frontend libraries that we'll use for this example; the Bootstrap framework (with one JavaScript and one CSS file) and the jQuery library (with one other JavaScript file).

As you will be writing a fair amount of JavaScript for this application, it is also useful to add another instance of a `js/app.js` file in which you can place your own JavaScript code to the <head> section of the HTML page:

```
<head>
  <title>Chat application</title>
  <script src="bower_components/jquery/dist/jquery.min.js"></script>
  <script
src="bower_components/bootstrap/dist/js/bootstrap.min.js"></script>
  <script src="js/app.js"></script>
  <link rel="stylesheet"
href="bower_components/bootstrap/dist/css/bootstrap.min.css"/>
</head>
```

You can then continue by building a minimalist chat window in the <body> section of your `index.html` file. All you need to get started is an input field for writing messages, a button for sending them, and an area for displaying other user's messages:

```
<div class="container">
  <div class="row">
    <div class="col-md-12">
      <div class="input-group">
        <input class="form-control" type="text" id="message"
placeholder="Your message..." />
        <span class="input-group-btn">
          <button id="submit" class="btn btn-primary">Send</button>
        </span>
      </div>
    </div>
  </div>
  <div class="row">
    <div id="messages"></div>
  </div>
</div>
```

The HTML file contains an input field (`id="message"`) in which a user can enter new chat messages, a button (`id="submit"`) to submit the message, and a (currently still empty) section (`id="messages"`) in which the messages received from other users can be displayed. The following screenshot shows how this page will be displayed in the browser:

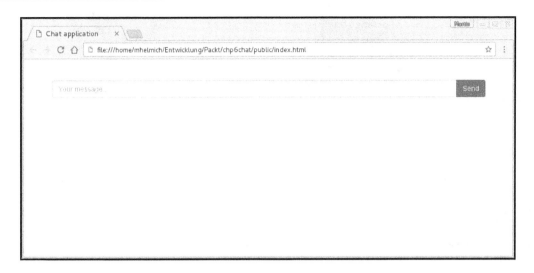

Of course, all of this will not be any good without the appropriate JavaScript to actually make the chat work. In JavaScript, you can open a WebSocket connection by using the WebSocket class.

On browser support

WebSockets are supported in all modern browsers and have been for quite some time. You may run into issues where you need to support older Internet Explorer versions (9 and below), which do not support WebSockets. In this case, you can use the web-socket-js library, which internally uses a fallback using Flash, which is also well supported by Ratchet.

In this example, we will be placing all our JavaScript code in the file js/app.js in the public/ directory. You can open a new WebSocket connection by instantiating the WebSocket class with the WebSocket server's URL as the first parameter:

```
var connection = new WebSocket('ws://localhost:8080/chat');
```

Just like the server-side component, the client-side WebSocket offers several events that you can listen on. Conveniently, these events are named similarly to the methods used by Ratchet, onopen, onclose, and onmessage, all of which you can (and should) implement in your own code:

```
connection.onopen = function() {
    console.log('connection established');
}

connection.onclose = function() {
```

```
        console.log('connection closed');
    }

connection.onmessage = function(event) {
    console.log('message received: ' + event.data);
}
```

Receiving messages

Each client connection will have a corresponding `ConnectionInterface` instance in the Ratchet server application. When you call a connection's `send()` method on the server, this will trigger the `onmessage` event on the client side.

Each time a new message is received; this message should be displayed in the chat window. For this, you can implement a new JavaScript method `appendMessage` that will display a new message in the previously created message container:

```
var appendMessage = function(message, sentByMe) {
    var text = sentByMe ? 'Sent at' : 'Received at';
     var html = $('<div class="msg">' + text + ' <span
class="date"></span>: <span
    class="text"></span></div>');

    html.find('.date').text(new Date().toLocaleTimeString());
    html.find('.text').text(message);

    $('#messages').prepend(html);
}
```

In this example, we are using a simple jQuery construct to create a new HTML element and populate it with the current date and time and the actual message text received. Be aware that a single message currently only consists of the raw message text and does not yet contain any kind of meta data, such as an author or other information. We'll get to that later.

 While creating HTML elements with jQuery is sufficient in this case, you might want to consider using a dedicated templating engine such as **Mustache** or **Handlebars** in a real-world scenario. Since this is not a JavaScript book, we will be sticking to the basics here.

You can then call the `appendMessage` method when a message is received:

```
connection.onmessage = function(event) {
    console.log('message received: ' + event.data);
    appendMessage(event.data, false);
}
```

The event's data property contains the entire received message as a string and you can use it as you see fit. Currently, our chat application is only equipped to handle plain text chat messages; whenever you need to transport more or structured data, using JSON encoding is probably a good option.

Sending messages

To send messages, you can (unsurprisingly) use the connection's `send()` method. Since you already have the respective user input fields in your HTML file, all it needs now to get the first version of our chat working is a little more jQuery:

```
$(document).ready(function() {
    $('#submit').click(function() {
        var message = $('#message').val();

        if (message) {
            console.log('sending message: "' + message + '"');
            connection.send(message);

            appendMessage(message, true);
        }
    });
});
```

As soon as the HTML page is loaded completely, we begin listening on the submit button's `click` event. When the button is clicked, the message from the input field is sent to the server using the connection's `send()` method. Each time a message is sent, Ratchet will call the `onMessage` event in the server-side component, allowing the server to react to that message and to dispatch it to other connected users.

Usually, a user will want to see messages that they sent themselves in the chat window, too. That is why we are calling the `appendMessage` that was implemented previously, which will insert the sent message into the message container, just as if it was received from a remote user.

Testing the application

When both containers (web server and WebSocket application) are running, you can now test the first version of your chat by opening the URL `http://localhost` in your browser (better yet, open the page twice in two different windows so that you can actually use the application to chat with yourself).

The following screenshot shows an example of the result that you should get when testing the application:

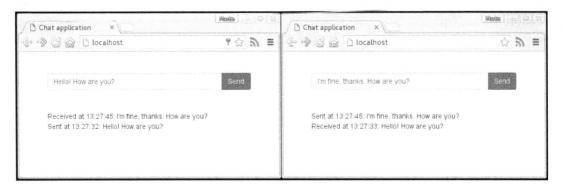

Testing the first version of the chat application with two browser windows

Keeping the connection from timing out

When you keep the test site open for more than a few minutes, you might notice that eventually the WebSocket connection will be closed. This is because most browsers will close a WebSocket connection when no messages were sent or received in a certain time frame (usually five minutes). As you are working with long-running connections, you will also need to consider connectivity issues-what if one of your users uses a mobile connection and temporarily disconnects while using your application?

The easiest way to mitigate this is to implement a simple re-connect mechanism-whenever the connection is closed, wait a few seconds and then try again. For this, you can start a timeout in the `onclose` event in which you open a new connection:

```
connection.onclose = function(event) {
    console.error(e);
    setTimeout(function() {
        connection = new WebSocket('ws://localhost:8080/chat');
    }, 5000);
}
```

This way, each time the connection is closed (due to a timeout, network connectivity problems, or any other reason); the application will try to re-establish the connection after a grace time of five seconds.

If you want to proactively prevent disconnects, you can also periodically send messages through the connection in order to keep the connection alive. This can be done by registering an interval function that periodically (in intervals smaller than the timeout) sends messages to the server:

```
var interval;

connection.onopen = function() {
    console.log('connection established');
    interval = setInterval(function() {
        connection.send('ping');
    }, 120000);
}

connection.onclose = function() {
    console.error(e);
    clearInterval(interval);
    setTimeout(function() {
        connection = new WebSocket('ws://localhost:8080/chat');
    }, 5000);
}
```

There are a few caveats to consider here: first of all, you should only start sending keep-alive messages after the connection was actually established (that is why we are registering the interval in the `onopen` event), and you should also stop sending keep-alives when the connection was closed (which can still happen, for example, when the network is not available), which is why the interval needs to be cleared in the `onclose` event.

Furthermore, you probably do not want keep-alive messages to be broadcast to the other connected clients; this means that these messages also need a special handling in the server-side component:

```
public function onMessage(ConnectionInterface $from, $msg)
{
    if ($msg == 'ping') {
        return;
    }

    echo "received message '$msg' from user {$from->remoteAddress}\n";
    foreach($this->users as $user) {
        if ($user != $from) {
            $user->send($msg);
        }
    }
}
```

Deployment options

As you have already noticed, Ratchet applications are not deployed like your typical PHP application, but in fact run their own HTTP server that can directly answer HTTP requests. Also, most applications will not *only* serve WebSocket connections, but also need to process regular HTTP requests, too.

> This section is meant to give you an overview on how to deploy a Ratchet application in a production environment. For the remaining sections of this chapter, we will continue using the Docker-based development setup (without load balancing and fancy process managers) for the sake of simplicity.

This will open an entire set of new problems to solve. One of them is scalability: by default, PHP runs single-threaded, so even when using the asynchronous event loop offered by `libev`, your application will never scale beyond a single CPU. While you could consider using the `pthreads` extension to enable threading in PHP (and to enter a whole new world of pain), it is usually easier to simply start the Ratchet application multiple times, have it listen on different ports, and use a load-balancer such as Nginx to distribute HTTP requests and WebSocket connections among them.

For processing regular (non-WebSocket) HTTP requests, you can still use a regular PHP process manager such as PHP-FPM or Apache's PHP module. You can then configure Nginx to dispatch those regular requests to FPM and all WebSocket requests to one of your running Ratchet applications.

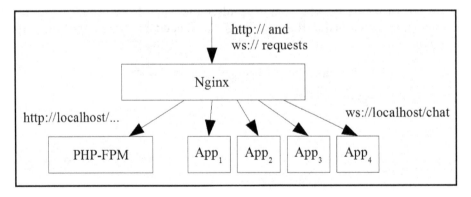

Deploying and load-balancing Ratchet applications using an Nginx load balancer

To achieve this, you first need to make the port that your application listens on so that it can be configured separately for each running process. As the application is started through the command line, the easiest way to make the port configurable per-process is a command-line parameter. You can use the getopt function to easily parse command-line parameters. While you're at it, you can also make the listen address configurable. Insert the following code into your server.php file:

```
$options = getopt('l:p:', ['listen:', 'port:']);
$port = $options['port'] ?? $options['p'] ?? 8080;
$addr = $options['listen'] ?? $options['l'] ?? '127.0.0.1';

$app = new \Ratchet\App('localhost', $port, $addr);
$app->route('/chat', new \Packt\Chp6\Chat\ChatComponent);
$app->run();
```

Next, you need to make sure your server actually automatically starts a sufficient number of processes. In a Linux environment, the **Supervisor** tool is usually a good choice for this. On Ubuntu or Debian Linux systems, you can install it from the system's package repositories using the following command:

```
$ apt-get install supervisor
```

You can then place a configuration file in /etc/supervisor/conf.d/ with the following contents:

```
[program:chat]
numprocs=4
command=php /path/to/application -port=80%(process_num)02d
process_name=%(program_name)s-%(process_num)02d
autostart=true
autorestart=unexpected
```

This will configure Supervisor to start four instances of the chat application on system boot. They will listen at the ports 8000 to 8003 and will automatically be restarted by Supervisor when they unexpectedly terminate-remember: a PHP fatal error may be relatively harmless in a FPM-managed environment, but in a standalone PHP process, a single fatal error will bring down your entire application for all users until someone restarts the process. For this reason, it's good to have a service like Supervisor that automatically restarts crashed processes.

Next, install an Nginx web server to serve as a load balancer for the four running chat applications. On Ubuntu or Debian, install Nginx as follows:

```
$ apt-get install nginx
```

After having installed Nginx, place a configuration file `chat.conf` in the directory `/etc/nginx/sites-enabled/` with the following contents:

```
upstream chat {
    server localhost:8000;
    server localhost:8001;
    server localhost:8002;
    server localhost:8003;
}
server {
    listen 80;
    server_name chat.example.com;

    location /chat/ {
        proxy_pass http://chat;
        proxy_http_version 1.1;
        proxy_set_header Upgrade $http_upgrade;
        proxy_set_header Connection "upgrade";
    }

    // Additional PHP-FPM configuration here
    // ...
}
```

This configuration will configure all four application processes as *upstream* servers for the Nginx load balancer. All HTTP requests starting with the `/chat/` path will be forwarded to one of the Ratchet applications running on the server. The `proxy_http_version` and `proxy_set_header` directives are necessary to allow Nginx to correctly forward the WebSocket handshake between server and client.

Bridging Ratchet and PSR-7 applications

Sooner or later, your chat application will also need to respond to regular HTTP requests (for example, this will become necessary as soon as you want to add an authentication layer with a login form and authentication processing).

As explained in the previous section, a common setup for WebSocket applications in PHP is to have a Ratchet application handle all WebSocket connections, and to direct all regular HTTP requests to a regular PHP-FPM setup. However, as a Ratchet application in fact also ships its own HTTP server, you can also respond to regular HTTP requests directly from your Ratchet application.

Just as you have used the Ratchet\MessageComponentInterface to implement
WebSocket applications, you can use the Ratchet\HttpServerInterface to implement a
regular HTTP server. As an example, consider the following class:

```
namespace Packt\Chp6\Http;

use Guzzle\Http\Message\RequestInterface;
use Ratchet\ConnectionInterface;
use Ratchet\HttpServerInterface;

class HelloWorldServer implements HttpServerInterface
{
    public function onOpen(ConnectionInterface $conn, RequestInterface
$request = null)
    {}

    public function onClose(ConnectionInterface $conn)
    {}

    public function onError(ConnectionInterface $conn, \Exception $e)
    {}

    public function onMessage(ConnectionInterface $from, $msg)
    {}
}
```

As you can see, the methods defined by the HttpServerInterface are similar to the
MessageCompomentInterface. The only difference is the $request parameter that is now
additionally passed into the onOpen method. This class is an instance of the
Guzzle\Http\Message\RequestInterface (which, unfortunately, does not implement
the PSR-7 RequestInterface) from which you can get the basic HTTP request properties.

You can now use the onOpen method to send a regular HTTP in response to a received
HTTP request:

```
public function onOpen(ConnectionInterface $conn, RequestInterface $request
= null)
{
    $conn->send("HTTP/1.1 200 OK\r\n");
    $conn->send("Content-Type: text/plain\r\n");
    $conn->send("Content-Length: 13\r\n");
    $conn->send("\r\n");
    $conn->send("Hello World\n");
    $conn->close();
}
```

As you can see, you'll have to send the entire HTTP response (including response headers!) in the onOpen method. This is a bit tedious, and we'll find a better way for that later, but it will suffice for the moment.

Next, register your HTTP server in your server.php the same way that you would register a new WebSocket server:

```
$app = new \Ratchet\App('localhost', $port, $addr);
$app->route('/chat', new \Packt\Chp6\Chat\ChatComponent);
$app->route('/hello', new \Packt\Chp6\Http\HelloWorldServer, ['*']);
$app->run();
```

Especially note the third parameter ['*'] here: this parameter will allow any request origin (not just localhost) for this route, as most browsers and command-line clients will not even send an origin header for regular HTTP requests.

After restarting your application, you can test the new HTTP route using any regular HTTP client, either on the command line or using your browser. As shown in the following screenshot:

Testing a Ratchet HTTP server using cURL

Building an HTTP response including headers by hand is a very tedious task-especially if at some point, your application contains multiple HTTP endpoints. For this reason, it would be nice to have a framework that handles all this stuff for you.

In the previous chapter, you've already worked with the **Slim** framework, which you can also integrate quite nicely with Ratchet. Unfortunately, Ratchet is not (yet) PSR-7 compliant, so you'll have to do some legwork to convert Ratchet's request interfaces to PSR-7 instances and pipe PSR-7 responses back into the ConnectionInterface.

Start by installing the Slim framework into your application using Composer:

```
$ composer require slim/slim
```

The goal of the remainder of this section will be to build a new implementation of the `HttpServerInterface` that takes a Slim application as a dependency and forwards all incoming requests to the Slim application.

Start by defining the class `Packt\Chp6\Http\SlimAdapterServer` that implements the `HttpServerInterface` and accepts a `Slim\App` as a dependency:

```php
namespace Packt\Chp6\Http;

use Guzzle\Http\Message\RequestInterface;
use Ratchet\ConnectionInterface;
use Ratchet\HttpServerInterface;
use Slim\App;

class SlimAdapterServer implements HttpServerInterface
{
    private $app;

    public function __construct(App $app)
    {
        $this->app = $app;
    }

    // onOpen, onClose, onError and onMessage omitted
    // ...
}
```

The first thing that you'll need to do is to map the `$request` parameter that Ratchet passes into the `onOpen` event to a PSR-7 request object (which you can then pass into the Slim application for processing). The Slim framework ships its own implementation of this interface: the class `Slim\Http\Request`. Start by adding the following code to your `onOpen` method, which maps the request URI to an instance of the `Slim\Http\Uri` class:

```php
$guzzleUri = $request->getUrl(true);
$slimUri = new \Slim\Http\Uri(
    $guzzleUri->getScheme() ?? 'http',
    $guzzleUri->getHost() ?? 'localhost',
    $guzzleUri->getPort(),
    $guzzleUri->getPath(),
    $guzzleUri->getQuery() . '',
    $guzzleUri->getFragment(),
    $guzzleUri->getUsername(),
    $guzzleUri->getPassword()
);
```

This will map the Guzzle request's URI object in a Slim URI object. These are largely compatible, allowing you to simply copy most of the properties into the `Slim\Http\Uri` class' constructor. Only the `$guzzleUri->getQuery()` return value needs to be forced into a string by concatenating it with an empty string.

Continue by building the HTTP request header object:

```
$headerValues = [];
foreach ($request->getHeaders() as $name => $header) {
    $headerValues[$name] = $header->toArray();
}
$slimHeaders = new \Slim\Http\Headers($headerValues);
```

After having built both the request URI and headers, you can create an instance of the `SlimRequest` class:

```
$slimRequest = new \Slim\Http\Request(
    $request->getMethod(),
    $slimUri,
    $slimHeaders,
    $request->getCookies(),
    [],
    new \Slim\Http\Stream($request->getBody()->getStream());
);
```

You can then use this request object to invoke the Slim application that you've passed as a dependency into the `SlimAdapterServer` class:

```
$slimResponse = new \Slim\Http\Response(200);
$slimResponse = $this->app->process($slimRequest, $slimResponse);
```

The `$this->app->process()` function will actually execute the Slim application. It works similar to the `$app->run()` method that you've worked with in the previous chapter, but directly accepts a PSR-7 request object and returns a PSR-7 response object for further processing.

The final challenge is now to use the `$slimResponse` object and return all data contained in it back to the client. Let's start by sending the HTTP headers:

```
$statusLine = sprintf('HTTP/%s %d %s',
    $slimResponse->getProtocolVersion(),
    $slimResponse->getStatusCode(),
    $slimResponse->getReasonPhrase()
);
$headerLines = [$statusLine];

foreach ($slimResponse->getHeaders() as $name => $values) {
```

```
    foreach ($values as $value) {
        $headerLines[] = $headerName . ': ' . $value;
    }
}

$conn->send(implode("\r\n", $headerLines) . "\r\n\r\n");
```

The `$statusLine` contains the first line of the HTTP response (usually, something like `HTTP/1.1 200 OK` or `HTTP/1.1 404 Not Found`). The nested `foreach` loops are used to collect all response headers from the PSR-7 response object and concatenate them into a string that can be used in an HTTP response (each header gets its own line, separated by both a **Carriage Return** (CR) and **Line Feed** (LF) newline). The double \r\n finally terminates the header and marks the beginning of the response body, which you'll output next:

```
$body = $slimResponse->getBody();
$body->rewind();

while (!$body->eof()) {
    $conn->send($body->read(4096));
}
$conn->close();
```

In your `server.php` file, you can now instantiate a new Slim application, pass it into a new `SlimAdapterServer` class, and register this server at the Ratchet application:

```
use Slim\App;
use Slim\Http\Request;
use Slim\Http\Response;

$slim = new App();
$slim->get('/hello', function(Request $req, Response $res): Response {
    $res->getBody()->write("Hello World!");
    return $res;
});
$adapter = new \Packt\Chp6\Http\SlimAdapterServer($slim);

$app = new \Ratchet\App('localhost', $port, $addr);
$app->route('/chat', new \Packt\Chp6\Chat\ChatComponent);
$app->route('/hello', $adapter, ['*']);
$app->run();
```

Integrating the Slim framework into your Ratchet application allows you to serve both WebSocket requests and regular HTTP requests with the same application. Serving HTTP requests from one continuously running PHP process presents interesting new opportunities, although you'll have to use these with care. You will need to worry about things like memory consumption (PHP does have a **Garbage Collector**, but if you do not pay attention, you may still create a memory leak that will cause your PHP process to run into the memory limit and crash and burn), but building applications like these may be an interesting alternative when you have high-performance requirements.

Accessing your application via the web server

In our development setup, we're currently running two containers, the application container itself, listening on port 8080 and an Nginx server listening on port 80 that serves static files such as the index.html and various CSS and JavaScript files. Exposing two different ports for static files and the application itself is often not recommendable in a production setup.

Because of this, we will now configure our web server container to serve a static file, when it's present (such as the index.html or CSS and JavaScript files), and to delegate the HTTP request to the application container when no actual file with the given name exists. For this, start by creating an Nginx configuration file that you can place anywhere in your project directory-for example, etc/nginx.conf:

```
map $http_upgrade $connection_upgrade {
    default upgrade;
    '' close;
}

server {
    location / {
        root /var/www;
        try_files $uri $uri/index.html @phpsite;
    }

    location @phpsite {
        proxy_http_version 1.1;
        proxy_set_header X-Real-IP   $remote_addr;
        proxy_set_header Host $host;
        proxy_set_header X-Forwarded-For $proxy_add_x_forwarded_for;
        proxy_set_header Upgrade $http_upgrade;
        proxy_set_header Connection $connection_upgrade;
```

```
        proxy_pass http://app:8080;
    }
}
```

This configuration will cause Nginx to look for files in the /var/www directory (when using Docker to start the Nginx web server, you can simply mount your local directory into the container's /var/www directory). There, it will first look for a direct filename match, then for an index.html inside a directory, and as a last option, pass the request to an upstream HTTP server.

> This configuration is also suitable for a production setup as described in the *Deployment options* section. When you have multiple instances of your application running, you will need to reference a dedicated upstream configuration with multiple upstream applications in your proxy_pass statement.

After creating the configuration file, you can re-create your Nginx container as follows (pay special attention to the --link flag of the docker run command):

```
$ docker rm -f chat-web
$ docker run -d --name chat-web --link chat-app:app -v $PWD/public:/var/www
-p 80:80 nginx
```

Adding authentication

Currently, our application is missing one crucial feature: anyone can post messages in the chat, and there is also no way to determine which user sent which message. Because of this, in the next step, we will add an authentication layer to our chat application. For this, we'll need a login form and some kind of authentication handler.

In this example, we will use a typical session-based authentication. After successfully authenticating the username and password, the system will create a new session for the user and store the (random and non-guessable) session ID in a cookie on the user's browser. On subsequent requests, the authentication layer can use the session ID from the cookie to look up the currently authenticated user.

Creating the login form

Let's start by implementing a simple class for managing sessions. This class will be named
`Packt\Chp6\Authentication\SessionProvider`:

```
namespace Packt\Chp6\Authentication;

class SessionProvider
{
    private $users = [];

    public function hasSession(string $sessionId): bool
    {
        return array_key_exists($sessionId, $this->users);
    }

    public function getUserBySession(string $sessionId): string
    {
        return $this->users[$sessionId];
    }

    public function registerSession(string $user): string
    {
        $id = sha1(random_bytes(64));
        $this->users[$id] = $user;
        return $id;
    }
}
```

This session handler is built extremely simple: it simply stores which user (by name) is
using which session ID; new sessions can be registered using the `registerSession`
method. As all HTTP requests will be served by the same PHP process, you do not even
need to persist these sessions in a database, but can simply keep them in-memory (however,
you will need database-backed session storage as soon as you have multiple processes
running in a load-balanced environment, as you cannot simply share memory between
different PHP processes).

On really random random numbers

In order to generate a cryptographically secure session ID, we're using the
`random_bytes` function which was added in PHP 7 and is now the
suggested way to obtain cryptographically secure random data (do not
use functions such as `rand` or `mt_rand` for this, ever).

In the following steps, we'll implement a few additional routes into our newly integrated Slim application:

1. The GET / route will serve the actual chat HTML site. Up until now, this was a static HTML page that was served directly by the web server. Using authentication, we will be needing a bit more login on this site (for example, redirecting a user to the login page when they are not logged in), which is why we're moving the index page into the application.

2. The GET /login route will serve a login form in which users can authenticate with a username and password. Provided credentials will be submitted to the…

3. POST /authenticate route. This route will verify credentials provided by a user and start a new session (using the previously-built SessionProvider class) when a user was successfully authenticated. After a successful authentication, the /authenticate route will redirect the user back to the / route.

Let's start by registering these three routes in the Ratchet application and connecting them to the previously created Slim adapter in the server.php file:

```
$app = new \Ratchet\App('localhost', $port, $addr);
$app->route('/chat', new \Packt\Chp6\Chat\ChatComponent);
$app->route('/', $adapter, ['*']);
$app->route('/login', $adapter, ['*']);
$app->route('/authenticate', $adapter, ['*']);
$app->run();
```

Continue by implementing the / route. Remember, this route is supposed to simply serve the index.html file that you have already created previously, but only if a valid user session exists. For this, you will have to check if there is an HTTP cookie with a session ID provided within the HTTP request and then verify that there is a valid user session with this ID. For this, add the following code to your server.php (also, remove the previously created GET /hello route, if still present). As shown in the following code:

```
$provider = new \Packt\Chp6\Authentication\SessionProvider();
$slim = new \Slim\App();
$slim->get('/', function(Request $req, Response $res) use ($provider):
Response {
    $sessionId = $req->getCookieParams()['session'] ?? '';
    if (!$provider->hasSession($sessionId)) {
        return $res->withRedirect('/login');
    }
    $res->getBody()->write(file_get_contents('templates/index.html'));
    return $res
        ->withHeader('Content-Type', 'text/html; charset=utf8');
});
```

This route serves the file `templates/index.html` to your users. Currently, this file should be located in the `public/` directory in your setup. Create the `templates/` directory in your project folder and move the `index.html` there from the `public/` directory. This way, the file will not be served by the Nginx web server anymore, and all requests to / will be directly forwarded to the Ratchet application (which will then either deliver the index view or redirect the user to the login page).

In the next step, you can implement the `/login` route. No special logic is required for this route:

```
$slim->get('/login', function(Request $req, Response $res): Response {
    $res->getBody()->write(file_get_contents('templates/login.html'));
    return $res
        ->withHeader('Content-Type', 'text/html;charset=utf8');
});
```

Of course, for this route to actually work, you will need to create the `templates/login.html` file. Start by creating a simple HTML document for this new template:

```html
<!DOCTYPE html>
<html lang="en">
<head>
    <meta charset="UTF-8">
    <title>Chap application: Login</title>
    <script src="bower_components/jquery/dist/jquery.min.js"></script>
    <script
src="bower_components/bootstrap/dist/js/bootstrap.min.js"></script>
    <link rel="stylesheet"
href="bower_components/bootstrap/dist/css/bootstrap.min.css"/>
</head>
<body>
</body>
</html>
```

This loads all required JavaScript libraries and CSS files required for the login form to work. In the <body> section, you can then add the actual login form:

```html
<div class="row" id="login">
    <div class="col-md-4 col-md-offset-4">
        <div class="panel panel-default">
            <div class="panel-heading">Login</div>
            <div class="panel-body">
                <form action="/authenticate" method="post">
                    <div class="form-group">
                        <label for="username">Username</label>
```

```
                       <input type="text" name="username" id="username"
placeholder="Username" class="form-control">
                  </div>
                  <div class="form-group">
                     <label for="password">Password</label>
                     <input type="password" name="password"
id="password" placeholder="Password" class="form-control">
                  </div>
                  <button type="submit" id="do-login" class="btn btn-
primary btn-block">
                     Log in
                  </button>
               </form>
            </div>
         </div>
      </div>
</div>
```

Pay special attention to the `<form>` tag: the form's action parameter is the `/authenticate` route; this means that all values that are entered into the form will be passed into the (still to-be-written) `/authenticate` route handler where you will be able to verify the entered credentials and create a new user session.

After saving this template file and restarting the application, you can test the new login form by simply requesting the `/` URL, either in your browser or using a command-line tool such as **HTTPie** or **curl**. As you do not have a login session yet, you should be redirected to the login form at once. As shown in the following screenshot:

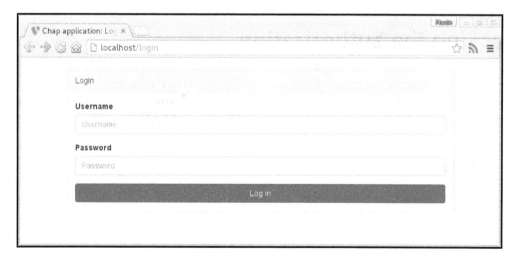

Unauthenticated users are now redirected to the login form

The one thing that's missing now is the actual /authenticate route. For this, add the following code in your server.php file:

```
$slim->post('/authenticate', function(Request $req, Response $res) use
($provider): Response {
    $username = $req->getParsedBodyParam('username');
    $password = $req->getParsedBodyParam('password');

    if (!$username || !$password) {
        return $res->withStatus(403);
    }

    if (!$username == 'mhelmich' || !$password == 'secret') {
        return $res->withStatus(403);
    }

    $session = $provider->registerSession($username);
    return $res
        ->withHeader('Set-Cookie', 'session=' . $session)
        ->withRedirect('/');
});
```

Of course, the actual user authentication is still extremely rudimentary in this example- we're only checking one hardcoded user/password combination. In a production setup, you can implement any kind of user authentication in this place (which will typically consist of looking up a user in a database collection and comparing the submitted password's hash with the user's stored password hash).

Checking the authorization

Now, all that's left is to extend the chat application itself to only allow authorized users to connect. Luckily, WebSocket connections start as regular HTTP connections (before being upgraded to a WebSocket connection). This means that the browser will transfer all cookies in a Cookie HTTP header which you can then access in your application.

In order to keep the authorization concern separated from the actual chat business logic, we will implement everything authorization-related in a special decorator class that also implements the Ratchet\MessageComponentInterface interface and wraps the actual chat application. We will call this class Packt\Chp6\Authentication\AuthenticationComponent. Start by implementing this class with a constructor that accepts both a MessageComponentInterface and a SessionProvider as dependencies:

```
namespace Packt\Chp6\Authentication;

use Ratchet\MessageComponentInterface;
use Ratchet\ConnectionInterface;

class AuthenticationComponent implements MessageComponentInterface
{
    private $wrapped;
    private $sessionProvider;

    public function __construct(MessageComponentInterface $wrapped,
SessionProvider $sessionProvider)
    {
        $this->wrapped         = $wrapped;
        $this->sessionProvider = $sessionProvider;
    }
}
```

Continue by implementing the methods that are defined by the
MessageComponentInterface. to begin, implement all these methods to simply delegate
to the respective method on the $wrapped object:

```
public function onOpen(ConnectionInterface $conn)
{
    $this->wrapped->onOpen($conn);
}

public function onClose(ConnectionInterface $conn)
{
    $this->wrapped->onClose($conn);
}

public function onError(ConnectionInterface $conn, \Exception $e)
{
    $this->wrapped->onError($conn, $e);
}

public function onMessage(ConnectionInterface $from, $msg)
{
    $this->wrapped->onMessage($from, $msg);
}
```

You can now add an authentication check to the following new `onOpen` method. In here, you can check if a cookie with a session ID is set, use the `SessionProvider` to check if the session ID is valid, and only accept the connection (meaning: delegate to the wrapped component) when a valid session exists:

```
public function onOpen(ConnectionInterface $conn)
{
    $sessionId = $conn->WebSocket->request->getCookie('session');
    if (!$sessionId || !$this->sessionProvider->hasSession($sessionId)) {
        $conn->send('Not authenticated');
        $conn->close();
        return;
    }

    $user = $this->sessionProvider->getUserBySession($sessionId);
    $conn->user = $user;

    $this->wrapped->onOpen($conn);
}
```

If no session ID is found or if the given session ID is not valid, the connection will be closed immediately. Otherwise, the session ID will be used to look up the associated user from the `SessionProvider` and added as a new property to the connection object. In the wrapped component, you can then simply access `$conn->user` again to get a reference to the currently authenticated user.

Connecting users and messages

You can now assert that only authenticated users can send and receive messages in the chat. However, the messages themselves are not yet associated with any specific user, so you'll still not know which user actually sent a message.

Up until now, we have worked with simple plain-text messages. As each message will now need to contain more information than the pure message text, we'll switch to JSON encoded messages. Each chat message will contain an `msg` property that is sent from the client to the server, and the server will add an `author` property filled with the username of the currently authenticated username. This can be done in the `onMessage` method of the `ChatComponent` that you've built earlier, as follows:

```
public function onMessage(ConnectionInterface $from, $msg)
{
    if ($msg == 'ping') {
        return;
    }
```

```
$decoded = json_decode($msg);
$decoded->author = $from->user;
$msg = json_encode($decoded);

foreach ($this->users as $user) {
    if ($user != $from) {
        $user->send($msg);
    }
}
}
```

In this example, we're first JSON-decoding the message received from the client. Then, we'll add an "author" property to the message, filled with the username of the authenticated user (remember, the $from->user property is set in the AuthenticationComponent that you built in the previous section). The message is then re-encoded and sent to all connected users.

Of course, our JavaScript frontend must also support these new JSON encoded messages. Start by changing the appendMessage function in your app.js JavaScript file to accept messages in the form of structured objects, instead of simple strings:

```
var appendMessage = function(message, sentByMe) {
    var text = sentByMe ? 'Sent at' : 'Received at';
  var html = $('<div class="msg">' + text + ' <span class="date"></span> by
<span class="author"></span>: <span class="text"></span></div>');

    html.find('.date').text(new Date().toLocaleTimeString());
    html.find('.author').text(message.author);
    html.find('.text').text(message.msg);

    $('#messages').prepend(html);
};
```

The appendMessage function is used by both the WebSocket connection's onmessage event and your submit button listener. The onmessage event needs to be modified to first JSON-decode incoming messages:

```
connection.onmessage = function(event) {
    var msg = JSON.parse(event.data);
    appendMessage(msg, false);
}
```

Also, the submit button listener needs to send JSON-encoded data to the WebSocket server, and also pass structured data into the modified `appendMessage` function:

```
$(document).ready(function () {
    $('#submit').click(function () {
        var text = $('#message').val();
        var msg = JSON.stringify({
            msg: text
        });
        connection.send(msg);

        appendMessage({
            author: "me",
            message: text
        }, true);
    })
});
```

Summary

In this chapter, you have learned about the basic principles of WebSocket applications and how to build them using the Ratchet framework. In contrast to most PHP applications, Ratchet apps are deployed as single, long-running PHP processes that do not require process managers such as FPM or web servers. This requires a quite different deployment, which we have also looked into in this chapter, both for development and for high-scale production environments.

In addition to simply serving WebSockets using Ratchet, we have also looked at how you can integrate Ratchet applications with other frameworks (for example, the Slim framework that you have already worked with in Chapter 5, *Creating a RESTful Web Service*) using the PSR-7 standard.

In Chapter 7, *Building an Asynchronous Microservice Architecture*, you will learn about yet another communication protocol that you can use to integrate applications. While WebSockets are still built on HTTP, the next chapter will feature the **ZeroMQ** protocol-which is completely different from HTTP and brings along a whole new set of challenges to be solved.

7
Building an Asynchronous Microservice Architecture

In this chapter, we will build an application consisting of a set of small and independent components that communicate with each other over network protocols. Often, these so-called **Microservice architectures** are built using HTTP-based communication procotols, often in the form of RESTful APIs, which we've already implemented in `Chapter 5`, *Creating a RESTful Web Service.*

Instead of focusing on REST, in this chapter we will explore an alternative communication protocol that focuses on asynchronicity, loose coupling, and high performance: **ZeroMQ**. We will use ZeroMQ to build a simple**checkout service** for an (entirely fictional) e-commerce scenario that will handle a wide range of concerns, beginning with e-mail messaging, order processing, inventory management, and more.

The target architecture

The central service of our Microservice architecture will be the checkout service. This service will offer an API for a checkout process that is common to many e-commerce systems. For each checkout process, we will require the following input data:

- A **cart** that can contain an arbitrary number of articles
- The customer's **contact data**

The checkout service will then be responsible for executing the actual checkout process, which will involve a number of additional services, each handling a single step or concern of the checkout process:

1. Our fictional e-commerce venture will handle physical goods (or more abstract goods, of which we can only have a limited quantity in stock). So, for each article in a cart, the checkout service will need to ensure that the desired quantity of said article is actually in stock, and if possible, reduce the available stock by that amount. This will be the responsibility of the **inventory service**.

2. After successfully completing a checkout process, the user needs to be notified via e-mail about the successful checkout. This will be the responsibility of the **mailing service**.

3. Also, after completing the checkout process, the order has to be forwarded to a shipping service that starts the shipping for this order.

The following diagram shows a high-level view of the desired target architecture for this chapter:

In this chapter, the focus will be on using ZeroMQ for implementing the communication patterns between the different services. We will not implement the entire business logic that would be required for such a checkout process to actually work (as you could very well fill another book with this). Instead, we will implement the actual services as simple stubs that offer the APIs that we want them to implement, but contain only a prototypical implementation of the actual business logic.

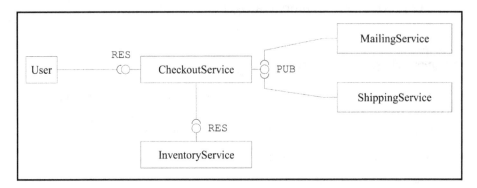

The target architecture of our application

The labels beside the depicted interfaces (**RES** and **PUB**) are the different ZeroMQ socket types that you'll learn about in this chapter.

ZeroMQ patterns

In this chapter, you will learn about the basic communication patterns that are supported by ZeroMQ. Do not worry if all that sound a bit theoretical; you will implement all of these patterns yourself throughout the chapter.

Request/reply pattern

The ZeroMQ library supports a variety of different communication patterns. For each of these, you will need different ZeroMQ socket types. The easiest communication pattern is the Request/reply pattern, in which a client opens an REQ socket and connects to a server listening on an REP socket. The client sends a request that is then replied to by the server.

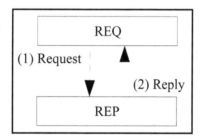

ZeroMQ Request/Reply sockets

It's important to know that REQ and REP sockets are always *synchronous*. Each REQ socket can be sending requests to a single REP socket at a time, and more importantly, each REP socket can also only be connected to a single REQ socket at a time. The ZeroMQ library even enforces this on the protocol level and triggers errors when an REQ socket tries to receive new requests before replying to the current one. There are advanced communication patterns to work around this limitation that we'll work with later.

Publish/subscribe pattern

The publish/subscribe pattern consists of a PUB socket on which messages can be published. To this socket, any number of SUB sockets can be connected. When a new message is published on a PUB socket, it will be forwarded to all connected SUB sockets.

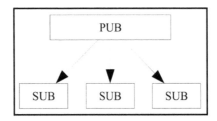

Publish/subscribe sockets

Each subscriber in a PUB/SUB architecture needs to specify at least one subscription – a string that works as a filter for each message. Messages will be filtered by the publisher so that each subscriber only receives messages that they have subscribed to.

Publish/Subscribe works strictly in one direction. Publishers cannot receive messages from the subscribers, and subscribers cannot send messages back to the publishers. However, just as multiple SUB sockets can be connected to a single PUB socket, a single SUB socket can also be connected to multiple PUB sockets.

Push/pull pattern

The push/pull pattern works similar to the publish/subscribe pattern. A PUSH socket is used to publish messages to any number of PULL sockets (just like with PUB/SUB, a single PULL sockets can also be connected to any number of PUSH sockets). In contrast to publish/subscribe patterns, however, each message that is sent on a PUSH socket is dispatched to only one of the connected PULL sockets. This behavior makes the PUSH/PULL patterns are ideal to implement worker pools that you can, for example, use to distribute tasks to any number of workers to process in parallel. Similarly, a PULL socket may also be used to collect results from any number of PUSH sockets (which may in turn be results that are sent back from a worker pool).

Using a PUSH/PULL socket to distribute tasks to a worker pool and then using a second PUSH/PULL layer to collect results from that pool in a single socket is also called *fan-out/fan-in*.

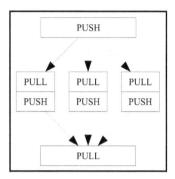

Using PUSH and PULL sockets to implement a fan-out/fan-in architecture

Bootstrapping the project

As usual, we will begin by bootstrapping our project for this chapter. For using the ZeroMQ library in PHP applications, you will need the **php-zmq extension** that you can install via PECL. You will also need the `libzmq-dev` package that contains the C header files for the ZeroMQ library. You can install it via your operating system's package manager. The following commands will work on both Ubuntu and Debian Linux:

```
$ apt-get install libmzq-dev
$ pecl install zmq-beta
```

As usual, we will be using composer to manage our PHP dependencies and Docker for managing the required system libraries. As our application will consist of multiple services that run in multiple processes, we will be working with multiple composer projects and multiple Docker images.

If you are using Windows and want to run your ZeroMQ/PHP applications natively without using Docker, you can download the ZeroMQ extension from the PECL website (`https://pecl.php.net/package/zmq/1.1.3/windows`)

All of our services will use the same software (PHP with the ZeroMQ extension installed). We'll start by implementing the inventory service, but you will be able to use the same Docker image (or at least the same Dockerfile) for all services that we will be creating in this example. Start by creating an `inventory/Dockerfile` file in your project directory with the following contents:

```
FROM php:7
RUN apt-get update && apt-get install -y libzmq-dev
RUN docker-php-ext-configure pcntl && \
    docker-php-ext-install pcntl && \
    pecl install ev-beta && docker-php-ext-enable ev && \
    pecl install zmq-beta && docker-php-ext-enable zmq
WORKDIR /opt/app
ONBUILD ADD . /opt/app
CMD ["/usr/local/bin/php", "server.php"]
```

You'll notice that we're also installing the `pcntl` and `ev` extensions. You've already worked with the `ev` extension in Chapter 6, *Building a Chat Application*. It offers an asynchronous event loop that works well with the `react/zmq` library that we will be using later in this chapter. The `pcntl` extension offers some features that will help you control the process state of long-running PHP processes later on.

To make life easier, you can also create a `docker-compose.yml` file in your project directory in order to use Docker compose to manage the multitude of containers in your application. We'll get to that once you have the first service that you can run in a container.

Building the inventory service

We will start by implementing the inventory service, as it will use a simple request/reply pattern for communication and it does not have any other dependencies.

Getting started with ZeroMQ REQ/REP sockets

Start by creating the service's `composer.json` file in the `inventory/` directory:

```
{
  "name": "packt-php7/chp7-inventory",
  "type": "project",
  "authors": [{
    "name": "Martin Helmich",
    "email": "php7-book@martin-helmich.de"
  }],
  "require": {
    "php": ">= 7.0",
    "ext-zmq": "*"
  },
  "autoload": {
    "psr-4": {
      "Packt\\Chp7\\Inventory": "src/"
```

```
        }
    }
}
```

After creating the `composer.json` file, install the project's dependencies using the `composer install` command on a command line within the `inventory/` directory.

Let's start by creating a `server.php` file for the inventory. Just like the Ratchet application from Chapter 6, *Building a Chat Application,* this file will later be our main server process – remember, in this example, we're not even using HTTP as a communication protocol, so there's no web server and no FPM involved anywhere.

The starting point of each ZeroMQ application is the context. The context stores all kind of states that the ZeroMQ library needs for maintaining sockets and communicating with other sockets. You can then use this context to create a new socket and bind this context to a port:

```
$args = getopt('p:', ['port=']);
$ctx = new ZMQContext();

$port = $args['p'] ?? $args['port'] ?? 5557;
$addr = 'tcp://*:' . $port;

$sock = $ctx->getSocket(ZMQ::SOCKET_REP);
$sock->bind($addr);
```

This code creates a new ZeroMQ REP socket (a socket that can reply to requests) and binds this socket to a configurable TCP port (5557 by default). You can now receive messages on this socket and reply to them:

```
while($message = $sock->recv()) {
    echo "received message '" . $message . "'\n";
    $sock->send("this is my response message");
}
```

As you can see, this loop will poll infinitely for new messages and then respond to them. The socket's `recv()` method will block the script execution until a new message has been received (you can later use the `react/zmq` library to easily implement non-blocking sockets, but this will suffice for now).

In order to test your ZeroMQ server, you can create a second file, `client.php`, in your `inventory/` directory in which you can use an REQ socket to send requests to the server:

```
$args = getopt('h', ['host=']);
$ctx = new ZMQContext();
```

```
$addr = $args['h'] ?? $args['host'] ?? 'tcp://127.0.0.1:5557';

$sock = $ctx->getSocket(ZMQ::SOCKET_REQ);
$sock->connect($addr);

$sock->send("This is my request");
var_dump($sock->recv());
```

When your server script is running, you can simply run the `client.php` script to connect to the server's REP socket, send a request, and wait for the server's reply. Just like with the REP socket, the REQ socket's `recv` method will also block until a reply has been received from the server.

If you are using Docker compose to manage the multitude of containers in your development environment (currently, it's only one, but there will be more), add the following section to your `docker-compose.yml` file:

```
inventory:
  build: inventory
  ports:
    - 5557
  volumes:
    - inventory:/usr/src/app
```

After adding the inventory service to the `docker-compose.yml` configuration file, you can start the container by simply running the following command on a command line:

```
$ docker-compose up
```

Using JsonRPC for communication

Now we have a server that can receive text messages from a client and then send responses back to that client. However, in order to build a working and maintainable Microservice architecture, we'll need some kind of protocol and format that these messages can follow and all services can agree upon. Often in Microservice architectures, this common denominator is HTTP, whose rich protocol semantics can be used to easily build REST web services. However, ZeroMQ as a protocol is much more low-level and does not concern itself with different request methods, headers, caching, and all the other features that come *for free* with HTTP.

Instead of a RESTful service, we will implement the inventory service as a simple **Remote Procedure Call** (**RPC**) service. A quick and easy format that can be used for this is JSON-RPC, which implements RPCs with JSON messages. Using JSON-RPC, a client can send a method call using the following JSON format:

```
{
    "jsonrpc": "2.0",
    "method": "methodName",
    "params": ["foo", "bar", "baz"],
    "id": "some-random-id"
}
```

The server can then respond to this message using the following format:

```
{
    "jsonrpc": "2.0",
    "id": "id from request",
    "result": "the result value"
}
```

Or alternatively, when an error occurred during processing:

```
{
    "jsonrpc": "2.0",
    "id": "id from request",
    "error": {
        "message": "the error message",
        "code": 1234
    }
}
```

This protocol is relatively simple and we can easily implement it on top of ZeroMQ. For this, start by creating a new `Packt\Chp7\Inventory\JsonRpcServer` class. This server will need a ZeroMQ socket and also an object that provides the methods that clients should be able to invoke using RPCs:

```
namespace Packt\Chp7\Inventory;

class JsonRpcServer
{
    private $socket;
    private $server;

    public function __construct(\ZMQSocket $socket, $server)
    {
        $this->socket = $socket;
        $this->server = $server;
    }
}
```

We can now implement a method that receives messages from the socket, tries to parse them as JSON-RPC messages, and invokes the respective method on the $server object and returns that method's result value:

```
public function run()
{
    while ($msg = $this->socket->recv()) {
        $resp = $this->handleMessage($msg);
        $this->socket->send($resp);
    }
}
```

As in the previous example, this method will run infinitely and will process any number of requests. Now, let's have a look at the handleMessage method:

```
private function handleMessage(string $req): string {
    $json   = json_decode($req);
    $method = [$this->server, $json->method];

    if (is_callable($method)) {
        $result = call_user_func_array($method, $json->params ?? []);
        return json_encode([
            'jsonrpc' => '2.0,
            'id'      => $json->id,
            'result'  => $result
        ]);
    } else {
        return json_encode([
            'jsonrpc' => '2.0',
            'id'      => $json->id,
            'error'   => [
                'message' => 'uncallable method ' . $json->method,
                'code'    => -32601
            ]
        ]);
    }
}
```

This method checks if the $this->server object has a callable method with the same name as the method property of the JSON-RPC request. If so, this method is invoked with the request's param property as arguments and the return value is incorporated into the JSON-RPC response.

Currently, this method is still missing some basic exception handling. As a single unhandled exception, a fatal error can terminate the entire server process, so we need to be extra careful here. First, we need to make sure that the incoming message is really a valid JSON string:

```
private function handleMessage(string $req): string {
    $json   = json_decode($req);
    if (json_last_error()) {
        return json_encode([
            'jsonrpc' => '2.0',
            'id'      => null,
            'error'   => [
                'message' => 'invalid json: ' .
json_last_error_msg(),
                'code'    => -32700
            ]
        ]);
    }
    // ...
}
```

Also, make sure that you catch anything that might be thrown from the actual service function. As we're working with PHP 7, remember that regular PHP errors are now also thrown, so it's important to not only catch exceptions, but errors as well. You can catch both exceptions and errors by using the `Throwable` interface in your `catch` clause:

```
if (is_callable($method)) {
    try {
        $result = call_user_func_array($method, $json->params ?? []);
        return json_encode(/* ... */);
    } catch (\Throwable $t) {
        return json_encode([
            'jsonrpc' => '2.0',
            'id'      => $json->id,
            'error'   => [
                'message' => $t->getMessage(),
                'code'    => $t->getCode()
            ]
        ]);
    }
} else { // ...
```

You can now continue by implementing the actual service containing the inventory service business logic. As we've spent a fair amount of time with low-level protocols until now, let's recapitulate the requirements for this service: the inventory service manages the inventories of articles in stock. During the checkout process, the inventory service needs to check if the required amount of an article is in stock, and if possible, reduce the inventory amount by the given amount.

We will implement this logic in the `Packt\Chp7\Inventory\InventoryService` class. Note that we'll try to keep the example simple and manage our article inventories simply in-memory. In a production setup, you'd probably use a database management system for storing your article data:

```php
namespace Packt\Chp7\Inventory\InventoryService;

class InventoryService
{
    private $stock = [
        1000 => 123,
        1001 => 4,
        1002 => 12
    ];

    public function checkArticle(int $articleNumber, int $amount = 1): bool
    {
        if (!array_key_exists($articleNumber, $this->stock)) {
            return false;
        }
        return $this->stock[$articleNumber] >= $amount;
    }

    public function takeArticle(int $articleNumber, int $amount = 1): bool
    {
        if (!$this->checkArticle($articleNumber, $amount) {
            return false;
        }

        $this->stock[$articleNumber] -= $amount;
        return true;
    }
}
```

In this example, we're starting off with three articles with the article numbers `1000` to `1002`. The `checkArticle` function tests if the required amount of a given article is in stock. The `takeArticle` function attempts to reduce the amount of articles by the required amount, if possible. If this was successful, the function returns `true`. If the required amount is not in stock, or the article is not known at all, the function will return `false`.

We now have a class that implements a JSON-RPC server and another class containing the actual business logic for our inventory service. We can now put both of these classes together in our `server.php` file:

```
$args = getopt('p:', ['port=']);
$ctx = new ZMQContext();

$port = $args['p'] ?? $args['port'] ?? 5557;
$addr = 'tcp://*:' . $port;

$sock = $ctx->getSocket(ZMQ::SOCKET_REP);
$sock->bind($addr);

$service = new \Packt\Chp7\Inventory\InventoryService();
$server = new \Packt\Chp7\Inventory\JsonRpcServer($sock, $service);
$server->run();
```

To test this service, at least until you have a first version of the checkout service up and running, you can adjust the `client.php` script that you've created in the previous section to also send and receive JSON-RPC messages:

```
// ...

$msg = [
    'jsonrpc' => '2.0',
    'method'  => 'takeArticle',
    'params'  => [1001, 2]
];

$sock->send(json_encode($msg));
$response = json_decode($sock->recv());

if (isset($response->error)) {
    // handle error...
} else {
    $success = $reponse->result;
    var_dump($success);
}
```

Each call of this script will remove two items of article #1001 from your inventory. In our example, we're working with a locally managed inventory that is always initialized with four items of this article, so the first two invocations of the `client.php` script will return true as a result, and all subsequent invocations will return false.

Making the inventory service multithreaded

Currently, the inventory service works in a single thread, and with a blocking socket. This means that it can handle only one request at a time; if a new request is received while other requests are being processed, the client will have to wait until all previous requests have finished processing. Obviously, this does not scale very well.

In order to implement a server that can handle multiple requests in parallel, you can employ ZeroMQ's **ROUTER/DEALER** pattern. A ROUTER is a special kind of ZeroMQ socket that behaves very much like a regular REP socket, with the only difference being that multiple REQ sockets can connect to in parallel. Likewise, a DEALER socket is another kind of socket that is similar to an REQ socket, only that it can be connected to multiple REP sockets. This allows you to construct a load balancer that simply consists of one ROUTER and one DEALER socket that pipes packages from a set of multiple clients to a set of multiple servers.

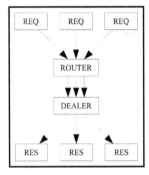

The ROUTER/DEALER pattern

As PHP does not support multithreading (at least, not very well), we will resort to using multiple processes in this example. Our multithreaded server will consist of one master process that handles the ROUTER and DEALER sockets, and multiple worker processes that each work with one REP socket. To implement this, you can fork a number of worker processes using the `pcntl_fork` function.

> For the `pcntl_fork` function to work, you need the `pcntl` extension enabled. In nearly all distributions, this extension is enabled by default; in the Dockerfile that you have built in the previous section, it is also explicitly installed. If you compiled PHP yourself, you will need the `--enable-pcntl` flag when calling the `configure` script.

In this example, our inventory service will consist of multiple ZeroMQ sockets: first a multitude of worker processes, each listening on a RES socket that responds to requests, and a master process with each ROUTER and DEALER socket that accepts and dispatches these requests. Only the ROUTER socket will be visible to outside services and reachable via TCP; for all other sockets, we will use UNIX sockets for communicating – they are faster and not reachable via network.

Start by implementing a worker function; create a new file called `server_multithreaded.php` for this:

```php
require 'vendor/autoload.php';

use Packt\Chp7\Inventory\InventoryService;
use Packt\Chp7\Inventory\JsonRpcServer;

function worker()
{
    $ctx = new ZMQContext();

    $sock = $ctx->getSocket(ZMQ::SOCKET_REP);
    $sock->connect('ipc://workers.ipc');

    $service = new InventoryService();

    $server = new JsonRpcServer($sock, $service);
    $server->run();
}
```

The `worker()` function creates a new REP socket and connects this socket to the UNIX socket `ipc://workers.ipc` (this will be created by the master process later). It then runs the usual `JsonRpcServer` that you've already worked with before.

You can now start any number (in this case, four) of these worker processes using the `pcntl_fork` function:

```php
for ($i = 0; $i < 4; $i ++) {
    $pid = pcntl_fork();
    if ($pid == 0) {
        worker($i);
        exit();
    }
}
```

In case you're not familiar with the `fork` function: it duplicates the currently running process. The forked process will continue to run at the same code location at which it was forked. However, in the parent process, the return value of `pcntl_fork()` will return the process ID of the newly created process. However, within the new process, this value will be 0. In this case, the child processes now become our worker processes and the actual master process will pass the loop without exiting.

After this, you can start the actual load balancer by creating a ROUTER and a DEALER socket:

```
$args = getopt('p:', ['port=']);
$ctx = new ZMQContext();

$port = $args['p'] ?? $args['port'] ?? 5557;
$addr = 'tcp://*:' . $port;

$ctx = new ZMQContext();

// Socket to talk to clients
$clients = $ctx->getSocket(ZMQ::SOCKET_ROUTER);
$clients->bind($addr);

// Socket to talk to workers
$workers = $ctx->getSocket(ZMQ::SOCKET_DEALER);
$workers->bind("ipc://workers.ipc");
```

The ROUTER socket is bound to the actual network address at which the service is intended to be reachable (in this case, a TCP socket, allowing the service to be reached via a network). The DEALER socket, on the other hand, is bound to a local UNIX socket that will not be exposed to the outside world. The only purpose of the UNIX socket `ipc://workers.ipc` is that the worker processes can connect their REP sockets to it.

After having created both the ROUTER and the DEALER socket, you can use the `ZMQDevice` class to pipe incoming packages from the ROUTER socket to the DEALER socket, which will then distribute equally to all connected REP sockets. Response packages that are sent back from the REP sockets will also be dispatched back to the original clients:

```
// Connect work threads to client threads via a queue
$device = new ZMQDevice($clients, $workers);
$device->run();
```

Changing the inventory service this way does not require any modification of the client code; the ROUTER socket that the load balancer is listening on behaves very much like a REP socket, and any REQ socket can connect to it in exactly the same way.

Building the checkout service

We now have a service that manages the inventory stock of your small, fictional e-commerce venture. In the next step, we will now implement a first version of the actual checkout service. The checkout service will offer an API for completing a checkout process, using a cart consisting of multiple articles and basic customer contact data.

Using react/zmq

For this, the checkout service will offer a simple REP ZeroMQ socket (or a ROUTER socket, in a concurrent setup). After receiving a checkout order, the checkout service will then communicate with the inventory service to check if the required items are available and to reduce the stock amount by the item amounts in the cart. If that was successful, it will publish the checkout order on a PUB socket that other services can listen on.

If a cart consists of multiple items, the checkout service will need to make multiple calls to the inventory service. In this example, you will learn how to make multiple requests in parallel in order to speed up execution. We will also use the react/zmq library, which offers an asynchronous interface for the ZeroMQ library and the react/promise library that will help you to better handle an asynchronous application.

Start by creating a new composer.json file in a new checkout/ directory and initialize the project with composer install:

```
{
  "name": "packt-php7/chp7-checkout",
  "type": "project",
  "authors": [{
    "name": "Martin Helmich",
    "email": "php7-book@martin-helmich.de"
  }],
  "require": {
    "php": ">= 7.0",
    "react/zmq": "^0.3.0",
    "react/promise": "^2.2",
    "ext-zmq": "*",
    "ext-ev": "*"
  },
  "autoload": {
    "psr-4": {
      "Packt\\Chp7\\Checkout": "src/"
    }
  }
}
```

This file is similar to the inventory service's `composer.json`; the only difference is the PSR-4 namespace and the additional requirements `react/zmq`, `react/promise`, and `ext-ev`. If you are using Docker for your development setup, you can simply copy your existing Dockerfile from the inventory service.

Continue by creating a `server.json` file in your `checkout/` directory. As with any React application (remember the Ratchet application from Chapter 6, *Building a Chat Application*), the first thing you need to do is to create an event loop that you can then run:

```php
<?php
use \React\ZMQ\Factory;
use \React\ZMQ\Context;

require 'vendor/autoload.php';

$loop = Factory::create();
$ctx  = new Context($loop);

$loop->run();
```

Note that we're using the `React\ZMQ\Context` class instead of the `ZMQContext` class now. The React context class offers the same interface, but extends its base class by some functionalities to better support asynchronous programming.

You can already start this program and it will run infinitely, but it will not actually do anything just yet. As the checkout service should offer a REP socket to which clients should send requests, you should continue by creating and binding a new REP socket before running the event loop:

```php
// ...
$ctx = new Context($loop);

$socket = $ctx->getSocket(ZMQ::SOCKET_REP);
$socket->bind('tcp://0.0.0.0:5557');

$loop->run();
```

ReactPHP applications are asynchronous; instead of just calling `recv()` on the socket to wait for the next incoming message, you can now register an event handler on the socket that will be called by ReactPHP's event loop as soon as a message is received:

```php
// ...

$socket = $ctx->getSocket(ZMQ::SOCKET_REP);
$socket->bind('tcp://0.0.0.0:5557');
$socket->on('message', function(string $msg) use ($socket) {
```

```
        echo "received message $msg.\n";
        $socket->send('Response text');
});

$loop->run();
```

This callback solution works similar to other asynchronous libraries that you will most commonly encounter when developing client-site JavaScript code. The basic principle is the same: the `$socket->on(...)` method simply registers an event listener that can be called at any later point in time whenever a new message is received. The execution of the code will continue immediately (in contrast to this, compare the regular `$socket->recv()` function that blocks until a new message is received) and the `$loop->run()` method is called. This call starts the actual event loop that is responsible for calling the registered event listener when new messages are received. The event loop will block until it is interrupted (for example, by a SIGINT signal that you can trigger with *Ctrl + C* on the command line).

Working with promises

When working with asynchronous code, it is often just a matter of time until you find yourself in "callback hell". Imagine you want to send two consecutive ZeroMQ requests (for example, first asking the inventory service if a given article is available and then actually instructing the inventory service to reduce the stock by the required amount). You can implement this using multiple sockets and the 'message' event that you have seen previously. However, this will quickly become an unmaintainable mess:

```
$socket->on('message', function(string $msg) use ($socket, $ctx) {
    $check = $ctx->getSocket(ZMQ::SOCKET_REQ);
    $check->connect('tcp://identity:5557');
    $check->send(/* checkArticle JSON-RPC here */);
    $check->on('message', function(string $msg) use ($socket, $ctx) {
        $take = $ctx->getSocket(ZMQ::SOCKET_REQ);
        $take->connect('tcp://identity:5557');
        $take->send(/* takeArticle JSON-RPC here */);
        $take->on('message', function(string $msg) use ($socket) {
            $socket->send('success');
        });
    });
});
```

The preceding code snippet is just an example of how complicated this might get; in our case, you would even need to consider that each checkout order can contain any number of articles, each of them requiring two new requests to the identity service.

To make life better, you can implement this functionality using promises (see the following box for a detailed explanation of the concept). A good implementation of promises is provided by the `react/promise` library that should already be declared in your `composer.json` file.

What are promises?

Promises (sometimes also called futures) are a concept commonly found in asynchronous libraries. They present an alternative to the regular callback-based approach.

Basically, a promise is an object that represents a value that is not yet available (for example, because the ZeroMQ request that was supposed to retrieve the value has not yet received a reply). In an asynchronous application, a promise may become available (fulfilled) at any time. You can then register functions that should be called whenever a promise was fulfilled, to further process the promised, and now resolved value:

```
$promise = $someService->someFunction();
$promise->then(function($promisedValue) {
    echo "Promise resolved: $promisedValue\n";
});
```

Each call of the `then()` function returns a new promise, this time for the value that will be returned by the callback passed to `then()`. This allows you to easily chain multiple promises together:

```
$promise
    ->then(function($value) use ($someService) {
        $newPromise =
$someService->someOtherFunc($value);
        return $newPromise;
    })
    ->then(function ($newValue) {
        echo "Promise resolved: $newValue\n";
    });
```

We can now put this principle to use by writing an asynchronous client class for communicating with our inventory service. As that service communicates using JSON-RPC, we will now implement the `Packt\Chp7\Checkout\JsonRpcClient` class. This class is initialized with a ZeroMQ context, and for convenience, also the remote service's URL:

```
namespace Packt\Chp7\Checkout;

use React\Promise\PromiseInterface;
use React\ZMQ\Context;

class JsonRpcClient
```

```
{
    private $context;
    private $url;

    public function __construct(Context $context, string $url)
    {
        $this->context = $context;
        $this->url     = $url;
    }

    public function request(string $method, array $params = []):
PromiseInterface
    {
    }
}
```

In this example, the class already contains a `request` method that accepts a method name and a set of parameters, and should return an implementation of `React\Promise\PromiseInterface`.

In the `request()` method, you can now open a new REQ socket and send a JSON-RPC request to it:

```
public function request(string $method, array $params = []):
PromiseInterface
{
    $body = json_encode([
        'jsonrpc' => '2.0',
        'method'  => $method,
        'params'  => $params,
    ]);
    $sock = $this->context->getSocket(\ZMQ::SOCKET_REQ);
    $sock->connect($this->url);
    $sock->send($body);
}
```

Since the `request()` method is supposed to work asynchronously, you cannot simply call the `recv()` method and block until a result is received. Instead, we will need to return a promise for the response value that can be resolved later, whenever a response message is received on the REQ socket. For this, you can use the `React\Promise\Deferred` class:

```
$body = json_encode([
    'jsonrpc' => '2.0',
    'method'  => $method,
    'params'  => $params,
]);
$deferred = new Deferred();
```

```
$sock = $this->context->getSocket(\ZMQ::SOCKET_REQ);
$sock->connect($this->url);
$sock->on('message', function(string $response) use ($deferred) {
    $deferred->resolve($response);
});
$sock->send($body);

return $deferred->promise();
```

This is a prime example of how promises work: you can use the Deferred class to create and return a promise for a value that is not yet available. Remember: the function passed into the $sock->on(...) method will not be called immediately, but at any later point in time when a response was actually received. As soon as this event occurs, the promise that was returned by the request function is resolved with the actual response value.

As the response message contains a JSON-RPC response, you need to evaluate this response before fulfilling the promise that you made to the caller of the request function. As a JSON-RPC response can also contain an error, it is worth noting that you can also reject a promise (for example, when an error occurred while waiting for the response):

```
$sock->on('message', function(string $response) use ($deferred) {
    $response = json_decode($response);
    if (isset($response->result)) {
        $deferred->resolve($response->result);
    } elseif (isset($response->error)) {
        $deferred->reject(new \Exception(
            $response->error->message,
            $response->error->code
        );
    } else {
        $deferred->reject(new \Exception('invalid response'));
    }
});
```

You can now use this JSON-RPC client class in your server.php to actually communicate with the inventory service on each incoming checkout request. Let's start with a simple example on how you can use the new class to chain two consecutive JSON-RPC calls together:

```
$client = new JsonRpcClient($ctx, 'tcp://inventory:5557');
$client->request('checkArticle', [1000])
    ->then(function(bool $ok) use ($client) {
        if ($ok) {
            return $client->request('takeArticle', [1000]);
        } else {
            throw new \Exception("Article is not available");
        }
```

```
    })
    ->then(function(bool $ok) {
        if ($ok) {
            echo "Successfully took 1 item of article 1000";
        }
    }, function(\Exception $error) {
        echo "An error occurred: ${error->getMessage()}\n";
    });
```

As you can see, the `PromiseInterface`'s `then` function accepts two parameters (each both a new function): the first function will be called as soon as the promise was resolved with an actual value; the second function will be called in case the promise was rejected.

If a function passed to `then(...)` returns a new value, the then function will return a new promise for this value. An exception to this rule is when the callback function returns a new promise itself (in our case, in which `$client->request` is called again within the `then()` callback). In this case, the returned promise replaces the original promise. This means that chained calls to the `then()` function actually listen on the second promise.

Let's put this to use in the `server.php` file. In contrast to the preceding example, you need to consider that each checkout order may contain multiple articles. This means that you will need to execute multiple `checkArticle` requests to the inventory service:

```
$client = new JsonRpcClient($ctx, 'tcp://inventory:5557');
$socket->on('message', function(string $msg) use ($socket, $client) {
    $request = json_decode($msg);
    $promises = [];
    foreach ($request->cart as $article) {
        $promises[] = $client->request('checkArticle',
[$article->articlenumber, $article->amount]);
    }
});
```

In this example, we assume that incoming checkout orders are JSON encoded messages that look like the following example:

```
{
  "cart": [
    "articlenumber": 1000,
    "amount": 2
  ]
}
```

In the current version of our `server.php`, we call the JSON-RPC client multiple times and collect the returned promises in an array. However, we do not actually do anything with them yet. You could now call the `then()` function on each of these promises with a callback that will be called for each article with a boolean parameter indicating whether this one article is available. However, for processing the order correctly, we need to know if all articles from the checkout order are available. So what you need to do is not to wait on each promise separately, but to wait until all of them are completed. This is what the `React\Promise\all` function is for: this function takes a list of promises as parameters and returns a new promise that is fulfilled as soon as all supplied promises are fulfilled:

```php
$request = json_decode($msg);
$promises = [];

foreach ($request->cart as $article) {
    $promises[] = $client->request('checkArticle',
[$article->articlenumber, $article->amount]);
}

React\Promise\all($promises)->then(function(array $values) use ($socket) {
    if (array_sum($values) == count($values)) {
        echo "all required articles are available";
    } else {
        $socket->send(json_encode([
            'error' => 'not all required articles are available'
        ]);
    }
}));
```

If not all required articles are available in the inventory service, you can answer the request early with an error message, as there is no need to continue any further. If all articles are available, you'll need a set of subsequent requests to actually reduce the inventory by the specified amounts.

The `array_sum($values) == count($values)` construct used in this example is a quick hack to ensure that an array of boolean values contains only true values.

In the next step, you can now extend your server to run the second set of requests to the inventory service after all of the `checkArticle` method calls have successfully returned. This can be done by following the same way as before using the `React\Promise\all` method:

```php
React\Promise\all($promises)->then(function(array $values) use ($socket,
$request) {
    $promises = [];
```

```
        if (array_sum($values) == count($values)) {
            foreach ($request->cart as $article) {
                $promises[] = $client->request('takeArticle',
[$article->articlenumber, $article->amount]);
            }
            React\Promise\all($promises)->then(function() use ($socket) {
                $socket->send(json_encode([
                    'result' => true
                ]);
            }
        }
    } else {
        $socket->send(json_encode([
            'error' => 'not all required articles are available'
        ]);
    }
});
```

In order to actually test this new server, let's write a short test script that tries to execute an example checkout order. For this, create a new `client.php` file in your `checkout/` directory:

```
$ctx  = new ZMQContext();
$sock = $ctx->getSocket(ZMQ::SOCKET_REQ);
$sock->connect('tcp://checkout:5557');
$sock->send(json_encode([
    'cart' => [
        ['articlenumber' => 1000, 'amount' => 3],
        ['articlenumber' => 1001, 'amount' => 2]
    ]
]));

$result = $sock->recv();
var_dump($result);
```

To run both the checkout service and the test script, you can extend your `docker-compose.yml` file in your project's root directory with the new checkout service:

```
checkout:
  build: checkout
  volumes:
    - checkout:/usr/src/app
  links:
    - inventory:inventory
inventory:
  build: inventory
  ports:
    - 5557
  volumes:
```

```
      - inventory:/usr/src/app
```

For the test script, add a second Compose configuration file, `docker-compose.testing.yml`:

```
test:
  build: checkout
  command: php client.php
  volumes:
    - checkout:/usr/src/app
  links:
    - checkout:checkout
```

Afterwards, you can test your checkout service using the following command line commands:

```
$ docker-compose up -d
$ docker-compose -f docker-compose.testing.yml run --rm test
```

The following screenshot shows an example output of both the test script and both server scripts (in this example, some additional `echo` statements have been added to make the server more verbose):

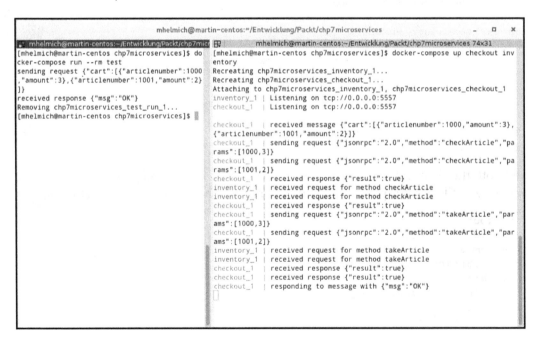

An example output of a checkout order being processed by the checkout and inventory services

Building the mailing service

In the next step, we will put a mailing service into our Microservice architecture. After a checkout was processed, the user should be notified via e-mail about the status of the checkout.

As mentioned before, the focus of this chapter is on building the communication patterns between individual services. Because of this, we will not implement the mailing service's actual mailing functionality in this section, but instead focus on how this service will communicate with other services. Have a look at Chapter 3, *Building a Social Newsletter Service*, to see how you can use PHP to actually send e-mails to other recipients.

In theory, you could implement the mailing service just as you did the inventory service – build a standalone PHP program that listens on a ZeroMQ REP socket, have the checkout service open an REQ socket, and send requests to the mailing service. However, the same can also be achieved using the publish/subscribe pattern.

Using the publish/subscribe pattern, the checkout service does not even need to know about the mailing service. Instead, the checkout service simply opens a PUB socket that other services can connect to. Any and all messages that are sent on the PUB socket are distributed to all connected (subscribing) services. This allows you to implement a very loosely coupled architecture that is also very extensible – you can add new functionality to your checkout process by having more and different services subscribe to the same PUB socket, without having to modify the checkout service itself.

This is possible, because in the case of the mailing service, communication does not need to be synchronous – the checkout service does not need to wait for the mailing service to complete its action before continuing with the process, nor does it need any kind of data that might be returned from the mailing service. Instead, messages can flow strictly in one direction – from checkout service to mailing service.

First, you need to open the PUB socket in the checkout service. For this, modify the checkout service's `server.php`, create a new PUB socket, and bind it to a TCP address:

```
$socket = $ctx->getSocket(ZMQ::SOCKET_REP);
$socket->bind('tcp://0.0.0.0:5557');

$pubSocket =
$ctx->getSocket(ZMQ::SOCKET_PUB);$pubSocket->bind('tcp://0.0.0.0:5558');

$client = new JsonRpcClient($ctx, 'tcp://inventory:5557');
```

After having successfully taken the required items from the inventory service, you can then publish a message on this socket. In this case, we'll simply resend the original message on the PUB socket:

```
$socket->on('message', function(string $msg) use ($client, $pubSocket) {
    // ...
    React\Promise\all($promises)->then(function(array $values) use
($socket, $pubSocket, $request) {
        $promises = [];
        if (array_sum($values) == count($values)) {
            // ...
            React\Promise\all($promises)->then(function() use ($socket,
$pubSocket, $request) {
            $pubSocket->send($request);
            $socket->send(json_encode([
                'result' => true
            ]);
        } else {
            $socket->send(json_encode([
                'error' => 'not all required articles are available'
            ]);
        }
    });
});

$loop->run();
```

Now that you have a PUB socket on which accepted checkout orders are published, you can write the actual mailing service that creates a SUB socket that subscribes to this PUB socket.

For this, start by creating a new directory, `mailing/`, in your project directory. Copy the Dockerfile from the previous examples and create a new `composer.json` file with the following contents:

```
{
    "name": "packt-php7/chp7-mailing",
    "type": "project",
    "authors": [{
        "name": "Martin Helmich",
        "email": "php7-book@martin-helmich.de"
    }],
    "require": {
        "php": ">= 7.0",
        "react/zmq": "^0.3.0"
    },
    "autoload": {
        "psr-4": {
```

```
        "Packt\\Chp7\\Mailing": "src/"
    }
  }
}
```

In contrast to the previous examples, the only difference is the new package name and the different PSR-4 autoloading namespace. Also, you will not need the `react/promise` library for the mailing service. As usual, continue by running `composer install` on a command line within the `mailing/` directory to download the required dependencies.

You can now create a new `server.php` file in the `mailing/` directory in which you create a new SUB socket that you can then connect to the checkout service:

```
require 'vendor/autoload.php';

$loop = \React\EventLoop\Factory::create();
$ctx  = new \React\ZMQ\Context($loop);

$socket = $ctx->getSocket(ZMQ::SOCKET_SUB);
$socket->subscribe('');
$socket->connect('tcp://checkout:5558');

$loop->run();
```

Pay attention to the `$socket->subscribe()` call. Each SUB socket can subscribe to a given *topic* or *channel*. A channel is identified by a string prefix that can be submitted as part of each published message. Clients will then only receive messages that match the channel that they have subscribed to. If you do not care about different channels on one PUB socket, you can simply subscribe to the empty channel by calling `$socket->subscribe` with an empty string to receive all messages that are published on the PUB socket. However, if you do not call the subscribe method; you will not receive any messages at all.

After the socket is connected, you can provide a listener function for the `'message'` event in which you decode the JSON-encoded message and process it accordingly:

```
$socket->connect('tcp://checkout:5558');
$socket->on('message', function(string $msg) {
    $data = json_decode($msg);
    if (isset($data->customer->email)) {
        $email = $data->customer->email;

        echo "sending confirmation email to $email.\n";
    }
});

$loop->run();
```

Also note that PUB and SUB sockets are strictly unidirectional: you send messages from the PUB sockets to any number of subscribing SUB sockets, but you cannot send a reply back to the publisher-at least, not on the same socket. If you really need some kind of feedback channel, you could have the publisher listening on a separate REP or SUB socket and the subscriber connecting with a new REQ or PUB socket. The following diagram illustrates two strategies to implement a feedback channel like this:

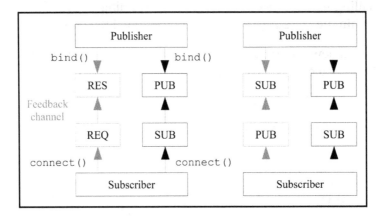

Different strategies for implementing feedback channels in a publish/subscribe architecture

To test the new mailing service, you can reuse the `client.php` script from the previous section. As the mailing service requires the checkout order to contain an e-mail address, you'll need to add one to the message body:

```php
$sock->send(json_encode([
    'cart' => [
        ['articlenumber' => 1000, 'amount' => 3],
        ['articlenumber' => 1001, 'amount' => 2]
    ],
    'customer' => [
        'email' => 'john.doe@example.com'
    ]
]));
```

Also, remember to add the new mailing service to the `docker-compose.yml` file:

```yaml
# ...
checkout:
  build: checkout
  volumes:
    - checkout:/usr/src/app
  links:
    - inventory:inventory
```

```
mailing:
  build: mailing
  volumes:
    - mailing:/usr/src/app
  links:
    - checkout:checkout
inventory:
  build: inventory
  ports:
    - 5557
  volumes:
    - inventory:/usr/src/app
```

After adding the new service to `docker-compose.yml`, start all services and run the test script again:

```
$ docker-compose up -d inventory checkout mailing
$ docker-compose run --rm test
```

After that, inspect the output of the separate containers to check if the checkout order was correctly processed:

```
$ docker-compose logs
```

Building the shipping service

In our small e-commerce example, we are still missing the shipping service. In real-world scenarios, this would be a really complex task, and you would often need to communicate with outside parties and maybe integrate with APIs of external transport service providers. For this reason, we will now build our shipping service as a worker pool using PUSH and PULL sockets and an arbitrary number of worker processes.

PUSH/PULL for beginners

A PUB socket publishes each message to all connected subscribers. ZeroMQ also offers the PUSH and PULL socket types – they work similar to PUB/SUB, but each message published on a PUSH socket is sent to only one of potentially many connected PULL sockets. You can use this to implement a worker pool into which you can push long-running tasks that are then executed in parallel.

For this, we will need one master process that uses a SUB socket to subscribe to completed checkout orders. The same process needs to offer a PUSH socket that the individual worker processes can connect to. The following diagram illustrates this architecture:

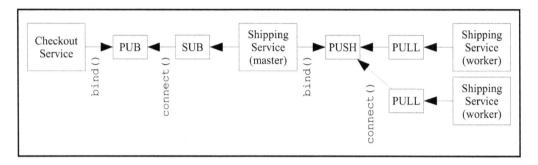

PUB/SUB and PUSH/PULL in combination

As usual, start by creating a new directory, `shipping/`, in your project folder. Copy the Dockerfile from one of the previous services, create a new `composer.json` file, and initialize the project with `composer install`:

```
{
    "name": "packt-php7/chp7-shipping",
    "type": "project",
    "authors": [{
        "name": "Martin Helmich",
        "email": "php7-book@martin-helmich.de"
    }],
    "require": {
        "php": ">= 7.0.0",
        "react/zmq": "^0.3.0"
    },
    "autoload": {
        "psr-4": {
            "Packt\\Chp7\\Shipping": "src/"
        }
    }
}
```

We'll start by implementing the master process. This master process needs to do three simple things:

- Open a SUB socket and connect this socket to the checkout service's PUB socket. This will allow the shipping service to receive all checkout orders that were accepted by the checkout service.

- Open a PUSH socket and bind this socket to a new TCP port. This will allow the worker processes to connect and receive checkout orders.
- Forward each message received on the SUB socket to the PUSH socket.

For this, create a new `master.php` file in your `shipping/` directory in which you can create a new event loop and create the two required sockets:

```
require 'vendor/autoload.php';

$loop = React\EventLoop\Factory::create();
$ctx  = new React\ZMQ\Context($loop);

$subSocket = $ctx->getSocket(ZMQ::SOCKET_SUB);
$subSocket->subscribe('');
$subSocket->connect('tcp://checkout:5558');

$pushSocket = $ctx->getSocket(ZMQ::SOCKET_PUSH);
$pushSocket->bind('tcp://0.0.0.0:5557');

$loop->run();
```

For actually processing messages that are received on the SUB socket, register a listener function on the `$subSocket` variable that sends each received message on the PUSH socket:

```
$pushSocket->bind('tcp://0.0.0.0:5557');

$subSocket->on('message', function(string $msg) use ($pushSocket) {
    echo 'dispatching message to worker';
    $pushSocket->send($msg);
});

$loop->run();
```

Next, create a new file, `worker.php`, also in the `shipping/` directory. In this file, you will create a PULL socket that receives messages from the PUSH socket opened in the master process:

```
require 'vendor/autoload.php';

$loop = React\EventLoop\Factory::create();
$ctx  = new React\ZMQ\Context($loop);

$pullSocket = $ctx->getSocket(ZMQ::SOCKET_PULL);
$pullSocket->connect('tcp://shippingmaster:5557');

$loop->run();
```

Again, attach a listener function to the $pullSocket in order to process incoming messages:

```
$pullSocket->connect('tcp://shippingmaster:5557');
$pullSocket->on('message', function(string $msg) {
    echo "processing checkout order for shipping: $msg\n";
    sleep(5);
});

$loop->run();
```

sleep(5), in this example, just simulates the execution of a shipping order which may take a longer amount of time. As usual in this chapter, we will not implement the actual business logic any more than we need to, to demonstrate the communication patterns between the individual services.

In order to test the shipping service, now add both the master process and the worker process to your docker-compose.yml file:

```
# ...

inventory:
  build: inventory
  volumes:
    - inventory:/usr/src/app

shippingmaster:
  build: shipping
  command: php master.php
  volumes:
    - shipping:/usr/src/app
  links:
    - checkout:checkout

shippingworker:
  build: shipping
  command: php worker.php
  volumes:
    - shipping:/usr/src/app
  links:
    - shippingmaster:shippingmaster
```

After this, you can start all containers and then follow their output using the following commands:

```
$ docker-compose up -d
```

By default, Docker compose will always start one instance of each service. However, you can start additional instances of each service by using the `docker-compose scale` command. This is a good idea for the `shippingworker` service, as the PUSH/PULL architecture that we've chosen for this service actually allows any number of instances of this service to be running in parallel:

```
$ docker-compose scale shippingworker=4
```

After having started some more instances of the `shippingworker` service, you can attach to all container's log output using the `docker-compose logs` command. Then, use a second terminal to start the client test script that you've created in the previous section:

```
$ docker-compose run --rm test
```

When you run this command multiple times, you will see that the debug output within the shipping worker process is printed by different instances of the container for subsequent invocations. You can see an example output in the following screenshot:

An example output, demonstrating a working push/pull architecture with multiple workers

Fan-out/fan-in

In addition to distributing time-consuming tasks to a number of worker processes, you can also use PUSH and PULL sockets to have the workers push results back to their master process. This pattern is called **fan-out/fan-in**. For this example, have the master process in the `master.php` file listen on a separate PULL socket:

```
$pushSocket = $ctx->getSocket(ZMQ::SOCKET_PUSH);
$pushSocket->bind('tcp://0.0.0.0:5557');

$pullSocket = $ctx->getSocket(ZMQ::SOCKET_PULL);
$pullSocket->bind('tcp://0.0.0.0:5558');
$pullSocket->on('message', function(string $msg) {
    echo "order $msg successfully processed for shipping\n";
});

$subSocket->on('message', function(string $msg) use ($pushSocket) {
    // ...
});

$loop->run();
```

In the `worker.php` file, you can now connect to this PULL socket with a new PUSH socket and send a message as soon as a checkout order has successfully been processed:

```
$pushSocket =
$ctx->getSocket(ZMQ::SOCKET_PUSH);$pushSocket->connect('tcp://shippingmaste
r:5558');

$pullSocket = $ctx->getSocket(ZMQ::SOCKET_PULL);
$pullSocket->connect('tcp://shippingmaster:5557');
$pullSocket->on('message', function(string $msg) use ($pushSocket) {
    echo "processing checkout order for shipping: $msg\n";
    sleep(5);
    $pushSocket->send($msg);
});

$loop->run();
```

This will push the message back to the master process as soon as it has been processed. Note that PUSH/PULL is used the other way around than in the previous section – before we had one PUSH socket and multiple PULL sockets; for the fan-in we have one PULL socket on the master process and multiple PUSH sockets on the worker processes.

Using bind() and connect()

In this section, we have used both the `bind()` and `connect()` method for both PUSH and PULL sockets. In general, `bind()` is used to have a socket listen on a new TCP port (or UNIX socket), while `connect()` is used to have a socket connect to another, already existing socket.

In general, you can use both `bind()` and `connect()` with any socket type. In some cases, like REQ/REP, you'll intuitively `bind()` the REP socket and then `connect()` the REQ socket, but both PUSH/PULL and PUB/SUB actually work both ways. You can have a PULL socket connect to a listening PUSH socket, but you can also have a PUSH socket connect to a listening PULL socket.

The following screenshot shows an example output of both the shipping service's master and worker processes handling multiple checkout orders in parallel. Note that the actual processing is done by different worker processes (`shippingworker_1` to `shippingworker_3` in this example), but are "fanned-in" back to the master process after that:

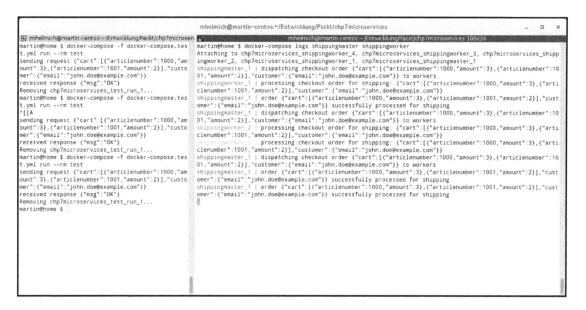

Fan-out/fan-in in action

Bridging ZeroMQ and HTTP

As you have seen in this chapter, ZeroMQ offers a lot of different possibilities for implementing communication between separate services. In particular, patterns such as publish/subscribe and push/pull are not that easy to implement with PHP's de-facto standard protocol, HTTP.

On the other hand, HTTP is more widely adopted and offers a richer set of protocol semantics, handling concerns such as caching or authentication already at the protocol-level. Because of this, especially when offering external APIs, you might prefer offering an HTTP-based API instead of a ZeroMQ-based API. Luckily, it's easy to bridge between the two protocols. In our example architecture, the checkout service is the only service that will be used by outside services. In order to offer a better interface for the checkout service, we will now implement an HTTP-based wrapper for the checkout service that can be used in a RESTful way.

For this, you can use the `react/http` package. This package offers a minimalist HTTP server that – just like `react/zmq` – works asynchronously and uses an event loop for handling requests. This means that a react-based HTTP server can even run in the same process using the same event loop as the REP ZeroMQ socket that is already offered by the checkout service. Start by installing the `react/http` package by running the following command in the `checkout/` folder in your project directory:

```
$ composer require react/http
```

Before extending the checkout service with an HTTP server, the `server.php` script needs a bit of refactoring. Currently, the `server.php` creates a REP ZeroMQ socket with an event listener function in which the request is processed. As our goal is now to add an HTTP API that triggers the same functionality, we'll need to extract this logic into a separate class. Start by creating the `Packt\Chp7\Checkout\CheckoutService` class:

```php
namespace Packt\Chp7\Checkout;

use React\Promise\PromiseInterface;

class CheckoutService
{
    private $client;

    public function __construct(JsonRpcClient $client)
    {
        $this->client = $client;
    }
```

```
        public function handleCheckoutOrder(string $msg): PromiseInterface
        {
        }
}
```

The `handleCheckoutOrder` method will be holding the logic that was previously implemented directly in the `server.php` file. As this method will later be used by both the ZeroMQ REP socket and the HTTP server, this method cannot directly send a response message, but will simply return a promise that can then be used in the `server.php`:

```
public function handleCheckoutOrder(string $msg): PromiseInterface
{
    $request = json_decode($msg);
    $promises = [];

    foreach ($request->cart as $article) {
        $promises[] = $this->client->request('checkArticle',
[$article->articlenumber, $article->amount]);
    }

    return \React\Promise\all($promises)
        ->then(function(array $values):bool {
            if (array_sum($values) != count($values)) {
                throw new \Exception('not all articles are in stock');
            }
            return true;
        })->then(function() use ($request):PromiseInterface {
            $promises = [];

            foreach ($request->cart as $article) {
                $promises[] = $this->client->request('takeArticle',
[$article->articlenumber, $article->amount]);
            }

            return \React\Promise\all($promises);
        })->then(function(array $values):bool {
            if (array_sum($values) != count($values)) {
                throw new \Exception('not all articles are in stock');
            }
            return true;
        });
}
```

The consistent use of promises and not caring about the return message actually allows some simplifications; instead of directly sending back an error message, you can simply throw an exception, which will cause the *promise* returned by this function to be automatically rejected.

The existing `server.php` file can now be simplified by quite a few lines of code:

```
$client            = new JsonRpcClient($ctx, 'tcp://inventory:5557');
$checkoutService = new CheckoutService($client);

$socket->on('message', function($msg) use ($ctx, $checkoutService,
$pubSocket, $socket) {
    echo "received checkout order $msg\n";

    $checkoutService->handleCheckoutOrder($msg)->then(function() use
($pubSocket, $msg, $socket) {
        $pubSocket->send($msg);
        $socket->send(json_encode(['msg' => 'OK']));
    }, function(\Exception $err) use ($socket) {
        $socket->send(json_encode(['error' => $err->getMessage()]));
    });
});
```

Next, you can get to work on the HTTP server. For this, you'll first need a simple socket server that you can then pass into the actual HTTP server class. This can be done at any point in the `server.php` before the event loop is run:

```
$httpSocket = new \React\Socket\Server($loop);
$httpSocket->listen(8080, '0.0.0.0');
$httpServer = new \React\Http\Server($httpSocket);

$loop->run();
```

The HTTP server itself has a `'request'` event for which you can register a listener function (similar to the `'message'` event of the ZeroMQ sockets). The listener function gets a request and a response object passed as a parameter. These are instances of the `React\Http\Request` respective `React\Http\Response` classes:

```
$httpServer->on('request', function(React\Http\Request $req,
React\Http\Response $res) {
    $res->writeHead(200);
    $res->end('Hello World');
});
```

Unfortunately, React HTTP's `Request` and `Response` classes are not compatible with the respective PSR-7 interfaces. However, if the need arises you can convert them relatively easily, as already seen in the section *Bridging Ratchet and PSR-7 applications* in Chapter 6, *Building a Chat Application*.

Within this listener function, you can first check for a correct request method and path, and send an error code, otherwise:

```
$httpServer->on('request', function(React\Http\Request $req,
React\Http\Response $res) {
    if ($request->getPath() != '/orders') {
        $msg = json_encode(['msg' => 'this resource does not exist']);
        $response->writeHead(404, [
            'Content-Type' => 'application/json;charset=utf8',
            'Content-Length' => strlen($msg)
        ]);
        $response->end($msg);
        return;
    }
    if ($request->getMethod() != 'POST') {
        $msg = json_encode(['msg' => 'this method is not allowed']);
        $response->writeHead(405, [
            'Content-Type' => 'application/json;charset=utf8',
            'Content-Length' => strlen($msg)
        ]);
        $response->end($msg);
        return;
    }
});
```

This is where it gets tricky. The ReactPHP HTTP server is so asynchronous, that when the `request` event is triggered the request body has not yet been read from the network socket. To get the actual request body, you need to listen on the request's `data` event. However, the request body is read in chunks of 4096 bytes, so for large request bodies, the data event may actually be called multiple times. The easiest way to read the full request body is to check the `Content-Length` header and check in the data event handler if exactly this amount of bytes has already been read:

```
$httpServer->on('request', function(React\Http\Request $req,
React\Http\Response $res) {
    // error checking omitted...

    $length = $req->getHeaders()['Content-Length'];
    $body   = '';
    $request->on('data', function(string $chunk) use (&$body) {
        $body .= $chunk;
        if (strlen($body) == $length) {
            // body is complete!
        }
    });
});
```

Of course, this won't work when the sender uses the so-called chunked transfer encoding in their request. However, reading a request body using chunked transfer would work a similar way; in this case, the exit condition is not dependent on the `Content-Length` header, but instead when the first empty chunk has been read.

After the complete request body has been read, you can then pass this body into the `$checkoutService` that you have already used before:

```
$httpServer->on('request', function(React\Http\Request $req,
React\Http\Response $res) use ($pubSocket, $checkoutService) {
    // error checking omitted...

    $length = $req->getHeaders()['Content-Length'];
    $body   = '';

    $request->on('data', function(string $chunk) use (&$body, $pubSocket,
$checkoutService) {
        $body .= $chunk;
        if (strlen($body) == $length) {
            $checkoutService->handleCheckoutOrder($body)
                ->then(function() use ($response, $body, $pubSocket) {
$pubSocket->send($body);
                    $msg = json_encode(['msg' => 'OK']);
                    $response->writeHead(200, [
                        'Content-Type' => 'application/json',
                        'Content-Length' => strlen($msg)
                    ]);
                    $response->end($msg);
                }, function(\Exception $err) use ($response) {
                    $msg = json_encode(['msg' => $err->getMessage()]);
                    $response->writeHead(500, [
                        'Content-Type' => 'application/json',
                        'Content-Length' => strlen($msg)
                    ]);
                    $response->end($msg);
                });
        }
    });
});
```

The `CheckoutService` class is used exactly the same way as before. The only difference now is how the response is sent back to the client; if the original request was received by the ZeroMQ REP socket, a respective response was sent to the REQ socket that sent the request. Now, if the request was received by the HTTP server, an HTTP response with the same content is sent.

You can test your new HTTP API using a command-line tool such as curl or HTTPie:

```
$ http -v localhost:8080/orders
cart:='[{"articlenumber":1000,"amount":3}]'
customer:='{"email":"john.doe@example.com"}'
```

The following screenshot shows an example output when testing the new API endpoint using the preceding HTTPie command:

Testing the new HTTP API

Summary

In this chapter, you have learned about ZeroMQ as a new communication protocol and how you can use it in PHP. In contrast to HTTP, ZeroMQ supports other and more complex communication patterns than the simple request/reply pattern. Especially the publish/subscribe and the push/pull pattern, which allow you to build loosely coupled architectures that are easily extensible by new functionalities and scale very well.

You have also learned how you can use the ReactPHP framework to build asynchronous services using event loops and how you can make asynchronicity manageable using promises. We have also discussed how you can integrate ZeroMQ-based applications with *regular* HTTP APIs.

While the previous chapters have all focused on different network communication patterns (RESTful HTTP in Chapter 5, *Creating a RESTful Web Service*, WebSockets in Chapter 6, *Building a Chat Application*, and now ZeroMQ), we will make a fresh start in the following chapter and learn how PHP can be used to build parsers for custom expression languages.

8
Building a Parser and Interpreter for a Custom Language

Extensibility and adaptability are often the required features in enterprise applications. Often, it is useful and practical-or even an actual feature requirement by users-to change an application's behavior and business rules at runtime. Imagine, for example, an e-commerce application in which sales representatives can configure business rules themselves; for example, when the system should offer free shipping for a purchase or should apply a certain discount when some special conditions are met (offer free shipping when the purchase amount exceeds 150 Euros , and the customer has already made two or more purchases in the past or has been a customer for more than a year).

By experience, rules such as these tend to get ridiculously complex (offer a discount when the customer is male and is older than 35 years and has two kids and a cat named Mr. Whiskers and placed the purchase order on a cloudless full-moon night) and may change frequently. For this reason, as a developer, you might actually be glad to offer your user a possibility to configure rules such as these for themselves, instead of having to update, test, and redeploy the application every time one of these rules changes. A feature like this is called **end-user development** and is often implemented using **domain-specific languages**.

Domain-specific languages are languages that are tailored for one specific application domain (in contrast to general-purpose languages, such as C, Java or-you guessed it-PHP). In this chapter, we will build our own parser for a small expression language that can be used to configure business rules in enterprise applications.

For this, we'll need to recapitulate how a parser works and how formal languages are described using formal grammars.

How interpreters and compilers work

Interpreters and compilers read programs that are formulated in a programming language. They either execute them directly (interpreters) or first convert them into a machine language or another programming language (compilers). Both interpreters and compilers usually have (among others) two components called **lexer** and **parser**.

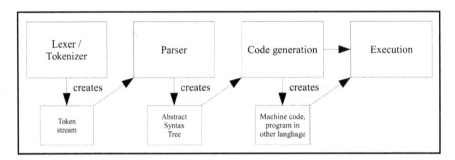

This is a basic architecture of a compiler or interpreter

An interpreter may omit the code generation and run the parsed program directly without a dedicated compilation step.

The **lexer** (also called **scanner** or **tokenizer**) dissects an input program into its smallest possible parts, the so-called tokens. Each token consists of a token class (for example, numerical value or variable identifier) and the actual token contents. For example, a lexer for a calculator given the input string 2 + (3 * a) might generate the following list of tokens (each having a token class and value):

1. Number ("2")
2. Addition operator ("+")
3. Opening bracket (" (")
4. Number ("3")
5. Multiplication operator ("*")
6. Variable identifier ("a")
7. Closing bracket (") ")

In the next step, the **parser** takes the token streams and tries to derive the actual program structure from this stream. For this, the parser needs to be programmed with a set of rules that describe the input language, a grammar. In many cases, a parser generates a data structure that represents the input program in a structured tree; the so-called syntax tree. For example, the input string 2 + (3 * a) generates the following syntax tree:

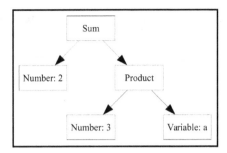

An Abstract Syntax Tree (AST) that can be generated from the expression 2 + (3 * a)

Note that there are programs that will pass the lexical analysis, but in the following step, they are recognized as syntactically wrong by the parser. For example, the input string called `2 + ( 1` would pass the lexer (and generate a token list such as `{Number(2), Addition Operator, Opening bracket, Number(1)}`), but it is obviously syntactically wrong as the opening bracket does not make any sense without a matching closing bracket (assuming that the parser uses the grammar universally recognized for mathematical expressions; in other grammars, `2+(1` might actually be a syntactically valid expression)

Languages and grammars

In order for a parser to be able to understand a program, it needs a formal description of that language-a grammar. In this chapter, we will work with a so-called **parsing expression grammar** (**PEG**). A PEG is (relatively) easy to define and there are libraries that can generate a parser for a given grammar automatically.

A grammar consists of **terminal symbols** and **non-terminal symbols**. A non-terminal symbol is a symbol that maybe composed of several other symbols, following certain rules (**production rules**). For example, a grammar could contain a *number* as non-terminal symbol. Each number could be defined as an arbitrary-length sequence of digits. As a digit could then be any of the characters from 0 to 9 (with each of the actual digits being a terminal symbol).

Let's try to describe the structure of numbers (and then building on this mathematical expressions in general) formally. Let's start by describing how a number looks like. Each number consists of one or more digits, so let's start by describing digits and numbers:

```
Digit: '0'|'1'|'2'|'3'|'4'|'5'|'6'|'7'|'8'|'9'
Number: Digit+
```

In this example, Digit is our first non-terminal symbol. The first rule of our grammar states that any of the characters 0 to 9 is a digit. In this example, the characters '0' to '9' are terminal symbols, the smallest possible building blocks.

> In practice, many Parser generators will allow you to use regular expressions to match terminal symbols. In the previous example, instead of enumerating all possible digits, you could then simply state this:
> `Digit: /[0-9]/`

The second rule of our grammar states that a Number (our second non-terminal symbol) consists of one or more Digit symbols (the + means repeat once or more). Using the same way, we could also expand the grammar to also support decimal numbers:

```
Digit: '0'|'1'|'2'|'3'|'4'|'5'|'6'|'7'|'8'|'9'
Integer: Digit+Decimal: Digit* '.' Digit+Number: Decimal | Integer
```

Here, we've introduced two new non-terminal symbols: Integer and Decimal. Integer is simply a sequence of digits, while a Decimal may start with any number of digits (or none at all, which means that a value such as .12 would also be a valid number), then a dot and then one or more digits. In contrast to the + operator ("repeat once or more") already used above, the * operator means "none or once or more". The production rule for Number now states that a number can either be a decimal number or an integer.

> Order is important here; given an input string of 3.14, the integer rule would match the 3 of this input string, while the Decimal rule would match the entire string. So, in this case it's safer to first try to parse the number as a decimal, and when that fails, parse the number as an integer.

Right now, this grammar describes only positive numbers. However, it can easily be modified to also support negative numbers:

```
Digit: '0'|'1'|'2'|'3'|'4'|'5'|'6'|'7'|'8'|'9'
Integer: '-'? Digit+
Decimal: '-'? Digit* '.' Digit+
Number: Decimal | Integer
```

The ? character used in this example states that a symbol is optional. This means that both an integer and a decimal number can now optionally start with a – character.

We can now continue to define more rules for our grammar. For example, we could add a new rule that describes a multiplication:

```
Product: Number ('*' Number)*
```

As a division is basically the same operation as a multiplication (and has the same operator precedence), we can treat both cases with the same rule:

```
Product: Number (('*'|'/') Number)*
```

As soon as you add a rule for sums to your grammar, it's important to consider the order of operations (multiplication first, then addition). Let's define a new rule called Sum (again, covering both addition and subtraction with one rule):

```
Sum: Product (('+'|'-') Product)*
```

This may seem counter intuitive, at first. After all, a sum does not really need to consist of two products. However, as our Product rule uses * as a quantifier, it will also match single numbers, allowing expressions such as 5 + 4 to be parsed as Product + Product.

For our grammar to become complete, we still need the ability to parse nested statements. As it is, our grammar is able to parse statements such as 2 * 3, 2 + 3. Even 2 + 3 * 4 will be parsed correctly as 2 + (3 * 4) (and not (2 + 3) * 4). However, a statement such as (2 + 3) * 4 does not match any rule of our grammar. After all, the Product rule states that a product is any number of Numbers joined by * characters; since a bracket-enclosed sum does not match the Number rule, the Product rule will not match either. To solve this problem, we'll introduce two new rules:

```
Expr: Sum
Value: Number | '(' Expr ')'
```

With the new Value rule, we can adjust the Product rule to match either regular numbers or bracket-enclosed exceptions:

```
Product: Value ('*' Value)*
```

Here, you will find a complete grammar necessary for describing mathematical expressions. It does not support any kind of variables or logical statements yet, but it will be a reasonable starting point for our own parser that we'll build in the remainder of this chapter:

```
Expr: Sum
Sum: Product (('+' | '-') Product)*
Product: Value (('*' | '/') Value)*
Value: Number | '(' Expr ')'
Number: (Decimal | Integer)
Decimal: '-'? Digit* '.' Digit+
Integer: '-'? Digit+
Digit: '0'|'1'|'2'|'3'|'4'|'5'|'6'|'7'|'8'|'9'
```

Your first PEG parser

Building a tokenizer and parser from scratch is a very tedious task. Luckily, many libraries exist that you can use to generate a parser automatically from some kind of formal grammar definition.

In PHP, you can use the `hafriedlander/php-peg` library to generate the PHP code for a parser for any kind of formal language that can be described by a parsing expression grammar. For this, create a new project directory and create a new `composer.json` file with the following contents:

```json
{
  "name": "packt-php7/chp8-calculator",
  "authors": [{
    "name": "Martin Helmich",
    "email": "php7-book@martin-helmich.de"
  }],

  "require": {
    "hafriedlander/php-peg": "dev-master"
  },
  "autoload": {
    "psr-4": {
      "Packt\\Chp8\\DSL": "src/"
    },
    "files": [
      "vendor/hafriedlander/php-peg/autoloader.php"
    ]
  }
}
```

Note that the `hafriedlander/php-peg` library does not use a PSR-0 or PSR-4 autoloader, but it ships its own class loader instead. Because of this, you cannot use composer's built-in PSR-0/4 class loader and need to manually include the package's autoloader.

Similar to the previous chapters, we'll be using `Packt\Chp8\DSL` as a base namespace for our PSR-4 class loader based in the `src/` directory. This means that a PHP class called `Packt\Chp8\DSL\Foo\Bar` should be located in the `src/Foo/Bar.php` file.

When working with PHP PEG, you write a parser as a regular PHP class that contains the grammar in a special kind of comment. This class is used as an input file for the actual parser generator, which then generates the actual parser source code. The file type for the parser input file is typically `.peg.inc`. The parser class has to extend the `hafriedlander\Peg\Parser\Basic` class.

Our parser will have the `Packt\Chp8\DSL\Parser\Parser` class name. It will be stored in the `src/Parser/Parser.peg.inc` file:

```
namespace Packt\Chp8\DSL\Parser;

use hafriedlander\Peg\Parser\Basic;

class Parser extends Basic
{
    /*!* ExpressionLanguage

    <Insert grammar here>

    */
}
```

Note the comment within the class that starts with the `/*!*` characters. This special comment block will be picked up by the parser generator and needs to contain the grammar from which the parser will be generated.

You can then build the actual parser (which will be stored in the file `src/Parser/Parser.php`, where it will be able to be picked up by the composer class loader) using the PHP-PEG CLI script:

```
$ php -d pcre.jit=0 vendor/hafriedlander/php-peg/cli.php
src/Parser/Parser.peg.inc > src/Parser/Parser.php
```

The `-d pcre.jit=0` flag is required to fix a PHP 7-related bug in the PEG package. Disabling the `pcre.jit` flag may have an impact on the program's performance; however this flag must only be disabled when the parser is generated. The generated parser will not be affected by the `pcre.jit` flag.

Currently, the parser generation will fail with an error, because the parser class does not yet contain a valid grammar. This can easily be changed; add the following lines to the special comment (starting with `/*!*`) in your parser input file:

```
/*!* ExpressionLanguage

Digit: /[0-9]/
Integer: '-'? Digit+
Decimal: '-'? Digit* '.' Digit+
Number: Decimal | Integer

*/
```

You will note that this is exactly the example grammar for matching numbers that we've used in the previous section. This means that after rebuilding the parser, you will have a parser that knows how numbers look like and can recognize them. Admittedly, this is not enough. But we can build on it.

Rebuild your parser by running the `cli.php` script as shown previously and continue by creating a test script called `test.php` in your project directory:

```
require_once 'vendor/autoload.php';

use \Packt\Chp8\DSL\Parser\Parser;

$result1 = new (Parser('-143.25'))->match_Number();
$result2 = new (Parser('I am not a number'))->match_Number();

var_dump($result1);
var_dump($result2);
```

Remember, the `Packt\Chp8\DSL\Parser\Parser` class was automatically generated from your `Parser.peg.inc` input file. The class inherits the `hafriedlander\Peg\Parser\Basic` class, which also provides the constructor. The constructor accepts an expression that the parser should parse.

For each non-terminal symbol that is defined in your grammar, the parser will contain a function named `match_[symbol name]()` (so, for example, `match_Number`) that will match the input string against the given rule.

In our example, `$result1` is the matching result against a valid number (or, in general, an input string that's matched by the parser's grammar), while the input string of `$result2` is obviously not a number and should not be matched by the grammar. Let's have a look at the output of this test script:

```
array(3) {
  '_matchrule' =>
  string(6) "Number"
  'name' =>
  string(6) "Number"
  'text' =>
  string(7) "-143.25"
}
bool(false)
```

As you can see, parsing the first input string returns an array that contains both the matching rule and the string that was matched by the rule. If the rule did not match (as for example in `$result2`), the `match_*` functions will always return `false`.

Let's continue by adding the remainder of the rules that we've already seen in the previous section. These will allow our parser to not only parse numbers but entire mathematical expressions:

```
/*!* ExpressionLanguage

Digit: /[0-9]/
Integer: '-'? Digit+
Decimal: '-'? Digit* '.' Digit+
Number: Decimal | Integer
Value: Number | '(' > Expr > ')'
Product: Value (> ('*'|'/') > Value)*
Sum: Product (> ('+'|'-') > Product)*
Expr: Sum


*/
```

Pay special attention to the > characters in this code example. Those are a special symbol provided by the parser generator that matches whitespace sequences of any length. In some grammars, whitespaces might matter, but when parsing mathematical expressions, you typically do not care if someone enters 2+3 or 2 + 3.

Rebuild your parser and adjust your test script to test these new rules:

```
var_dump((new Parser('-143.25'))->match_Expr());
var_dump((new Parser('12 + 3'))->match_Expr());
var_dump((new Parser('1 + 2 * 3'))->match_Expr());
var_dump((new Parser('(1 + 2) * 3'))->match_Expr());
var_dump((new Parser('(1 + 2)) * 3'))->match_Expr());
```

Pay special attention to the last line. Obviously, the (1 + 2)) * 3 expression is syntactically wrong, because it contains more closing brackets than opening brackets. However, the output of the match_Expr function for this input statement will be the following:

```
array(3) {
  '_matchrule' =>
  string(4) "Expr"
  'name' =>
  string(4) "Expr"
  'text' =>
  string(7) "(1 + 2)"
}
```

As you can see, the input string still matched the Expr rule, just not the entire string. The first part of the string, (1 + 2), is syntactically correct and mated by the Expr rule. This is very important to keep in mind when working with the PEG parser. If a rule does not match the entire input string, the parser will still match as much of the input as it can. It's up to you, as a user of this parser, to determine if a partial match is a good thing or not (in our case, this should probably trigger an error, as a partially matched expression would result in very strange results and undoubtedly be very surprising for a user).

Evaluating expressions

Up until now, we've only used our custom-built PEG parser to check if an input string conforms to a given grammar (meaning, we can *tell* if an input string contains a valid mathematical expression or not). The next logical step is to actually evaluate these expressions (for example, determining that '(1 + 2) * 3' evaluates to '9').

As you have already seen, each match_* function returns an array with additional information on the matched string. Within the parser, you can register custom functions that will be called when a given symbol is matched. Let's start with something simple and try to convert numbers that are matched by our grammar to actual PHP integer or float values. For this, start by modifying the Integer and Decimal rules in your grammar as follows:

```
Integer: value:('-'? Digit+)
    function value(array &$result, array $sub) {
        $result['value'] = (int) $sub['text'];
    }

Double: value:('-'? Digit* '.' Digit+)
    function value(array &$result, array $sub) {
        $result['value'] = (float) $sub['text'];
    }
```

Let's have a look at what's happening here. In each rule, you can specify names for subpatterns within the rule. For example, the pattern Digit+ in the Integer rule gets the name called value assigned. As soon as the parser finds a string matching this pattern, it will call the function with the same name supplied below the Integer rule. The function will be called with two parameters: the &$result parameter will be the array returned by the actual match_Number function later. As you can see, the parameter is passed as reference and you can modify it within the value function. The $sub parameter contains the result array of the subpattern (which, in any case, contains a property text from which you can access the actual text contents of the matched subpattern).

In this case, we simply use PHP's built-in functions to convert the number within the text to an actual `int` or `float` variable. However, this is only possible because our custom grammar and PHP coincidentally represent numbers the same way, allowing us to use the PHP interpreter to convert these values to actual numeric values.

If you are using a non-terminal symbol in one of your rules, it is not necessary to explicitly specify a subpattern name; you can simply use the symbol name as a function name. This can be done in the `Number` rule:

```
Number: Decimal | Integer
    function Decimal(array &$result, array $sub) {
        $result['value'] = $sub['value'];
    }
    function Integer(array &$result, array $sub) {
        $result['value'] = $sub['value'];
    }
```

Again, the `$sub` parameter contains the result array from matching the subpattern. In this case, this means the result array returned by the `match_Decimal` and `match_Integer` functions that you've modified yourself previously.

This will get a little more complex with the `Product` and `Sum` rules. Start by adding labels to the individual parts of your `Product` rule:

```
Product: left:Value (operand:(> operator:('*'|'/') > right:Value))*
```

Continue by adding the respective rule functions to the rule:

```
Product: left:Value (operand:(> operator:('*'|'/') > right:Value))*
    function left(array &$result, array $sub) {
        $result['value'] = $sub['value'];
    }
    function right(array &$result, array $sub) {
        $result['value'] = $sub['value'];
    }
    function operator(array &$result, array $sub) {
        $result['operator'] = $sub['text'];
    }
    function operand(array &$result, array $sub) {
        if ($sub['operator'] == '*') {
            $result['value'] *= $sub['value'];
        } else {
            $result['value'] /= $sub['value'];
        }
    }
```

The Sum rule can be modified respectively:

```
Sum: left:Product (operand:(> operator:('+'|'-') > right:Product))*
    function left(array &$result, array $sub) {
        $result['value'] = $sub['value'];
    }
    function right(array &$result, array $sub) {
        $result['value'] = $sub['value'];
    }
    function operator(array &$result, array $sub) {
        $result['operator'] = $sub['text'];
    }
    function operand(array &$result, array $sub) {
        if ($sub['operator'] == '+') {
            $result['value'] += $sub['value'];
        } else {
            $result['value'] -= $sub['value'];
        }
    }
```

Lastly, you still need to modify the Value and Expr rules:

```
Value: Number | '(' > Expr > ')'
    function Number(array &$result, array $sub) {
        $result['value'] = $sub['value'];
    }
    function Expr(array &$result, array $sub) {
        $result['value'] = $sub['value'];
    }
Expr: Sum
    function Sum(array &$result, array $sub) {
        $result['value'] = $sub['value'];
    }
```

Using these new functions in your parser, it will now be able to evaluated parsed expressions on the fly (note that we're not following the *traditional* compiler architecture here, as parsing and execution are not treated as separate steps, but rather both be done in the same pass). Re-build your parser class using the cli.php script and adjust your test script to test some expressions:

```
var_dump((new Parser('-143.25'))->match_Expr()['value']);
var_dump((new Parser('12 + 3'))->match_Expr()['value']);
var_dump((new Parser('1 + 2 * 3'))->match_Expr()['value']);
var_dump((new Parser('(1 + 2) * 3'))->match_Expr()['value']);
```

Running your test script will provide the following output:

```
double(-143.25)
int(15)
int(7)
int(9)
```

Building an Abstract Syntax Tree

Currently, our parser interprets the input code and evaluates it in the same pass. Most compilers and interpreters; however, create an intermediate data structure before actually running the program: an **Abstract Syntax Tree** (**AST**). Using an AST offers some interesting possibilities; for example, it provides you with a structured representation of your program that you can then analyze. Also, you can use the AST and transform it back into a text-based program (maybe of another language).

An AST is a tree that represents the structure of a program. The first step to building an AST-based parser is to design the tree's object model: which classes are needed and in which way are they associated to another. The following figure shows the first draft for an object model that can be used to describe mathematical expressions:

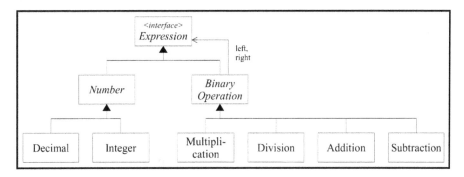

The (preliminary) object model for our Abstract Syntax Tree

In this model, nearly all classes implement the `Expression` interface. This interface prescribes the `evaluate()` method, which can be provided by the implementations of this interface to actually execute the operation modeled by the respective tree node. Let's start by implementing the `Packt\Chp8\DSL\AST\Expression` interface:

```
namespace Packt\Chp8\DSL\AST;

interface Expression
{
```

```
        public function evaluate()
    }
```

The next step is the `Number` class with its two subclasses: `Integer` and `Decimal`. As we're going to be using PHP 7's type hinting feature, and both the `Integer` and `Decimal` classes work exclusively with either the `int` or `float` variables; we cannot make much use of inheritance, forcing us to leave the `Number` class empty:

```
namespace Packt\Chp8\DSL\AST;

abstract class Number implements Expression
{}
```

The `Integer` class can be initialized with a PHP integer value. As this class models a literal integer value; the only thing that the `evaluate()` method needs to do in this class is to return this value again:

```
namespace Packt\Chp8\DSL\AST;

class Integer extends Number
{
    private $value;

    public function __construct(int $value)
    {
        $this->value = $value;
    }

    public function evaluate(): int
    {
        return $this->value;
    }
}
```

The `Decimal` class can be implemented the same way; in this case, simply use `float` instead of `int` as type hints:

```
namespace Packt\Chp8\DSL\AST;

class Decimal extends Number
{
    private $value;

    public function __construct(float $value)
    {
        $this->value = $value;
    }
```

```
    public function evaluate(): float
    {
        return $this->value;
    }
}
```

For the classes `Addition`, `Subtraction`, `Multiplication` and `Division`, we'll be using a common base class, `Packt\Chp8\DSL\AST\BinaryOperation`. This class will hold the constructor that you then won't have to implement over and over again:

```
namespace Packt\Chp8\DSL\AST;

abstract class BinaryOperation implements Expression
{
    protected $left;
    protected $right;

    public function __construct(Expression $left, Expression $right)
    {
        $this->left  = $left;
        $this->right = $right;
    }
}
```

Implementing the actual classes modeling the operations becomes easy. Let's consider the `Addition` class as an example:

```
namespace Packt\Chp8\DSL\AST;

class Addition extends BinaryOperation
{
    public function evaluate()
    {
        return $this->left->evaluate() + $this->right->evaluate();
    }
}
```

The remaining classes called `Subtraction`, `Multiplication` and `Division` can be implemented in a way similar to the `Addition` class. For the sake of brevity, the actual implementation of these classes is left as an exercise for you.

What's left now is to actually build the AST in the parser. This is relatively easy, as we can now simply modify the already existing hook functions that are called by the parser when individual rules are matched.

Let's start with the rules for parsing numbers:

```
Integer: value:('-'? Digit+)
    function value(array &$result, array $sub) {
        $result['node'] = new Integer((int) $sub['text']);
    }

Decimal: value:('-'? Digit* '.' Digit+)
    function value(array &$result, array $sub) {
        $result['node']  = new Decimal((float) $sub['text']);
    }

Number: Decimal | Integer
    function Decimal(&$result, $sub) {
        $result['node']  = $sub['node'];
    }
    function Integer(&$result, $sub) {
        $result['node']  = $sub['node'];
    }
```

When the `Integer` or `Decimal` rule matches, we create a new AST node of the `Integer` or `Decimal` class and save it in the return array's node property. When the `Number` rule matches, we simply take over the already created node stored in the matched symbol.

We can adjust the `Product` rule in a similar way:

```
Product: left:Value (operand:(> operator:('*'|'/') > right:Value))*
    function left(array &$result, array $sub) {
        $result['node']  = $sub['node'];
    }
    function right(array &$result, array $sub) {
        $result['node']  = $sub['node'];
    }
    function operator(array &$result, array $sub) {
        $result['operator'] = $sub['text'];
    }
    function operand(array &$result, array $sub) {
        if ($sub['operator'] == '*') {
            $result['node'] = new Multiplication($result['node'],
$sub['node']);
        } else {
            $result['node'] = new Division($result['node'], $sub['node']);
        }
    }
```

As our AST model treats operations such as multiplications strictly as binary operations, the parser will deconstruct input expressions such as 1 * 2 * 3 * 4 into a chain of binary multiplications (similar to 1 * (2 * (3 * 4))) as shown in the following figure):

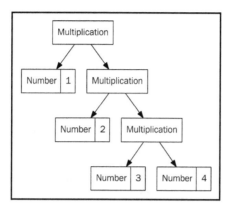

The expression 1 * 2 * 3 * 4 as a syntax tree

Continue by adjusting your Sum rule in the same way:

```
Sum: left:Product (operand:(> operator:('+'|'-') > right:Product))*
    function left(&$result, $sub) {
        $result['node'] = $sub['node'];
    }
    function right(&$result, $sub) {
        $result['node'] = $sub['node'];
    }
    function operator(&$result, $sub) { $result['operator'] = $sub['text'];
}
    function operand(&$result, $sub) {
        if ($sub['operator'] == '+') {
            $result['node'] = new Addition($result['node'], $sub['node']);
        } else {
            $result['node'] = new Subtraction($result['node'],
$sub['node']);
        }
    }
}
```

Now, all that's left is to read the created AST node in the Value and Expr rules is follows:

```
Value: Number | '(' > Expr > ')'
    function Number(array &$result, array $sub) {
        $result['node'] = $sub['node'];
    }
```

```
Expr: Sum
    function Sum(array &$result, array $sub) {
        $result['node'] = $sub['node'];
    }
```

In your test script, you can now test if the AST is correctly built by extracting the `node` property from the `match_Expr()` function's return value. You can then get the expression's result by calling the `evaluate()` method on the AST's root node:

```
$astRoot = (new Parser('1 + 2 * 3'))->match_Expr()['node'];
var_dump($astRoot, $astRoot->evaluate());

$astRoot = (new Parser('(1 + 2) * 3'))->match_Expr()['node'];
var_dump($astRoot, $astRoot->evaluate());
```

Note that the two expressions in this test script should yield two different syntax trees (both shown in the following figure) and evaluate to 7 and 9, respectively.

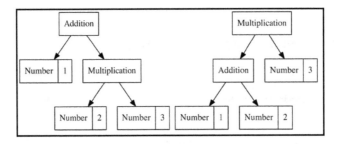

The two syntax trees resulting from parsing the 1+2*' and (1+2)*' expressions

Building a better interface

Right now, the parser that we have built is not really easy to use. In order to use the parser correctly, a user (in this context, read "user" as "another developer that uses your parser") has to call the `match_Expr()` method (which is just one of many public `match_*` functions offered by the parser that are not actually supposed to be called by external users), extract the `node` property from the returned array, and then call the evaluate function on the root node contained in this property. Also, the parser also matches partial strings (remember the example `(1 + 2)) * 3`, which was recognized as partially correct by our parser), which might really surprise some users.

This reason is enough to extend our project by a new class that encapsulates these quirks and to offer a cleaner interface to our parser. Let's create a new class, `Packt\Chp8\DSL\ExpressionBuilder`:

```
namespace Packt\Chp8\DSL\ExpressionBuilder;

use Packt\Chp8\DSL\AST\Expression;
use Packt\Chp8\DSL\Exception\ParsingException;
use Packt\Chp8\DSL\Parser\Parser;

class ExpressionBuilder
{
    public function parseExpression(string $expr): Expression
    {
        $parser = new Parser($expr);
        $result = $parser->match_Expr();

        if ($result === false || $result['text'] !== $expr) {
            throw new ParsingException();
        }

        return $result['node'];
    }
}
```

In this example, we're checking if the entire string could be parsed by asserting that the matched string returned by the parser is actually equal to the input string (and not just a substring). If this is the case (or if the expression could not be parsed at all, and the result is just false), an instance of `Packt\Chp8\DSL\Exception\ParsingException` is thrown. This exception class is not yet defined; for now, it can simply inherit the base exception class and does not need to contain any custom logic:

```
namespace Packt\Chp8\DSL\Exception;

class ParsingException extends \Exception
{}
```

The new `ExpressionBuilder` class now offers you a more concise way to parse and evaluate expressions. For example, you can now use the following construct in your `test.php` script:

```
$builder = new \Packt\Chp8\DSL\ExpressionBuilder;

var_dump($builder->parseExpression('12 + 3')->evaluate());
```

Evaluating variables

So far, our parser can evaluate static expressions, starting with simple ones such as 3 (which evaluates, what a surprise, to 3) up to arbitrarily complicated ones such as (5 + 3.14) * (14 + (29 - 2 * 3.918)) (which, by the way, evaluates to 286.23496). However, all of these expressions are static; they will always evaluate to the same result.

In order to make this more dynamic, we will now extend our grammar to allow variables. An example of an expression with variables is 3 + a, which could then be evaluated multiple times with different values for a.

This time, let's start by modifying the object model for the syntax tree. First, we'll need a new node type, Packt\Chp8\DSL\AST\Variable, allowing for example the 3 + a expression to generate the following syntax tree:

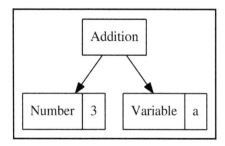

The syntax tree generated from the expression 3 + a

There's also a second problem: contrary to the Number nodes or arithmetic operations that use **Number** nodes, we cannot simply compute the numeric value of a **Variable** node (after all, it could have any value – that's the point of a variable). So when evaluating an expression, we'll also need to pass information on which variables exists and what values they have. For this, we'll simply extend the evaluate() function defined in the Packt\Chp8\DSL\AST\Expression interface by an additional parameter:

```
namespace Packt\Chp8\DSL\AST;

interface Expression
{
    public function evaluate(array $variables = []);
}
```

Changing the interface definition necessitates changing all classes that implement this interface. In the `Number` subclasses (`Integer` and `Decimal`), you can add the new parameter and simply ignore it. The value of a static number does not depend on the values of any variables at all. The following code example shows this change in the `Packt\Chp8\DSL\AST\Integer` class, but it remembers to change the `Decimal` class in the same way as well:

```
class Integer
{
    // ...
    public function evaluate(array $variables = []): int
    {
        return $this->value;
    }
}
```

In the `BinaryOperation` subclasses (`Addition`, `Subtraction`, `Multiplication`, and `Division`), the values of defined variables also do not really matter. But we need to pass them to the subnodes of these nodes. The following example shows this change in the `Packt\Chp8\DSL\AST\Addition` class, but it remembers to also change the `Subtraction`, `Multiplication`, and `Division` classes:

```
class Addition
{
    public function evaluate(array $variables = [])
    {
        return $this->left->evaluate($variables)
            + $this->right->evaluate($variables);
    }
}
```

Finally, we can now declare our `Packt\Chp8\DSL\AST\Variable` class:

```
namespace Packt\Chp8\DSL\AST;

use Packt\Chp8\DSL\Exception\UndefinedVariableException;

class Variable implements Expression
{
    private $name;

    public function __construct(string $name)
    {
        $this->name = $name;
    }
```

```
public function evaluate(array $variables = [])
{
    if (isset($variables[$this->name])) {
        return $variables[$this->name];
    }
    throw new UndefinedVariableException($this->name);
}
}
```

Within this class' `evaluate()` method, you can look up the actual value that this variable currently has. If a variable is not defined (read: does not exist in the `$variables` argument), we'll raise an instance of the (not-yet-implemented) `Packt\Chp8\DSL\Exception\UndefinedVariableException` to let the user know something's wrong.

How you handle undefined variables in your custom language is completely up to you. Instead of triggering errors, you could also change the `Variable` class' `evaluate()` method to return a default value such as 0 (or anything else) when an undefined variable is evaluated. However, using an undefined variable is probably unintentional, and simply continuing with a default value would probably be very surprising for your users.

The `UndefinedVariableException` class can simply extend the regular `Exception` class:

```
namespace Packt\Chp8\DSL\Exception;

class UndefinedVariableException extends \Exception
{
    private $name;

    public function __construct(string $name)
    {
        parent::__construct('Undefined variable: ' . $name);
        $this->name = $name;
    }
}
```

Finally, we need to adjust the parser's grammar to actually recognize variables in expressions. For this, our grammar needs two additional symbols:

```
Name: /[a-zA-z]+/
Variable: Name
    function Name(&$result, $sub) {
        $result['node'] = new Variable($sub['name']);
    }
```

Next, you'll need to extend the `Value` rule. Currently, `Value` can be either a `Number` symbol, or an `Expr` wrapped in braces. Now, you need to also allow variables:

```
Value: Number | Variable | '(' > Expr > ')'
    function Number(array &$result, $sub) {
        $result['node'] = $sub['node'];
    }
    function Variable(array &$result, $sub) {
        $result['node'] = $sub['node'];
    }
    function Expr(array &$result, $sub) {
        $result['node'] = $sub['node'];
    }
```

Rebuild your parser using PHP-PEG's `cli.php` script, and add a few calls to your `test.php` script to test this new feature:

```
$expr = $builder->parseExpression('1 + 2 * a');
var_dump($expr->evaluate(['a' => 1]));
var_dump($expr->evaluate(['a' => 14]));
var_dump($expr->evaluate(['a' => -1]));
```

These should evaluate to 3, 29, and -1 respectively. You can also try evaluating the expression without passing any variables, which should (rightfully so) result in an `UndefinedVariableException` being thrown.

Adding logical expressions

Currently, our language only supports numerical expressions. Another useful addition would be to support Boolean expressions that do not evaluate to numeric values but to *true* or *false*. Possible examples would include expressions such as $3 = 4$ (which would always evaluate to *false*), $2 < 4$ (which would always evaluate to *true*), or $a <= 5$ (which depends on the value of variable a).

Comparisons

As before, let's start by extending the object model of our syntax tree. We'll start with an **Equals** node that represents an equality check between two expressions. Using this node, the 1 + 2 = 4 – 1 expression would produce the following syntax tree (and should of course eventually evaluate to *true*):

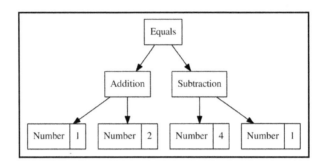

The syntax tree that should result from parsing the 1 + 2 = 4 – 1 expression

For this, we will implement the Packt\Chp8\DSL\AST\Equals class. This class can inherit the BinaryOperation class that we implemented earlier:

```
namespace Packt\Chp8\DSL\AST;

class Equals extends BinaryOperation
{
    public function evaluate(array $variables = [])
    {
        return $this->left->evaluate($variables)
            == $this->right->evaluate($variables);
    }
}
```

While we're at it, we can also implement the NotEquals node at the same time:

```
namespace Packt\Chp8\DSL\AST;

class NotEquals extends BinaryOperation
{
    public function evaluate(array $variables = [])
    {
        return $this->left->evaluate($variables)
            != $this->right->evaluate($variables);
    }
}
```

In the next step, we'll need to adjust our parser's grammar. First, we need to change the grammar to differentiate between numerical and Boolean expressions. For this, we'll rename the `Expr` symbol to `NumExpr` in the entire grammar. This affects the `Value` symbol:

```
Value: Number | Variable | '(' > NumExpr > ')'
    function Number(array &$result, array $sub) {
        $result['node'] = $sub['node'];
    }
    function Variable(array &$result, array $sub) {
        $result['node'] = $sub['node'];
    }
    function NumExpr(array &$result, array $sub) {
        $result['node'] = $sub['node'];
    }
```

Of course, you'll also need to change the `Expr` rule itself:

```
NumExpr: Sum
    function Sum(array &$result, array $sub) {
        $result['node'] = $sub['node'];
    }
```

Next, we can define a rule for equality (and also non-equality):

```
ComparisonOperator: '=' | '|='
Comparison: left:NumExpr (operand:(> op:ComparisonOperator >
right:NumExpr))
    function left(&$result, $sub) {
        $result['leftNode'] = $sub['node'];
    }
    function right(array &$result, array $sub) {
        $result['node'] = $sub['node'];
    }
    function op(array &$result, array $sub) {
        $result['op'] = $sub['text'];
    }
    function operand(&$result, $sub) {
        if ($sub['op'] == '=') {
            $result['node'] = new Equals($result['leftNode'],
$sub['node']);
        } else {
            $result['node'] = new NotEquals($result['leftNode'],
$sub['node']);
        }
    }
```

Note that this rule got a bit more complicated in this case, as it supports multiple operators. However, these rules are now relatively easy to be extended by more operators (when we're checking non-equality things such as "greater than" or "smaller than" might be the next logical steps). The `ComparisonOperator` symbol, which is defined first, matches all kinds of comparison operators and the `Comparison` rule that uses this symbol to match the actual expressions.

Lastly, we can add a new `BoolExpr` symbol, and also define the `Expr` symbol again:

```
BoolExpr: Comparison
    function Comparison(array &$result, array $sub) {
        $result['node'] = $sub['node'];
    }

Expr: BoolExpr | NumExpr
    function BoolExpr(array &$result, array $sub) {
        $result['node'] = $sub['node'];
    }
    function NumExpr(array &$result, array $sub) {
        $result['node'] = $sub['node'];
    }
```

When calling the `match_Expr()` function, our parser will now match both numeric and Boolean expressions. Rebuild your parser using PHP-PEG's `cli.php` script, and add a few new calls to your `test.php` script:

```
$expr = $builder->parseExpression('1 = 2');
var_dump($expr->evaluate());

$expr = $builder->parseExpression('a * 2 = 6');
var_dump($expr->evaluate(['a' => 3]));
var_dump($expr->evaluate(['a' => 4]));
```

These expressions should evaluate to *false*, *true*, and *false* respectively. The numeric expressions that you've added before should continue to work as before.

Similar to this, you could now add additional comparison operators, such as >, >=, <, or <= to your grammar. Since the implementation of these operators would be largely identical to the = and |= operations, we'll leave it as an exercise for you.

The "and" and "or" operators

Another important feature in order to fully support logical expressions is the ability to combine logical expressions via the "and" and "or" operators. As we are developing our language with an end user in mind, we'll build our language to actually support `and` and `or` as logical operators (in contrast to the ubiquitous `&&` and `||` that you find in many general-purpose programming language that are derived from the C syntax).

Again, let's start by implementing the respective node types for the syntax tree. We will need node types modeling both the `and` and `or` operation so that a statement such as `a = 1 or b = 2` will be parsed into the following syntax tree:

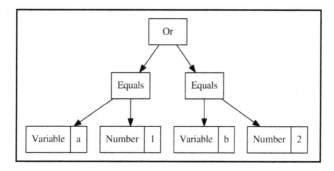

The syntax tree resulting from parsing a=1 or b=2

Begin by implementing the `Packt\Chp8\DSL\AST\LogicalAnd` class (we cannot use *And* as a class name, because that's a reserved word in PHP):

```
namespace Packt\Chp8\DSL\AST;

class LogicalAnd extends BinaryOperation
{
    public function evaluate(array $variables=[])
    {
        return $this->left->evaluate($variables)
            && $this->right->evaluate($variables);
    }
}
```

For the `or` operator, you can also implement the `Packt\Chp8\DSL\AST\LogicalOr` class the same way.

When working with the `and` and `or` operators, you will need to think about operator precedence. While operator precedence is well defined for arithmetic operations, this is not the case for logical operators. For example, the statement `a and b or c and d` could be interpreted as `(((a and b) or c) and d)` (same precedence, left to right), or just as well as `(a and b) or (c and d)` (precedence on `and`) or `(a and (b or c)) and d` (precedence on `or`). However, most programming languages treat the `and` operator with the highest precedence, so barring any other convention it makes sense to stick with this tradition.

The following figure shows the syntax trees that result from applying this precedence on the `a=1 and b=2 or b=3` and `a=1 and (b=2 or b=3)` statements:

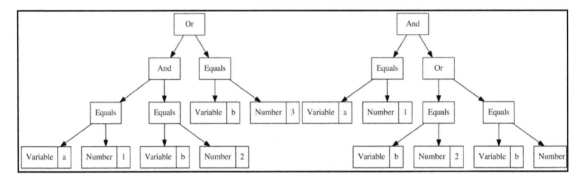

The syntax trees resulting form parsing a=1 and b=2 or b=3 and a=1 and (b=2 or b=3)

We will need a few new rules in our grammar for this. First of all, we need a new symbol representing a Boolean value. For now, such a Boolean value may either be a comparison or any Boolean expression wrapped in brackets.

```
BoolValue: Comparison | '(' > BoolExpr > ')'
    function Comparison(array &$res, array $sub) {
        $res['node'] = $sub['node'];
    }
    function BoolExpr(array &$res, array $sub) {
        $res['node'] = $sub['node'];
    }
```

Do you remember how we implemented operator precedence previously using the `Product` and `Sum` rules? We can implement the `And` and `Or` rules the same way:

```
And: left:BoolValue (> "and" > right:BoolValue)*
    function left(array &$res, array $sub) {
        $res['node'] = $sub['node'];
    }
```

```
    function right(array &$res, array $sub) {
        $res['node'] = new LogicalAnd($res['node'], $sub['node']);
    }

Or: left:And (> "or" > right:And)*
    function left(array &$res, array $sub) {
        $res['node'] = $sub['node'];
    }
    function right(array &$res, array $sub) {
        $res['node'] = new LogicalOr($res['node'], $sub['node']);
    }
```

After this, we can extend the `BoolExpr` rule to also match `Or` expressions (and since a single `And` symbol also matches the `Or` rule, a single `And` symbol will also be a `BoolExpr`):

```
BoolExpr: Or | Comparison
    function Or(array &$result, array $sub) {
        $result['node'] = $sub['node'];
    }
    function Comparison(array &$result, array $sub) {
        $result['node'] = $sub['node'];
    }
```

You can now add a few new test cases to your `test.php` script. Play around with variables and pay special attention to how operator precedence is resolved:

```
$expr = $builder->parseExpression('a=1 or b=2 and c=3');
var_dump($expr->evaluate([
    'a' => 0,
    'b' => 2,
    'c' => 3
]);
```

Conditions

Now that our language supports (arbitrarily complex) logical expressions, we can use these to implement another important feature: conditional statements. Our language currently supports only expressions that evaluate to a single numeric or the Boolean value; we'll now implement a variant of the ternary operator, which is also known in PHP:

```
($b > 0) ? 1 : 2;
```

As our language is targeted at end users, we'll use a more readable syntax, which will allow statements such as `when <condition> then <value> else <value>`. In our syntax tree, constructs such as these will be represented by the `Packt\Chp8\DSL\AST\Condition` class:

```php
<?php
namespace Packt\Chp8\DSL\AST;

class Condition implements Expression
{
    private $when;
    private $then;
    private $else;

    public function __construct(Expression $when, Expression $then,
Expression $else)
    {
        $this->when = $when;
        $this->then = $then;
        $this->else = $else;
    }

    public function evaluate(array $variables = [])
    {
        if ($this->when->evaluate($variables)) {
            return $this->then->evaluate($variables);
        }
        return $this->else->evaluate($variables);
    }
}
```

This means that, for example, the `when a > 2 then a * 1.5 else a * 2` expression should be parsed into the following syntax tree:

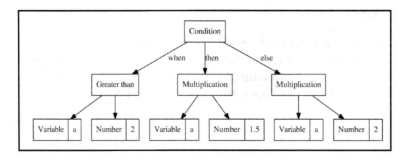

In theory, our language should also support complex expressions in the condition or the then/else part, allowing statements such as when (a > 2 or b = 2) then (2 * a + 3 * b) else (3 * a - b) or even nested statements such as when a=2 then (when b=2 then 1 else 2) else 3:

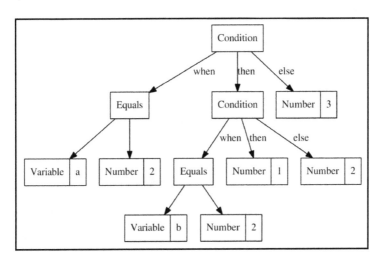

Continue by adding a new symbol and rule to your parser's grammar:

```
Condition: "when" > when:BoolExpr > "then" > then:Expr > "else" > else:Expr
    function when(array &$res, array $sub) {
        $res['when'] = $sub['node'];
    }
    function then(array &$res, $sub) {
        $res['then'] = $sub['node'];
    }
    function else(array &$res, array $sub) {
        $res['node'] = new Condition($res['when'], $res['then'],
$sub['node']);
    }
```

Also, adjust the BoolExpr rule to also match conditions. In this case, the order is important: if you're putting the Or or Comparison symbol first in the BoolExpr rule, the rule might interpret when as a variable name, instead of a conditional expression.

```
BoolExpr: Condition | Or | Comparison
    function Condition(array &$result, array $sub) {
        $result['node'] = $sub['node'];
    }
    function Or(&$result, $sub) {
        $result['node'] = $sub['node'];
```

```
    }
    function Comparison(&$result, $sub) {
        $result['node'] = $sub['node'];
    }
```

Again, rebuild your parser using PHP-PEG's **cli.php** script, and add a few test statements to your test script to test the new grammar rules:

```
$expr = $builder->parseExpression('when a=1 then 3.14 else a*2');
var_dump($expr->evaluate(['a' => 1]));
var_dump($expr->evaluate(['a' => 2]));
var_dump($expr->evaluate(['a' => 3]));
```

These test cases should evaluate to 3.14, 4, and 6 respectively.

Working with structured data

So far, our custom expression language has only supported very simple variables-numbers and Boolean values. However, in real applications, this is often not so simple. When using an expression language to offer programmable business rules, you will often be working with structured data. For example, consider an e-commerce system in which a back-office user has the possibility to define under which conditions a discount should be offered to a user and what amount of a purchase should be discounted (the following figure shows a hypothetical example of how such a feature might actually look in an application).

Typically, you do not know beforehand how a user is going to use this feature. Using only numerical variables, you'd have to pass a whole set of variables when evaluating the expression, on the off chance that the user might be using one or two of them. Alternatively, you could pass an entire domain object (for example, a PHP object representing a shopping cart and maybe another one representing the customer), as variable into the expression and give the user the option to access properties or call methods of these objects.

A feature such as this would allow a user to use expressions such as `cart.value` in an expression. When evaluating this expression, this could be translated to either a direct property access (if the `$cart` variable does have a publicly accessible `$value` property), or a call to a `getValue()` method:

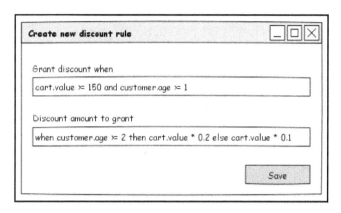

An example of how structured data could be used as variables in an enterprise e-commerce application

For this, we'll need to modify our AST object model a bit. We'll introduce a new node type, `Packt\Chp8\DSL\AST\PropertyFetch`, which models a named property being fetched from a variable. However, we need to consider that these property fetches need to be chained, for example, in expressions such as `cart.customer.contact.firstname`. This expression should be parsed into the following syntax tree:

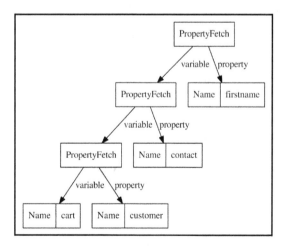

For this, we'll redefine the `Variable` node type that we added before. Rename the `Variable` class to `NamedVariable` and add a new interface named `Variable`. This interface can then be implemented by both the `NamedVariable` class and the `PropertyFetch` class. The `PropertyFetch` class can then accept a `Variable` instance as its left operator.

Start by renaming the `Packt\Chp8\DSL\AST\Variable` class to `Packt\Chp8\DSL\AST\NamedVariable`:

```
namespace Packt\Chp8\DSL\AST;

use Packt\Chp8\DSL\Exception\UnknownVariableException;

class NamedVariable implements Variable
{
    private $name;

    public function __construct(string $name)
    {
        $this->name = $name;
    }

    public function evaluate(array $variables = [])
    {
        if (isset($variables[$this->name])) {
            return $variables[$this->name];
        }
        throw new UnknownVariableException();
    }
}
```

Then, add the new interface called `Packt\Chp8\DSL\AST\Variable`. It does not need to contain any code; we'll use it just for type hinting:

```
namespace Packt\Chp8\DSL\AST;

interface Variable extends Expression
{
}
```

Continue by adding the `Packt\Chp8\DSL\AST\PropertyFetch` new class:

```
namespace Packt\Chp8\DSL\AST;

class PropertyFetch implements Variable
{
    private $left;
```

```
    private $property;

    public function __construct(Variable $left, string $property)
    {
        $this->left = $left;
        $this->property = $property;
    }

    public function evaluate(array $variables = [])
    {
        $var = $this->left->evaluate($variables);
        return $var[$this->property] ?? null;
    }

}
```

Lastly, modify the `Variable` rule in your parser's grammar:

```
Variable: Name ('.' property:Name)*
    function Name(array &$result, array $sub) {
        $result['node'] = new NamedVariable($sub['text']);
    }
    function property(&$result, $sub) {
        $result['node'] = new PropertyFetch($result['node'], $sub['text']);
    }
```

Using this rule, the `Variable` symbol can consist of multiple property names chained together with the `.` character. The rule functions will then build a `NamedVariable` node for the first property name, and then work this node into a chain of the `PropertyFetch` nodes for subsequent properties.

As usual, rebuild your parser and add a few lines to your test script:

```
$e = $builder->parseExpression('foo.bar * 2');
var_dump($e->evaluate(['foo' => ['bar' => 2]]));
```

Working with objects

Getting end users to grasp the concept of data structures is no easy task. While the concept of *objects* having *properties* (for instance, a customer having a first name and a last name) is usually easy to convey, you probably would not bother end users with things like data encapsulation and object methods.

Because of this, it might be useful to hide the intricacies of data access from your end user; if a user want to access a customer's first name, they should be able to write customer.firstname, even if the actual property of the underlying object is protected, and you would usually need to call a getFirstname() method to read this property. Since getter functions typically follow certain naming patterns, our parser can automatically translate expressions such as customer.firstname to method calls such as $customer->getFirstname().

To implement this feature, we need to extend the evaluate method of PropertyFetch by a few special cases:

```
public function evaluate(array $variables = [])
{
    $var = $this->left->evaluate($variables);
    if (is_object($var)) {
        $getterMethodName = 'get' . ucfirst($this->property);
        if (is_callable([$var, $getterMethodName])) {
            return $var->{$getterMethodName}();
        }           $isMethodName = 'is' . ucfirst($this->property);
        if (is_callable([$var, $isMethodName])) {
            return $var->{$isMethodName}();
        }
        return $var->{$this->property} ?? null;
    }
    return $var[$this->property] ?? null;
}
```

Using this implementation, an expression such as customer.firstname will first check if the customer object implements a getFirstname() method that can be called. Should this not be the case, the interpreter will check for an isFirstname() method (which does not make sense in this case, but could be useful as getter functions, for Boolean properties are often named isSomething instead of getSomething). If no isFirstname() method exists either, the interpreter will look for an accessible property named firstname, and then as a last resort simply return null.

Optimizing the interpreter by adding a compiler

Our parser now works as it should, and you could use it in any kind of application to offer very flexible customization options to the end user. However, the parser does not work very efficiently. In general, parsing expressions are computationally expensive, and in most use cases, it is reasonable to assume that the actual expressions that you're working with do not change with every request (or at least, are evaluated more often than they are changed).

Because of this, we can optimize the parser's performance by adding a caching layer to our interpreter. Of course, we cannot cache the actual evaluation results of an expression; after all, these could change when they are interpreted with different variables.

What we're going to do in this section is add a compiler feature to our parser. For each parsed expression, our parser generates an AST that represents the structure of this expression. You can now use this syntax tree to translate the expression into any other programming language, for example, to PHP.

Consider the 2 + 3 * a expression. This expression generates the following syntax tree:

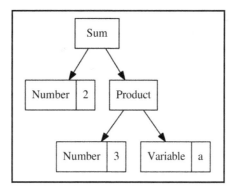

In our AST model, this corresponds to an instance of the `Packt\Chp8\DSL\AST\Addition` class, holding a reference to an instance of the `Packt\Chp8\DSL\AST\Number` class and the `Packt\Chp8\DSL\AST\Product` class (and so forth).

We cannot implement a compiler feature to translate this expressions back into PHP code (after all, PHP does support simple arithmetic operations, too), which might look like this:

```
use Packt\Chp8\DSL\AST\Expression;

$cachedExpr = new class implements Expression
{
```

```php
    public function evaluate(array $variables=[])
    {
        return 2 + (3 * $variables['a']);
    }
}
```

The PHP code that is generated in this way could then be saved in files for later lookup. If the parser gets passed an expression that is already cached, it could simply load the saved PHP files in order to not actually parse the expression again.

To implement this feature, we'll need to have the possibility to convert each node in a syntax tree into a corresponding PHP expression. For this, let's start by extending our `Packt\Chp8\DSL\AST\Expression` interface by a new method:

```php
namespace Packt\Chp8\DSL\AST;

interface Expression
{
    public function evaluate(array $variables = []);

    public function compile(): string;
}
```

The downside of this approach is that you'll now need to implement this method for each and every single one of the classes that implement this interface. Let's start with something simple: the `Packt\Chp8\DSL\AST\Number` class. As each `Number` implementation will always evaluate to the same number (3 will always evaluate to 3 and never to 4), we can simply return the numeric value:

```php
namespace Packt\Chp8\DSL\AST;

abstract class Number implements Expression
{
    public function compile(): string
    {
        return var_export($this->evaluate(), true);
    }
}
```

As for the remaining node types, we'll need methods that return an implementation of each expression type in PHP. For example, for the `Packt\Chp8\DSL\AST\Addition` class, we could add the following `compile()` method:

```php
namespace Packt\Chp8\DSL\AST;

class Addition extends BinaryOperation
{
```

```
// ...

    public function compile(): string
    {
        return '(' . $this->left->compile() . ') + (' .
$this->right->compile() . ')';
    }
}
```

Proceed similarly for the remaining arithmetic operations: Subtraction, Multiplication, and Division, and also the logical operations such as Equals, NotEquals, And, and Or.

For the Condition class, you can use PHP's ternary operator:

```
namespace Packt\Chp8\DSL\AST;

class Condition implements Expression
{
    // ...

    public function compile(): string
    {
        return sprintf('%s ? (%s) : (%s)',
            $this->when->compile(),
            $this->then->compile(),
            $this->else->compile()
        );
    }
}
```

The NamedVariable class is difficult to adjust; the class' evaluate() method currently throws UnknownVariableException when a non-existing variable is referenced. However, our compile() method needs to return a single PHP expression. And looking up a value and also throwing an exception cannot be done in a single expression. Luckily, you can instantiate classes and call methods on them:

```
namespace Packt\Chp8\DSL\AST;

use Packt\Chp8\DSL\Exception\UnknownVariableException;

class NamedVariable implements Variable
{
    // ...

    public function evaluate(array $variables = [])
    {
```

```
        if (isset($variables[$this->name])) {
            return $variables[$this->name];
        }
        throw new UnknownVariableException();
    }

    public function compile(): string
    {
        return sprintf('(new %s(%s))->evaluate($variables)',
            __CLASS__,
            var_export($this->name, true)
        );
    }
}
```

Using this workaround, the a * 3 expression would be compiled to the following PHP code:

```
(new \Packt\Chp8\DSL\AST\NamedVariable('a'))->evaluate($variables) * 3
```

This just leaves the PropertyFetch class. You might remember that this class was a bit more complex than the other node types, as it implemented quite a few different contingencies on how to look up properties from objects. In theory, this logic could be implemented in a single expression using ternary operators. This would result in the foo.bar expression being compiled to the following monstrosity:

```
is_object((new
\Packt\Chp8\DSL\AST\NamedVariable('foo'))->evaluate($variables)) ?
((is_callable([(new
\Packt\Chp8\DSL\AST\NamedVariable('foo'))->evaluate($variables), 'getBar'])
? (new
\Packt\Chp8\DSL\AST\NamedVariable('a'))->evaluate($variables)->getBar() :
((is_callable([(new
\Packt\Chp8\DSL\AST\NamedVariable('foo'))->evaluate($variables), 'isBar'])
? (new
\Packt\Chp8\DSL\AST\NamedVariable('a'))->evaluate($variables)->isBar() :
(new \Packt\Chp8\DSL\AST\NamedVariable('a'))->evaluate($variables)['bar']
?? null)) : (new
\Packt\Chp8\DSL\AST\NamedVariable('foo'))->evaluate($variables)['bar']
```

In order to prevent the compiled code from getting overly complicated, it's easier to refactor the PropertyFetch class a little bit. You can extract the actual property lookup method in a static method that can be called from both the evaluate() method and the compiled code:

```
<?php
namespace Packt\Chp8\DSL\AST;
```

```php
class PropertyFetch implements Variable
{
    private $left;
    private $property;

    public function __construct(Variable $left, string $property)
    {
        $this->left = $left;
        $this->property = $property;
    }

    public function evaluate(array $variables = [])
    {
        $var = $this->left->evaluate($variables);
        return static::evaluateStatic($var, $this->property);
    }

    public static function evaluateStatic($var, string $property)
    {
        if (is_object($var)) {
            $getterMethodName = 'get' . ucfirst($property);
            if (is_callable([$var, $getterMethodName])) {
                return $var->{$getterMethodName}();
            }
            $isMethodName = 'is' . ucfirst($property);
            if (is_callable([$var, $isMethodName])) {
                return $var->{$isMethodName}();
            }
            return $var->{$property} ?? null;
        }
        return $var[$property] ?? null;
    }
    public function compile(): string
    {
        return __CLASS__ . '::evaluateStatic(' . $this->left->compile() .
', ' . var_export($this->property, true) . ')';
    }
}
```

This way, the `foo.bar` expression will simply evaluate to this:

```
\Packt\Chp8\DSL\AST\PropertyFetch::evaluateStatic(
    (new \Packt\Chp8\DSL\AST\NamedVariable('foo'))->evaluate($variables),
    'bar'
)
```

In the next step, we can add an alternative to the previously introduced
ExpressionBuilder class that transparently compiles expressions, saves them in a cache,
and reuses the compiled versions when necessary.

We'll call this class Packt\Chp8\DSL\CompilingExpressionBuilder:

```php
<?php
namespace Packt\Chp8\DSL;

class CompilingExpressionBuilder
{
    /** @var string */
    private $cacheDir;
    /**
     * @var ExpressionBuilder
     */
    private $inner;

    public function __construct(ExpressionBuilder $inner, string $cacheDir)
    {
        $this->cacheDir = $cacheDir;
        $this->inner = $inner;
    }
}
```

As we don't want to re-implement the ExpressionBuilder's parsing logic, this class
takes an instance of ExpressionBuilder as a dependency. When a new expression is
parsed that is not yet present in the cache, this inner expression builder will be used to
actually parse this expression.

Let's continue by adding a parseExpression method to this class:

```php
public function parseExpression(string $expr): Expression
{
    $cacheKey = sha1($expr);
    $cacheFile = $this->cacheDir . '/' . $cacheKey . '.php';
    if (file_exists($cacheFile)) {
        return include($cacheFile);
    }

    $expr = $this->inner->parseExpression($expr);

    if (!is_dir($this->cacheDir)) {
        mkdir($this->cacheDir, 0755, true);
    }

    file_put_contents($cacheFile, '<?php return new class implements
```

```
'.Expression::class.' {
        public function evaluate(array $variables=[]) {
            return ' . $expr->compile() . ';
        }
        public function compile(): string {
            return ' . var_export($expr->compile(), true) . ';
        }
    };');
    return $expr;
}
```

Let's have a look at what happens in this method: first, the actual input string is used to calculate a hash value, uniquely identifying this expression. If a file with this name exists in the cache directory, it will be included as a PHP file, and the file's return value will return as the method's return value:

```
$cacheKey = sha1($expr);
$cacheFile = $this->cacheDir . '/' . $cacheKey;
if (file_exists($cacheFile)) {
    return include($cacheFile);
}
```

As the method's type hint specified that the method needs to return an instance of the `Packt\Chp8\DSL\AST\Expression` interface, the generated cache files also need to return an instance of this interface.

If no compiled version of the expression could be found, the expression is parsed as usual by the inner expression builder. This expression is then compiled to a PHP expression using the `compile()` method. This PHP code snippet is then used to write the actual cache file. In this file, we're creating a new anonymous class that implements the expression interface, and in its `evaluate()` method contains the compiled expression.

> Anonymous classes are a feature added in PHP 7. This feature allows you to create objects that implement an interface or extend an existing class without needing to explicitly define a named class for this. Syntactically, this feature can be used as follows:
> ```
> $a = new class implements SomeInterface {
>     public function test() {
>         echo 'Hello';
>     }
> };
> $a->test();
> ```

This means that the `foo.bar * 3` expression would create a cache file with the following PHP code as its contents:

```php
<?php
return new class implements Packt\Chp8\DSL\AST\Expression
{
    public function evaluate(array $variables = [])
    {
        return (Packt\Chp8\DSL\AST\PropertyFetch::evaluateStatic(
            (new
Packt\Chp8\DSL\AST\NamedVariable('foo'))->evaluate($variables),
            'bar'
        )) * (3);
    }

    public function compile(): string
    {
        return '(Packt\\Chp8\\DSL\\AST\\PropertyFetch::evaluateStatic((new
Packt\\Chp8\\DSL\\AST\\NamedVariable('foo'))->evaluate($variables),
'bar'))*(3)';
    }
};
```

Interestingly, the PHP interpreter itself works much the same way. Before actually executing PHP code, the PHP interpreter compiles the code into an intermediate representation or Bytecode, which is then interpreted by the actual interpreter. In order to not parse the PHP source code over and over again, the compiled bytecode is cached; this is how PHP's opcode cache works.

As we're saving our compiled expressions as PHP code, these will also be compiled into PHP bytecode and cached in the opcode cache for even more performance again. For example, the previous cached expression's evaluate method evaluates to the following PHP bytecode:

```
                            docker run --rm -it -v $PWD:/work php:7-vld          _ □ ×
                          docker run --rm -it -v $PWD:/work php:7-vld 136x29
Class class@anonymous:
Function evaluate:
Finding entry points
Branch analysis from position: 0
Jump found. Position 1 = -2
filename:       /work/cache/8eff4943aab9d2a72bd1c3a83bf588a2209b8c87.php
function name:  evaluate
number of ops:  14
compiled vars:  !0 = $variables
line    #* E I O op                         fetch        ext  return  operands
-------------------------------------------------------------------------------
   3    0  E >   RECV_INIT                                     !0      <array>
   5    1        INIT_STATIC_METHOD_CALL                               'Packt%5CChp8%5CDSL%5CAST%5CPropertyFetch', 'evaluateStatic'
   6    2        NEW                                           $1      :-1
        3        SEND_VAL_EX                                           'foo'
        4        DO_FCALL                    0
        5        INIT_METHOD_CALL                                      $1, 'evaluate'
        6        SEND_VAR_EX                                           !0
        7        DO_FCALL                    0     $3
        8        SEND_VAR_NO_REF             4                         $3
   7    9        SEND_VAL_EX                                           'bar'
       10        DO_FCALL                    0     $4
   8   11        MUL                               ~5             $4, 3
       12      > RETURN                                          ~5
   9   13*     > RETURN                                          null

branch: #  0; line:      3-   9; sop:    0; eop:    13
path #1: 0,
End of function evaluate
```

The PHP bytecode generated by the PHP interpreter

Verifying performance improvements

The motivation for implementing the compilation to PHP was to increase the parser's performance. As a last step, we'll now try to verify that the caching layer does actually increase the performance of the parser.

For this, you can use the **PHPBench** package that you can install using composer:

```
$ composer require phpbench/phpbench
```

PHPBench offers a framework for benchmarking single units of code in isolation (in that respect being similar to PHPUnit, only for benchmarks instead of tests). Each benchmark is a PHP class that contains scenarios as methods. The name of each scenario method needs to start with bench.

Start by creating a bench.php file in your root directory with the following contents:

```
require 'vendor/autoload.php';

use Packt\Chp8\DSL\ExpressionBuilder;
use Packt\Chp8\DSL\CompilingExpressionBuilder;
```

```
class ParserBenchmark
{
    public function benchSimpleExpressionWithBasicParser()
    {
        $builder = new ExpressionBuilder();
        $builder->parseExpression('a = 2')->evaluate(['a' => 1]);
    }
}
```

You can then run this benchmark using the following command:

vendor/bin/phpbench run bench.php --report default

This should generate a report such as the following one:

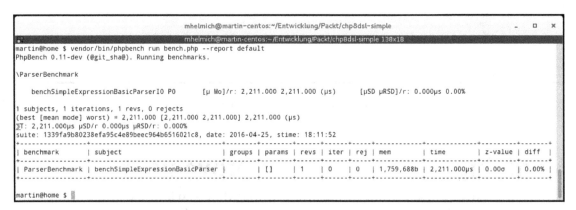

Currently, PHPBench runs the benchmark function exactly once and measures the time that it took to execute this function. In this case, it is about 2 milliseconds. This is not very precise, because micro-measurements such as these can vary quite a lot, depending on other things happening on your computer at the same time. For this reason, it's usually better to execute the benchmark function multiple times (let's say, a few hundred or thousand times) and then compute the average execution time. Using PHPBench, you can do this easily by adding a @Revs(5000) annotation to your benchmark class' DOC comment:

```
/**
 * @Revs(5000)
 */
class ParserBenchmark
{
    // ...
}
```

This annotation will cause PHPBench to actually run this benchmark function 5000 times and then compute the average runtime.

Let's also add a second scenario in which we're using the new
`CompilingExpressionBuilder` with the same expression:

```
/**
 * @Revs(5000)
 */
class ParserBenchmark
{
    public function benchSimpleExpressionWithBasicParser()
    {
        $builder = new ExpressionBuilder();
        $builder->parseExpression('a = 2')->evaluate(['a' => 1]);
    }

    public function benchSimpleExpressionWithCompilingParser()
    {
        $builder = new CompilingExpressionBuilder();
        $builder->parseExpression('a = 2')->evaluate(['a' => 1]);
    }
}
```

Run the benchmark again; this time benchmarking both parsers and with 5000 iterations:

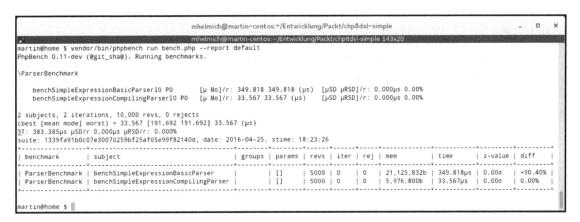

As you can see here, parsing and evaluating the a = 2 expression takes our regular parser
about 349 microseconds, on average (and about 20 megabytes of RAM). Using the
compiling parser takes only about 33 microseconds (that's a runtime reduction of about
90%) and only 5 MB's of RAM (or about 71%).

Now, a=2 might not really be the most representative benchmark, because actual
expressions used in a real-life use case might get a little more complex.

For a more realistic benchmark, let's add two more scenarios, this time with a more complex expression:

```php
public function benchComplexExpressionBasicParser()
{
    $builder = new ExpressionBuilder();
    $builder
        ->parseExpression('when (customer.age = 1 and cart.value = 200)
then cart.value * 0.1 else cart.value * 0.2')
        ->evaluate(['customer' => ['age' => 1], 'cart' => ['value' =>
200]]);
}

public function benchComplexExpressionCompilingParser()
{
    $builder = new CompilingExpressionBuilder(new ExpressionBuilder(),
'cache/auto');
    $builder
        ->parseExpression('when (customer.age = 1 and cart.value = 200)
then cart.value * 0.1 else cart.value * 0.2')
        ->evaluate(['customer' => ['age' => 1], 'cart' => ['value' =>
200]]);
}
```

Run the benchmark again and have a new look at the results:

That's even better than before! Using the regular parser for parsing the `when (customer.age = 1 and cart.value = 200) then cart.value * 0.1 else cart.value * 0.2` expression takes about 2.5 milliseconds (remember we were talking about *microseconds* in the last benchmark), while only 50 microseconds are using the optimized parser! That's an improvement of about 98%.

Summary

In this chapter, you learned how to use the PHP-PEG library to implement a parser, interpreter, and compiler for a custom expression language. You also learned how to define grammars for such languages and how you can use them to develop domain-specific languages. These can be used to offer end-user development features in large software systems, which allow users to customize their software's business rules to a large extent.

Dynamically modifying a program using domain-specific languages can be a strong selling point, especially in enterprise systems. They allow users to modify a program's behavior by themselves, without having to wait for a developer to change a business rule and trigger a lengthy release process. This way, new business rules can be implemented quickly and allow your customers to react quickly to changing requirements.

Reactive Extensions in PHP

9

In this chapter, we'll talk about Reactive extensions in PHP, a PHP library that allows PHP programmers to work with PHP in a reactive manner, and how to use in event, also known as publish-subscribe programming. We'll also discuss the idea of functional programming in PHP and how to program in a more succinct way. We will also discuss the following topics:

- Map
- Reduce
- Defer
- Reactive extensions in the following use cases:
  - Data analysis of logs (parsing Apache logs)
  - Queueing systems (asynchronously working through a queue of tasks)
  - Events

Reactive extensions are a way to code in a functional way using PHP. They are a set of libraries (available on GitHub at `https://github.com/ReactiveX/RxPHP`) that can help you compose event-based programs by using observable collections and LINQ-style query operators in PHP.

An introduction to observables

In short, you will be doing event-driven programming, where you will work with what's called as the event loop, and attaching (hooking up) events to do your bidding.

Installation is a simple composer that is required is all.

How does Reactive PHP work? In PHP, there is no such way to create a server except when running the code `php -S localhost:8000`. PHP will treat the current directory as the basis of the public directory (in Apache, usually this is `/var/www` or `C:/xampp/htdocs` when using **XAMPP**). This, by the way, has been available since PHP 5.4.0 only and also works with PHP 7.x.

There is no programmable way to control how that PHP command-line interface's server actually works.

Every time you send a request to that server, PHP server will be in charge of handling whether it's a valid request, and handle the event by itself. In short, every request is a new request-there's no streaming or events that get involved.

RxPHP works by creating an event loop by creating a PHP stream under the hood, which has added functions that help make **Reactive Programming** possible. The stream basically has a recursive function (a function that keeps calling itself and creates a loop of commands, in essence). An event loop is basically a programming construct that runs an infinite loop, which simply waits for events and be able to react (in other words, run some function) to each of those events.

Introduction to event loop and ReactiveX

The best way to get acquainted with event loop is through a popular library in the JavaScript world, that is, jQuery.

If you have experience working with jQuery, you can simply create (or chain) events to a simple DOM selector and then write code to handle those specific events. For example, you could create an `onClick` event by attaching it to a specific link and then code what will happen when that link is clicked.

If you're familiar with jQuery, the code to control a link that has the ID `someLink` would look something like the following:

HTML:

```
< a href="some url" id="someLink">
```

JavaScript:

```
$("#someLink").on('click', function() {
   //some code here
});
```

In the preceding code snippet, every time jQuery finds an element with an ID of `someLink`, it will do something on each click event.

As it is in an event loop, it will loop over each *iteration* of the event loop and work on what needs to be done.

However, it is a little bit different in Reactive Programming, which is a form of functional programming. Functional programming is about keeping functions as pure as possible and does not have side effects. Another aspect of functional programming is immutability, but we'll discuss that in another part.

In Reactive Programming, we basically have the concept of **Observables** and **Observers**.

An Observable emits events in the form of data, and an Observer subscribes to the Observable in order to receive its events.

The point of programming using Reactive extensions is to be able to program in a more *functional* manner. Instead of programming a `while`, `for` loop we instead invoke an event loop, which will track the Observers and their Observables (subscribers). The good thing about programming in this way is that there is a way to treat data as data that streams into your program over time. By feeding information this way, we can now make event-based or event-driven programs, where your code will react.

With this you can create programs that run forever in the background and just Reactive extensions.

Let's discuss some available functions of Reactive extensions:

- delay
- defer
- scheduler
- recursive-scheduler
- `map` and `flatMap`
- reduce
- toArray
- merge
- do
- scan
- zip

delay

The `delay` function in RxPHP is used as follows:

```php
<?php
require_once __DIR__ . '/../bootstrap.php';

$loop = new \React\EventLoop\StreamSelectLoop();

$scheduler = new \Rx\Scheduler\EventLoopScheduler($loop);

\Rx\Observable::interval(1000, $scheduler)
    ->doOnNext(function ($x) {
        echo "Side effect: " . $x . "\n";
    })
    ->delay(500)
    ->take(5)
    ->subscribe($createStdoutObserver(), $scheduler);

$loop->run();
```

In the preceding code, we create an `EventLoopScheduler`, which will help us schedule the execution of code by an interval of 1,000 milliseconds. The delay function is given 500 milliseconds to execute, and a take function will only take 5 milliseconds before finally subscribing.

defer

The `defer` function waits for X number of iterations before doing what is to be done:

```php
<?php

require_once __DIR__.'/../bootstrap.php';


$source = \Rx\Observable::defer(function () {
    return \Rx\Observable::just(42);
});

$subscription = $source->subscribe($stdoutObserver);
?>
```

In the preceding code, we create an Observable object, which will return 42 when the `defer` function is called. The `defer` function s a type of promise and returns an Observable, and the code inside it will be executed in an asynchronous manner. When the Observable is subscribed to, the functions are in a way *tied* together or *bound* to each other and then get *invoked* or *triggered*.

What is an Observable, you might ask? In ReactiveX, an Observer subscribes to an Observable. An Observer then reacts to whatever item or sequence of items that the Observable emits.

This means that when you have a bunch of events that are being sent to your application, but handle them in an asynchronous manner, meaning not necessarily in the order that they may have come in.

In the preceding code, `stdoutObserver` is an observer that puts out whatever is in the event loop or the Observable into the `stdout` or console log.

Scheduler

Schedulers work with three main components: an execution context, which is the ability to *do* the job given to it; the execution policy is *how* it will be ordered; and there's the clock or timer or the underlying system which measures time, which is needed to schedule *when* it will be executed.

The scheduler code is used as follows:

```
$loop     = \React\EventLoop\Factory::create();
$scheduler = new \Rx\Scheduler\EventLoopScheduler($loop);
```

It basically creates an `eventScheduler`, which executes the event loop and parameterizes the concurrency level. A simple scheduler within RxPHP is used in the preceding delay.

recursive-scheduler

This is how the recursive-scheduler function is used:

```
<?php

require_once __DIR__ . '/../bootstrap.php';

use Rx\Observable;
```

```
class RecursiveReturnObservable extends Observable
{
    private $value;

    /**
     * @param mixed $value Value to return.
     */
    public function __construct($value)
    {
        $this->value = $value;
    }

    public function subscribe(\Rx\ObserverInterface $observer, $scheduler =
null)
    {
        return $scheduler->scheduleRecursive(function ($reschedule) use
($observer) {
            $observer->onNext($this->value);
            $reschedule();
        });
    }
}

$loop      = React\EventLoop\Factory::create();
$scheduler = new Rx\Scheduler\EventLoopScheduler($loop);

$observable = new RecursiveReturnObservable(42);
$observable->subscribe($stdoutObserver, $scheduler);

$observable = new RecursiveReturnObservable(21);
$disposable = $observable->subscribe($stdoutObserver, $scheduler);

$loop->addPeriodicTimer(0.01, function () {
    $memory    = memory_get_usage() / 1024;
    $formatted = number_format($memory, 3) . 'K';
    echo "Current memory usage: {$formatted}\n";
});

// after a second we'll dispose the 21 observable
$loop->addTimer(1.0, function () use ($disposable) {
    echo "Disposing 21 observable.\n";
    $disposable->dispose();
});

$loop->run();
```

The preceding code works by adding several scheduler timers, which then recursively or repeatedly return an Observable and then subscribe to it afterward. The preceding code will generate 21 Observables.

Here's what happens after 1 second:

```
//Next value: 21
//Next value: 42
//Next value: 21
//Next value: 42
//Next value: 21
```

After this, it will dispose the Observables and finally print out the memory usage:

```
//Disposing 21 observable.
//Next value: 42
//Next value: 42
//Next value: 42
//Next value: 42
//Next value: 42
//Current memory usage: 3,349.203K
```

map and flatMap

A `map` is a simple function that takes another function and loops through or iterates through a bunch of elements (an Array), and applies or invokes the function passed into each of those elements.

A `flatMap`, on the other hand, subscribes to the Observable as well, meaning that you no longer have to take care of.

reduce

The `reduce` function simply applies a function to Observables coming in. In short, it takes a bunch of Observables and applies a function to all of them in a sequential manner, applying one to the next result.

Here is an example of how to use a `reduce` function:

```php
<?php

require_once __DIR__ . '/../bootstrap.php';
```

```php
//Without a seed
$source = \Rx\Observable::fromArray(range(1, 3));

$subscription = $source
    ->reduce(function ($acc, $x) {
        return $acc + $x;
    })
    ->subscribe($createStdoutObserver());
```

toArray

The `toArray` function lets you manipulate Observables and create an array from them. The code to use `toArray` looks like this:

```php
<?php

use Rx\Observer\CallbackObserver;

require_once __DIR__ . '/../bootstrap.php';

$source = \Rx\Observable::fromArray([1, 2, 3, 4]);

$observer = $createStdoutObserver();

$subscription = $source->toArray()
    ->subscribe(new CallbackObserver(
        function ($array) use ($observer) {
            $observer->onNext(json_encode($array));
        },
        [$observer, "onError"],
        [$observer, "onCompleted"]
    ));
```

In the preceding code, we first create an Observable based on the Array [1,2,3,4].

This allows us to work with the values of an array and subscribe to them using the Observer. In ReactiveX programming, every Observer only works with Observables. In short, the `toArray` function allows us to create Observers that subscribe to a source array.

merge

The `merge` function is simply an operator that combines multiple Observables into one by merging their emissions.

Any `onError` notification from any of the source Observables will be immediately passed through to the Observers. This will terminate the merged Observable:

```php
<?php

require_once __DIR__ . '/../bootstrap.php';

$loop      = React\EventLoop\Factory::create();
$scheduler = new Rx\Scheduler\EventLoopScheduler($loop);

$observable        = Rx\Observable::just(42)->repeat();
$otherObservable   = Rx\Observable::just(21)->repeat();
$mergedObservable = $observable
    ->merge($otherObservable)
    ->take(10);

$disposable = $mergedObservable->subscribe($stdoutObserver, $scheduler);

$loop->run();
```

do

The `do` function simply registers an action to take upon a variety of Observable life cycle events. Basically, you will register callbacks that ReactiveX will call only when certain events take place in the Observable. The callbacks will be called independently from the normal set of notifications. There are various operators that RxPHP have designed to allow this:

```php
<?php

require_once __DIR__ . '/../bootstrap.php';

$source = \Rx\Observable::range(0, 3)
    ->doOnEach(new \Rx\Observer\CallbackObserver(
        function ($x) {
            echo 'Do Next:', $x, PHP_EOL;
        },
        function (Exception $err) {
            echo 'Do Error:', $err->getMessage(), PHP_EOL;
        },
```

```php
    function () {
        echo 'Do Completed', PHP_EOL;
    }
));

$subscription = $source->subscribe($stdoutObserver);
```

scan

The `scan` operator applies a function to each item that an Observable emits. It applies this sequentially and emits each successive value:

```php
<?php

require_once __DIR__ . '/../bootstrap.php';

//With a seed
$source = Rx\Observable::range(1, 3);

$subscription = $source
    ->scan(function ($acc, $x) {
        return $acc * $x;
    }, 1)
    ->subscribe($createStdoutObserver());
```

Here is an example of `scan` without a seed:

```php
<?php

require_once __DIR__ . '/../bootstrap.php';

//Without a seed
$source = Rx\Observable::range(1, 3);

$subscription = $source
    ->scan(function ($acc, $x) {
        return $acc + $x;
    })
    ->subscribe($createStdoutObserver());
```

zip

The `zip` method returns an Observable and applies a function of your choosing to the combination of items emitted in sequence. The results of this function will become the items emitted by the returned Observable:

```php
<?php

require_once __DIR__ . '/../bootstrap.php';

//With a result selector
$range = \Rx\Observable::fromArray(range(0, 4));

$source = $range
    ->zip([
        $range->skip(1),
        $range->skip(2)
    ], function ($s1, $s2, $s3) {
        return $s1 . ':' . $s2 . ':' . $s3;
    });

$observer = $createStdoutObserver();

$subscription = $source->subscribe($createStdoutObserver());
```

In the following sample code, we use `zip` without a result selector:

```php
<?php

use Rx\Observer\CallbackObserver;

require_once __DIR__ . '/../bootstrap.php';

//Without a result selector
$range = \Rx\Observable::fromArray(range(0, 4));

$source = $range
    ->zip([
        $range->skip(1),
        $range->skip(2)
    ]);

$observer = $createStdoutObserver();

$subscription = $source
    ->subscribe(new CallbackObserver(
        function ($array) use ($observer) {
```

```
                    $observer->onNext(json_encode($array));
        },
        [$observer, "onError"],
        [$observer, "onCompleted"]
    ));
```

Parsing logs through a Reactive scheduler

It is difficult to just have theoretical knowledge of Reactive extensions and functional programming techniques and not be able to know when it can be used. In order to apply our knowledge, let's take a look at the following scenario.

Let's assume we have to read an Apache log file in an asynchronous manner.

An Apache log line looks like this:

```
111.222.333.123 HOME - [01/Feb/1998:01:08:39 -0800] "GET /bannerad/ad.htm
HTTP/1.0"
200 198 "http://www.referrer.com/bannerad/ba_intro.htm""Mozilla/4.01
(Macintosh; I; PPC)"

111.222.333.123 HOME - [01/Feb/1998:01:08:46 -0800] "GET /bannerad/ad.htm
HTTP/1.0"
200 28083 "http://www.referrer.com/bannerad/ba_intro.htm""Mozilla/4.01
(Macintosh; I; PPC)"
```

Let's dissect the parts of each line.

First, we have the IP address. It has three dots in between some numbers. Second, we have the field that logs the domain of the server.

Third, we have the date and time. Then we get the string, which says what was accessed and using what HTTP protocol. The status is 200, followed by the process ID and, finally, the name of the requestor, also known as the referrer.

When reading the Apache logs, we just want the IP address, the URL, and the date and time of access, and we also want to know what browser was used.

We know we can dissect the data into the spaces between them, so let's just change the logs into arrays split by the following method:

```php
<?php
function readLogData($pathToLog) {
$logs = [];
$data = split('\n', read($pathToLog);) //log newlines
```

```
foreach($data as line) {
$logLine = split('',$line);
  $ipAddr = $logLine[0];
  $time = $logLine[3];
$accessedUrl = $logLine[6];
  $referrer = $logLine[11];
  $logs[] = [
'IP' => $ipAddr,
'Time' => $time,
'URL' => $accessedUrl,
'UserAgent' => $referrer
  ];

}
return $logs;
}
```

Let's add an Observable so that we can execute the preceding function asynchronously, meaning it will work by reading the log file every hour.

The code would look like this:

```
$loop       = React\EventLoop\StreamSelectLoop;
$scheduler = new Rx\Scheduler\EventLoopScheduler($loop);


$intervalScheduler = \Rx\Observable::interval(3600000, $scheduler);

//execute function to read logFile:
$intervalScheduler::defer(function() {
readLogData('/var/log/apache2/access.log');
})->subscribe($createStdoutObserver());
```

Event queues with ReactiveX

An event queue would simply ensure that things that are to be done in a synchronous manner or in a first-in first-out manner. Let's define first what a queue is.

A queue is basically a list of things to do, which will get executed one by one until all the things in the queue have been finished.

In Laravel, for example, there is already a concept of queues, where we go through the elements of the queue. You can find the documentation at https://laravel.com/docs/5./queues.

Queues are usually used in systems that need to do some tasks in order and not in an asynchronous function. In PHP, there is already the `SplQueue` class, which provides the main functionalities of a queue implemented using a doubly linked list.

In general, queues are executed in the order that they come in. In ReactiveX, things are more of an asynchronous nature. In this scenario, we will implement a priority queue, where each task has corresponding levels of priority.

This is what a simple `PriorityQueue` code in ReactiveX would look like:

```
use \Rx\Scheduler\PriorityQueue;

Var $firstItem = new ScheduledItem(null, null, null, 1, null);

var $secondtItem = new ScheduledItem(null, null, null, 2, null);
$queue           = new PriorityQueue();
$queue->enqueue($firstItem);
$queue->enqueue($secondItem);
//remove firstItem if not needed in queue
$queue->remove($firstItem);
```

In the preceding code, we used the `PriorityQueue` library of RxPHP. We set some schedulers and queued them in a `PriorityQueue`. We gave each scheduled item a priority or time to spend in execution with 1 and 2. In the preceding scenario, the first item will execute first because it is the first priority and has the shortest time (1). Finally, we remove the `ScheduledItem` just to show what's possible with `PriorityQueue` in the RxPHP library.

Summary

You learned to work with the Reactive extensions library, RxPHP. Reactive Programming is all about using Observables and Observers, which is similar to working with subscribers and publishers.

You learned how to use `delay`, `defer`, `map`, and `flatMap`, among other operators, and how to use a scheduler.

You also learned how to read an Apache log file and schedule it to read after every hour and how to work with RxPHP's `PriorityQueue` class.

Index

I

ILog 95
ingestion workhorse 90
input data, checkout process
  cart 195
  contact data 195
interface
  building 256, 257
interpreter
  optimizing, by adding compiler 275, 282
  working 240
inventory service
  about 196
  building 200
  JsonRPC, used for communication 202, 203,
   204, 206
  making multithreaded 208, 209, 210
  ZeroMQ REQ/REP sockets, using 200
inverted index 89

J

JavaScript Object Notation (JSON)
  about 91
  decoding 93
  messages, encoding 93

K

key components, RESTful Web Service
  addressability 116
  decoupling of resources and representation 116
  statelessness 116
  uniform interface 116
Kibana dashboard 94

L

languages 241, 242, 243
lexer 240
Line Feed (LF) 183
localStorage 106
logical expressions
  adding 261
  and operator 265, 266
  comparisons 262, 264
  conditions 267, 268, 269

or operator 266
or operators 265
Logstash agent 84
Logstash
  about 89
  configuration, setting up 91
  installing 90
  reference link 90

M

mailing service
  about 196
  building 221
marketers dashboard
  about 58
  administration system, for managing marketers
   59, 60, 61
  AJAX Socket chat for support 68
  custom template, creating for newsletter 62, 63,
   64
  link tracking system 65, 66
  marketers dashboard 68
  reference link 60
Microservice architectures 195
Monolog 92
MySQL
  reference link 54

N

Nginx 158
non-terminal symbols 241
null coalesce operator 8
Number nodes 258

O

Oauth
  reference link 49
objects
  working with 273, 274
observables 289, 291
Observers 291

P

parser 240

www.ingramcontent.com/pod-product-compliance
Lightning Source LLC
Chambersburg PA
CBHW062106050326
40690CB00016B/3222